For my wife, whose persistent love, support, and
faith allow me to fulfill my life's purpose. And for
my daughter, whose pure spirit continues to fill my
days with love, joy, and happiness.

TREATING AND BEATING
Fibromyalgia and
Chronic Fatigue Syndrome

THE DEFINITIVE GUIDE FOR
PATIENTS AND PHYSICIANS

Dr. Rodger H. Murphree II, DC, CNS

4

Many manufacturers and sellers claim trademarks on their unique products. When these trademarks appear in this book and we are aware of them, we have used initial capital letters (e.g., Prozac) for designation.

Endnotes designated in the text of this book can be found at the end of each corresponding chapter. Patient testimonials are based on actual experiences as observed by the author. Patient names have been changed to protect privacy.

ISBN 0-9728938-0-6

SECOND EDITION
Copyright © 2003 by Rodger H. Murphree II

Printed in the United States of America.
Harrison and Hampton Publishing, Inc.
825 Conroy Road, Birmingham, AL 35222

Cover design by Dana Coester
Editing and book design by Betsy Stokes
Set in 10-point Century Schoolbook

Contact Dr. Murphree
Inquiries concerning content of this book should be addressed to the author at 3401 Independence Dr. Suite 121, Birmingham, AL, 35209. Phone: (205) 879-2383   Fax: (205) 879-2381

Visit us at www.drrodger.com.

This book and the advice given are not intended to take the place of your physician. Please consult with your health care professional before discontinuing any medication.

The author is deeply indebted to: "all the patients who have trusted me with their health challenges, my peers for their wisdom and guidance, Doctors Wendy Arthur and Ginger Campbell for their ongoing support, and Hugh and Sue Weeks for their unwavering encouragement."

Treating and Beating FMS and CFS

6

Foreword

By Doctors Wendy Arthur, MD, and Ginger Campbell, MD

Millions of people in the US suffer from fibromyalgia and chronic fatigue syndrome, yet mainstream medicine offers them little hope beyond marginal control of their symptoms. Friends, family, and even physicians may think a patient's problems are "all in her head" as she watches her life dissolve into constant pain, overwhelming fatigue, depression, and— maybe *most* disabling—mental confusion ("fibro fog").

In *Treating and Beating Fibromyalgia and Chronic Fatigue Syndrome,* Dr. Murphree provides an extensive investigation into these debilitating conditions. His holistic approach slowly transforms the mind, body, and spirit, restoring normal sleep, decreasing pain, and improving energy. In the past, my (Dr. Arthur's) patients had seen mild to moderate improvement. But with Dr. Murphree's comprehensive approach, I'm seeing energy levels tripled and pain reduced to the point where prescription medicine can be discontinued.

Dr. Murphree's program is grounded in his own clinical experience and passion for nutrition research. Most importantly, it works! Some of the changes he recommends are challenging, but they succeed because they utilize the body's innate healing abilities.

This is a book about medicine, not miracles, though sometimes Dr. Murphree seems to tap into a little of both. *Treating and Beating* is destined to inspire and educate millions of Americans who just want to feel good again, and their physicians who care for and about them.

8

Introduction

Peeling Away the Layers

Like an onion, chronic illness is the result of many layers, each building on the one before. To get to the center of your healing, we must peel back these layers, one by one, together.

You hold in your (perhaps aching) hands a detailed description of proven treatments and even possibly, your cure. Make this book your partner in medicine. Apply its step-by-step recommendations, and I assure you, you will feel better—probably than you have felt in years.

WHAT THIS BOOK WILL TEACH YOU

If you suffer from FMS or CFS, you have likely read much on the topic. Why is this book special? Because it's not merely a collection of facts gathered by a researcher. It is a first-hand success story of real-life solutions, not textbook theories or fluffy coping strategies. Read on to discover:

- why traditional medicine alone isn't successful in treating FMS and CFS.

- why you can't sleep and how to safely and consistently solve this problem with natural supplements.

- a proven program to eliminate your symptoms and then *stay* well.

- why you're in pain and how to reduce or eliminate chronic muscle aches.

- why you're so tired.

- why thyroid tests are usually inaccurate.

- who is most likely to be a victim of chronic illness.
- at what point in life chronic illness usually strikes.
- how FMS and CFS are diagnosed.
- the underlying conditions that contribute to them.
- what tests should be performed and how to interpret these tests.
- what dysautonomia is and how to effectively treat it.
- why you have "fibro fog" and how to correct it.
- how to accurately and easily test your thyroid at home.
- how to treat and correct hypothyroid.
- how prolonged stress eventually overwhelms your adrenal glands.
- how to accurately and easily test for low adrenal function.
- what is "leaky gut" and how it can cause food allergies, pain, inflammation, and chronic infections.
- why people become depressed and how over-the-counter amino acids are often more effective than prescription medications.
- how diet affects your health.
- how to successfully treat allergies and sensitivities.
- what causes irritable bowel, yeast overgrowth, and digestive disturbances, and how to treat them.
- why you've gained unwanted weight and how increasing your metabolism will allow you to lose it.
- why you have adverse reactions to certain chemicals, including medications.
- why you have chronic sinus infections and how to stop them once and for all.
- how to get your memory back and think clearly.
- how to stop anxiety, end depression, and overcome subconscious barriers to getting well.
- how to stop chronic pain and feel good again!

I know the frustration, confusion, fear, and despair that go along with these illnesses. There's hope for you, so don't give up.

When I began practicing ten years ago, I'd never heard of fibromyalgia or chronic fatigue syndrome. They were never mentioned in our medical textbooks. But seven years ago, I had a patient referred to me who changed my life forever. Sheila Hansen was suffering from a strange collection of symptoms: diffuse pain throughout her body, headaches, menstrual irregularities, allergies, chronic infections, insomnia, depression, digestive problems, and unrelenting fatigue. After several years of being passed from one doctor to the next, she had recently been diagnosed with fibromyalgia by a local rheumatologist.

The doctor couldn't provide her much information on this illness, nor could he offer her much hope of ever feeling well again. She had read all she could about fibromyalgia (there wasn't much) and knew that traditional medicine had little to offer: mostly just covering up various symptoms. Another patient of mine had told her about me, and she had come to me in desperation. Her symptoms were getting worse, and no one seemed able to help her.

I was tempted to dismiss her as a chronic hypochondriac, as did many of the other physicians she had seen. But then she said something that changed my mind:

Dr. Murphree, I know I sound crazy. I know you've probably not heard of or treated anyone with this thing called fibromyalgia. I've been to eight different doctors and had endless medical tests, and no one has helped me. I've been sick for almost seven years now, and I want to feel good again. I used to be healthy. I worked part-time in a job I loved. I played golf with my husband twice a week and tennis with friends on a regular basis. My husband and I have raised and married off two wonderful children. We're blessed with a great family, financial security, and supportive friends. I just want to enjoy life again.

Mrs. Hansen didn't have anything to gain from being sick. She wasn't crazy, and she had a real desire to be well. I told her I didn't know anything about fibromyalgia and didn't know if I could help her. She had already been to some of the best medical specialists in the state. What did I have to offer? But I told her I would do my best.

I knew I had to learn everything I could about this new, mysterious disease. I read everything I could find on fibromyalgia syndrome (FMS) and chronic fatigue syndrome

(CFS). I was not aware that there was "no cure" for fibromyalgia. I just did what I had been doing with all of my patients; I treated the whole person from the inside out.

Sheila's body was not properly communicating with itself (this is known as dysautonomia). Her regulatory system was broken. Repair the regulatory system, I concluded, and she would get better.

I began by analyzing her diet and placing her on an allergy-elimination diet. She improved. I ran some functional medical tests that revealed she wasn't digesting her food well. She had intestinal permeability, also known as "leaky gut," and yeast overgrowth. I started her on natural yeast medications and diet restrictions to repair her damaged gut. She continued to get better. I didn't know a fraction of what I know today about chronic illness. Still, she kept improving. I prescribed vitamins, minerals, and amino acids. She got better still. I developed specific chiropractic adjustments and physical therapies to accommodate her severe musculoskeletal pain. The gentler I was with her, the better she fared.

Three months later, Sheila was totally well. She no longer had pain, insomnia, fatigue, allergies, or any other symptoms. She was ecstatic, and so was I.

Soon, whether I liked it or not, I began seeing dozens of fibromyalgia and chronic fatigue syndrome patients. I continued to learn, refine, and update my treatment protocol. Some patients got well; some didn't. Although I was happy with my successes, I was disturbed about the failures. Why did some patients get well while others remained ill? I continued to search for answers. I found other chiropractors, nutritionists, massage therapists, and medical doctors who were also searching for answers. It became clear to me that "out-of-the-box" thinking was essential in treating FMS and CFS. They were not a neatly packaged set of symptoms that fit into an insurance code book.

A NEW KIND OF MEDICINE

It didn't take long to realize that my patients needed the best of traditional *and* alternative medicine: an integrated approach. Natural nutritional and physical therapies allowed me to correct nutritional deficiencies and structural illnesses, while judicious use of prescription medications helped to temporarily relieve symptoms. This was the beginning of our integrative clinic located in Birmingham, Alabama. There, we specialize in combining traditional and natural medicine to treat FMS, CFS, and other chronic illnesses.

Word of our unique approach began to spread. I spoke at dozens of cities throughout Alabama. Local and regional newspapers wrote articles about us, and patients arrived eagerly, first from all over the Southeast, and now from around the country.

Today, we offer hope to those who thought there was none. Our commitment to learning as much as we can about FMS and CFS has allowed us to help the majority of those who seek our care. We've put in thousands of study hours, and we've been in the trenches with our patients. Not only have we helped them get well, but we've dialogued with their primary physicians, educated their family members, and assured them that they're not crazy. We've cried with many of them and celebrated wellness with hundreds!

Equally important, we've failed sometimes! But this only makes us dig deeper and try harder. We continue to refine protocols, keeping what consistently works and eliminating what doesn't. Unlike theorists, we have been fighting and winning the battle against FMS and CFS for several years now.

14

1

Fibromyalgia

"I'm losing my mind! Some days I can't even remember the names of my children. And I can't escape the aching pain. My tests come back normal, but I know I'm sick." —Michelle

Fibromyalgia and chronic fatigue syndrome patients not only deal with the misery of their illness, but they also face an uphill battle trying to convince others that their illness even exists. They are often told by spouses, family, friends, and doctors that they just need to exercise, lose weight, eat better, or take antidepressant drugs. Some are told that it's all their heads. In many ways, it *is* all in their heads, but not as a psychologically manifested disease. Their brains just are not working properly; they don't make enough of the right brain chemicals. Many have free-radical damage that affects how they think and act.

Healthy people (a relative term)—including spouses—often can't understand how someone could be so sick and yet not be dying. Normal lab tests and baffled doctors can cause suspicion and lack of compassion in loved ones. Meanwhile, passing from one specialist to another, the patient can develop a co-dependence on medical physicians and on a growing number of prescription medications. There have been many occasions when I've cried along with a desperate patient whose husband didn't understand how sick she truly was. "I've been sick for so long. No one has been able to tell me why, and everyone thinks I'm crazy. Could you explain all this to my husband? He doesn't believe I'm really sick."

I know physicians who still don't believe there is such a thing as fibromyalgia or CFS. To me, this is like saying, "I don't believe the world is round." Science and astute observation have proven that the world is in fact round. Science and clinical observation have also proven the existence of FMS and CFS. How can normally intelligent, rational doctors turn their backs to the millions of patients suffering with FMS and CFS? I invite these doctors to follow *our* physicians for a day. They would hear the frustration our patients share of going from one doctor to another, searching first for the right diagnosis and then for meaningful treatment. The average FMS patient has seen 12 doctors and waited seven years before being diagnosed with FMS.

Each patient has her own story. Typically she is referred to a neurologist for testing, an internist for diagnosing, and finally a rheumatologist for treatment. The rheumatologist has to break the news that there is no cure. He recommends many of the drugs the patient has already tried: anti-inflammatories, pain meds, muscle relaxers, antidepressants, and others. Is it any wonder these patients think they are crazy?

It really doesn't matter what you call these symptoms shared by over 2% of the population. The symptoms exist. The syndromes are real, and the individuals who suffer are real. FMS and CFS are dreadful illnesses and far more insidious than many other chronic conditions that can be tested for and treated with prescription medication. They drain a person's life slowly. At first they are mostly a nuisance. But slowly they become the core of someone's life. They gradually take over, affecting not only health but social life, livelihood, marriage, and sometimes even desire to live.

ALL IN YOUR HEAD

You might have been told that "it's all in your head." Well, as stated before, part of the problem *is* in your head—or more accurately, your brain. Those with FMS don't produce enough of the brain chemical serotonin. Serotonin is an inhibitory neurotransmitter. Neurotransmitters are what carry brain messages from one nerve cell to another. These chemical messengers relay information that helps regulate our moods, sleep, mental acuity, pain level, and other important bodily functions. Some of these neurotransmitters cause excitatory reactions. Others, like serotonin, are inhibitory (calming) in nature. Neurotransmitters are made from amino acids—in association with certain co-factors, including magnesium (usually deficient in FMS and CFS patients) and vitamins B1, B6, and B3. These co-factors (and others) combine with amino acids to produce the brain chemicals serotonin, epinephrine, norepinephrine, and dopamine. These then help control our energy, immune system, digestion, and reaction to stress—basically, how we feel, sleep, think, and act.

Numerous studies have shown that those suffering from FMS are deficient in serotonin, and serotonin is very important. It is involved in the initiation and maintenance of deep, restorative sleep. Serotonin helps regulate the perception of pain; the higher the serotonin level, the higher the pain threshold. Low serotonin and poor sleep can cause mental fatigue and confusion, known to FMS sufferers as "fibro fog."

WHAT IS FIBRO FOG?

> *I can't remember half the things my husband tells me. I make little lists of what I'm supposed to do that day, and then I can't remember where I put the lists. I feel like I'm in a fog most of the time. My brain won't work right. Sometimes I can't remember what I was going to say in mid-sentence. I often feel like a total idiot. What is wrong with me?* —Alice

Normal brain activity decreases or even ceases when there is a deficiency in the chemicals needed for proper function (neurotransmitters/hormones). So without adequate levels of serotonin, the brain doesn't "fire on all cylinders." Mental functions, including rational thinking and short-term memory, begin to suffer.

We'll see in later chapters why using prescription antidepressants like Prozac, Celexa, and Zoloft often fail to correct neurotransmitter deficiencies. But for now, please realize that there is a reason for your brain fog, and it can be corrected.

Symptoms of Fibromyalgia Syndrome

Fibromyalgia Syndrome is characterized by diffuse muscle pain, poor sleep, and unrelenting fatigue. Other symptoms associated with FMS include poor memory, depression, irritable bowel, chemical sensitivities, allergies, chronic infections, and headaches. Leading FMS researchers estimate that 2–4% of the general population suffer from this syndrome. Ninety percent of those diagnosed with FMS are women. The stiffness and pain associated with FMS usually appear gradually and become worse with additional physical, emotional, or mental fatigue. The soft tissue and muscles of the neck, shoulders, chest and rib cage, lower back, and thighs are especially vulnerable. This pain can be mild and annoying, or severe and disabling.

FMS shares some of the symptoms of chronic fatigue syndrome (CFS). In fact, 70% of patients diagnosed with FMS also meet all of the diagnostic criteria for CFS.

Those with FMS tend to have more muscle pain, while CFS patients report disabling fatigue as their main complaint. Although both illnesses have their own unique symptoms and separate diagnostic criteria, they're really different sides of the same coin. A patient's symptoms can fall anywhere on the scale between FMS and CFS. Most patients share some of the symptoms associated with both syndromes and fall somewhere in the middle.

A Tragic Cycle

FMS involves localized pain. Chronic localized pain leads to poor sleep, which leads to a constant state of fatigue and consequent inactivity. When muscles aren't used, they become even more sensitive to pain. So decreased activity increases pain and insomnia, which further causes fatigue. Ultimately, many sufferers become depressed and develop headaches and flu-like symptoms caused by chronic inflammation. This cycle of pain and fatigue can seem impossible to correct.

In addition, FMS sufferers already have a lower-than-average pain threshold (allodynia), so they perceive pain that would normally not be felt by healthy individuals.

WHY "SYNDROME"?

In medicine, a disease is an illness with very specific symptoms and reproducible laboratory findings. Examples of diseases are diabetes, arthritis, and asthma. FMS and CFS, though, have a wide variety of symptoms and very few (if any) agreed upon, reproducible lab findings.

Because these two illnesses have such a myriad of symptoms and conditions (irritable bowel, insomnia, headache, muscle pain, allergies, etc.), they are considered syndromes rather than diseases. A syndrome is a collection of signs and symptoms that characterize a particular abnormal condition.

HISTORY OF FMS

Fibromyalgia and similar conditions have been reported for hundreds of years. Symptoms similar to those associated with FMS were reported as early as 1736 by Guillaume de Baillou, who used the term "rheumatism" to describe muscle aches and pain, as well as rheumatic fever. In 1951, Dr. Theron Randolph demonstrated that "allergic myalgia" was widespread and that severe muscle pain could be reproduced using ingested allergic foods. In 1952, Dr. Janet Travell first used the term "myofascial pain syndrome." She wrote several definitive books on recognizing and treating myofascial pain. In the early 1980s, fibromyalgia started receiving attention as an independent condition.

DIAGNOSIS OF FMS

Though some laboratory markers do exist, there is currently no agreed-upon test to positively identify FMS. A diagnosis is made, then, by first ruling out other conditions that may mimic its symptoms—thyroid disease, lupus, Lyme disease, rheumatoid arthritis. Current diagnosis criteria, proposed by the American College of Rheumatology (ACR), is then referenced. A diagnosis of FMS requires that all three of the major criteria and four or more of the minor criteria be present:

MAJOR CRITERIA:

- generalized aches or stiffness of at least three anatomical sites for at least three months
- six or more typical, reproducible tender points
- exclusion of other disorders that can cause similar symptoms

MINOR CRITERIA:

- generalized fatigue
- chronic headache
- sleep disturbance
- neurological and psychological complaints
- numbing or tingling sensations
- irritable bowel syndrome
- variation of symptoms in relation to activity, stress, and weather changes
- depression

Although only 2% of the population are reported to have FMS, the figure should be much larger. Diagnoses have been missed because of shortcomings of the ACR criteria. Most important, many individuals with FMS meet some of the criteria but not all of them. Most of these individuals have other symptoms associated with FMS not explicitly outlined in the ACR criteria. They might have insomnia, irritable bowel, fatigue, mental confusion, and only four of the 18 tender points. Or they might have insomnia, fatigue, and five reproducible tender points. Although the minor criteria represent the most frequent and usual symptoms associated with FMS, they don't account for all of the various conditions seen in FMS patients.

In our clinic we like to say, "anything that can go wrong in a FMS patient, will." That's because FMS patients are special. They have a wide variety of problems, and some of these problems can be quite bizarre: "Dr. Murphree, have you ever heard of getting dizzy when eating bagels?" "I tingle all over, including my tongue. Am I just crazy?" The symptoms of FMS and CFS don't fit neatly into a medical how-to book, and this frustrates many doctors and their patients.

POTENTIAL SYMPTOMS OF FMS

- **Sleep disturbances:** Sufferers might not feel refreshed, despite getting adequate amounts of sleep. They might also have difficulty falling or staying asleep.

- **Stiffness:** Body stiffness is present in most patients. Weather changes and remaining in one position for a long period of time contribute to the problem. Stiffness might also be present upon awakening.

- **Headaches and facial pain:** Headaches may be caused by associated tenderness in the neck and shoulder area or in the soft tissue around the temporomandibular joint (TMJ).

- **Abdominal discomfort:** Irritable bowel syndrome, with such symptoms as digestive disturbances, abdominal pain and bloating, constipation, and diarrhea, might be present.

- **Irritable bladder:** Patients might have an increase in urinary frequency and a greater urgency to urinate may be present.

- **Numbness (parathesia):** Symptoms include a prickling, tingling, or burning sensation in the extremities.

- **Chest pain:** Muscular pain at the point where the ribs meet the chest bone might occur.

- **Cognitive disorders:** The symptoms of cognitive disorders may vary from day to day. They can include "spaciness," memory lapses, difficulty concentrating, word mix-ups when speaking or writing, and clumsiness.

- **Chemical (environmental) sensitivity:** Sensitivities to light, noise, odor, and weather are often present, as are allergic reactions to a variety of substances (see below).

- **Disequilibrium:** Difficulties in orientation may occur when standing, driving, or reading. Dizziness and balance problems might also be present.

CHEMICAL SENSITIVITY

Substantial overlap exists among chemical sensitivity, fibromyalgia, and chronic fatigue syndrome. FMS and CFS often include chemical sensitivity in their symptoms. Certain chemicals are more likely than others to cause the onset of chemical sensitivity and chronic illness. These include gasoline, kerosene, natural gas, pesticides (especially chlordane and chlorpyrifos), certain solvents, new carpet, paints, glues, fiberglass, carbonless copy paper, fabric softeners, formaldehyde, carpet shampoos and other cleaning agents, combustion products (from poorly vented gas heaters, overheated batteries, etc.), perfumes, deodorants, and various medications. A sluggish detoxification system, allergic reactions, neurological-mediated sensitivities, and opportunistic pathogens may all also contribute to chemical sensitivity. For more information, see chapter 18, "Toxic Waste Sites."

CAUSES OF FMS

There is no one cause of fibromyalgia. Likewise, there is no quick remedy. Some physicians believe fibromyalgia to be a result of poor diet, trauma, stress, infection, immune dysfunction, hormonal imbalance, and/or genetics. But the truth is, we really don't know for sure what initiates the onset of FMS. Myriad factors have been linked to FMS, including prolonged stress, chemical sensitivities, trauma, allergies, sleep disturbances, poor posture, hormonal disturbances, and environmental toxins. It's not unreasonable to suggest that all of these triggers and others not mentioned may contribute.

FMS IS NOT ARTHRITIS

Because rheumatologists were the first group to officially acknowledge and classify FMS, they were considered the medical experts on the syndrome. And since rheumatologists treat many patients with arthritis, FMS may erroneously be presumed to be joint arthritis or an autoimmune connective disorder. However, unlike arthritis, FMS doesn't involve joint pain or inflammation. Instead, FMS sufferers have generalized muscle and soft tissue pain.

Conditions Associated with FMS

Carol Jessop, M.D. reports that a sample of close to 1,000 of her FMS patients shows that they suffer or suffered from the following:

- muscular pain (100%)

- poor sleep and fatigue (nearly 100%)

- depression (nearly 100%)

- cold hands and feet with poor circulation, known as Raynaud's syndrome (40%)

- anxiety (24%)

- elevated temperature (10%)

- low temperature, suggesting low thyroid and metabolism (65%)

- low blood pressure, suggesting dysautonomia and poor adrenal function (86%)

- white spots on their nails, suggesting low zinc and poor digestion or malabsorption (85%)

- tender thyroid (40%)

- swollen lymph nodes, suggesting an immune dysfunction (18%). (We at Advanced Family Medicine have a larger percentage of patients with this.)

- irritable bowel syndrome (73%)

- severe headaches, usually associated with low magnesium and low thyroid and adrenal hormones (50%)

- dry eyes, suggestive of allergies (18%)

- osteoarthritis (12%)

- rheumatoid arthritis (7%)

- yeast in the stool (82%)

- parasites in the stool (30%)

- irregular periods, suggestive of poor nutrition (60%)

- temporomandibular joint (TMJ) syndrome (25%)

- endometriosis, suggestive of estrogen dominance and/or liver dysfunction (15%)

- restless leg syndrome, suggestive of low magnesium (30%)

- multiple chemical sensitivities, suggestive of liver dysfunction (40%)
- interstitial cystitis (25%)
- irritable bladder (15%)
- mitral valve prolapse (75%)

Just as interesting are the symptoms her patients had *before* developing FMS:

- constipation (58%)
- bloating, gas, and/or indigestion (80%)
- heartburn (40%)
- irritable bowel syndrome (89%)[1]

The symptoms that presented before FMS suggest chronic malabsorption, a digestive problem. This condition, as discussed later, can lead to all sorts of deficiencies in essential nutrients. And these deficiencies can cause a variety of unwanted symptoms.

It's easy to see how doctors could be skeptical of FMS. Some physicians rationalize that only a psychosomatic (mental) illness could produce so many different and seemingly unrelated symptoms—in spite of the ACR guidelines and other notable studies published in distinguished medical journals. Other physicians accept FMS as an entity but don't want anything to do with those victimized by it. Fortunately though, through publications like this one, physicians can become more knowledgeable about FMS. And with persistence, you can receive compassionate, effective care.

Notes

[1]From author's notes: Fibromyalgia Workshop. Speaker: Leon Chaitow, 2000.

2

Chronic Fatigue Syndrome

"Don't tell me to get more sleep. I sleep all the time as it is. It's like I have the flu from hell and just can't shake it. I'm too tired to clean, exercise, even drive."—Willa

There are many similarities between chronic fatigue syndrome (CFS) and FMS. Several studies have suggested that they are the same illness. One study comparing 50 CFS patients with 50 FMS patients showed the following symptoms to be the same for both groups: low-grade fever (28%), swollen lymph nodes (33%), rash (47%), cough (40%), and recurrent sore throat (54%). Another study comparing CFS patients with FMS patients showed that the brain wave patterns, tender points, pain, and fatigue were virtually identical in both groups.[1]

A 1997 study by Allen N. Tyler, MD, ND, DC, muddies the water even further. Ten patients, all of whom met the ACR criteria for FMS, were selected at random for blood testing. They were tested for influenza type-B antibodies, and three of the ten tested positive. Another randomly selected group of ten FMS patients (meeting all the ACR criteria) were tested for antibodies to influenza type-A. Nine of them tested positive.[2]

Why are these results significant? Because positive blood tests for influenza type-A normally only occur for up to one year after exposure. But these test subjects had likely been exposed to influenza years before. The continuing presence of antibodies suggests a compromised immune system. And since a compromised immune system is generally accepted as a part of chronic fatigue, the fact that these FMS patients showed signs of depleted immunity links them even tighter with CFS.

DIAGNOSTIC CRITERIA FOR CFS[3]

Major Criteria

- new onset of fatigue causing 50% reduction in activity for at least six months
- exclusion of other illnesses that can cause fatigue

Minor Criteria

- presence of eight of 11 symptoms, or
- presence of six of 11 symptoms and two of three signs:

Symptoms

1. mild fever
2. recurrent sore throat
3. painful lymph nodes
4. muscle weakness
5. muscle pain
6. migratory joint pain
7. prolonged fatigue after exercise
8. recurrent headaches
9. neurological or psychological complaints, such as
   - depression
   - excessive irritability
   - forgetfulness
   - sensitivity to bright light
   - confusion
   - inability to concentrate

10. sleep disturbances

11. sudden onset of symptom complex

Signs

1. low-grade fever

2. non-exudative pharyngitis

3. palpable or tender lymph nodes

SPECT SCAN STUDIES

Chronic fatigue syndrome affects the mind differently than FMS does. Free radicals (oxidative stress) poison the brain, interfering with delicate neuronal functions. Sophisticated single photon emission computerized tomography (SPECT) scans have demonstrated dysfunctional areas in the brain of those suffering from CFS. Sadly, the longer they've had the disease, the worse the damage.

CFS and FMS do have enough in common to be considered the same syndrome. But to say that there is no distinction between the two illnesses suggests an ignorance on the part of those physicians who theorize about CFS and FMS but don't actively treat them. Modern medicine always wants to label a disease, systematically categorize each sign or symptom, then agree upon diagnostic tests to measure the presence of the disease. In short: label it, assign an insurance code, and list it in the Merck Manual. But many doctors today have learned the hard way (through trial and error) that a number of chronic illnesses just don't respond to this conventional approach.

CFS AND THE EPSTEIN-BARR VIRUS

Several studies have focused on identifying an infectious agent as the cause of CFS. The Epstein-Barr virus (EBV) has received the most attention over the last two decades. In 1985, reports published in the Annals of Internal Medicine discussed a mysterious, severe viral epidemic that gripped the Lake Tahoe region in California. Initially, CFS was presumed to be caused by the EBV, because research at the National Institutes of Health (NIH) confirmed elevated levels of antibodies against EBV present in afflicted people. As time passed, EBV was deemed just one of many viruses associated with CFS.

EBV is a member of the herpes group of viruses, which includes herpes simplex types 1 and 2, varicella zoster virus, cytomegalovirus, and psuedorabies virus. A common aspect of these viruses is their ability to establish lifelong, latent infection after an initial infection. Fortunately, this latent condition is kept in check by a healthy immune system. But when the immune system is weakened, opportunistic infections— especially latent viruses like EBV—are able to multiply. A normally dormant virus can rear its ugly head and be reactivated into a chronic infection.

We know that EBV causes the debilitating teenage disease infectious mononucleosis, or "mono." But not everyone who carries this virus develops mono symptoms. In fact, over 90% of Americans have been exposed to EBV by age 20. Some of them develop infectious mononucleosis; others simply experience flu-like symptoms for a few days. But most show no symptoms at all. Whatever its effect, EBV remains in the body for life.

How and when EBV re-emerges depends upon a number of factors, most prominently the strength of the individual's immune system. Stephen Straus, a leading virologist and EBV researcher, has stated that the reservoir of latent EBV in a person's blood acts as a "barometer of immunocompetence" and concludes that chronic illness is often "an indicator of faulty immune containment of EBV."[4]

Persons with a compromised immune system are susceptible to latent infections, including EBV. What's more, the infection itself can be the cause of the compromised immunity.

A variety of immune system abnormalities have been observed in EBV cases. The most consistent abnormality is a decreased number or activity of natural killer (NK) cells. NK cells are normally used by the body to destroy cells infected with cancerous or viral toxins.

THE EPSTEIN-BARR VIRUS AND MONONUCLEOSIS

Infectious mononucleosis is a condition marked by debilitating fatigue, fever, sore throat, and swollen lymph glands. It is caused by the Epstein-Barr virus and usually lasts from three to six weeks. But intimate exposure to the virus by adults does not always result in infection (and therefore, symptoms). The key to remaining symptom-free is a powerful and vigilant immune system.

Until recently, it was thought that mononucleosis patients always produced sufficient antibodies to keep them immune from future EBV infection. But recent research has helped change this line of thinking. Interestingly, it's now believed that individuals who have exhibited symptoms of mononucleosis are slightly *more* susceptible to recurrent EBV infection than the general population.

So how is EBV related to CFS? Physicians and researchers began to recognize the incidence of recurrent mononucleosis as early as 1948. Reports continued to appear throughout the 1950s and '60s, but it wasn't until the late '70s that studies were published describing long-term EBV infection characterized by intermittent fever, muscle and joint aches, sore throats, and debilitating fatigue.

In the mid '80s, numerous studies seemed to correlate these symptoms directly with reactivation of latent EBV. This disorder was therefore referred to as chronic Epstein-Barr virus syndrome (CEBV). Unlike mononucleosis, CEBV did not seem to be self-limiting. It would come and go, or never fully go away. Patients described it as "the flu from hell" and experienced feelings of physical and mental exhaustion. Symptoms varied but usually included extreme fatigue, weakness, depression, muscle and joint aches, sore throat, swollen lymph glands, headache, and low-grade afternoon fever. In addition, many patients reported impaired memory, difficulty concentrating, disturbed balance, anxiety, irritability, and insomnia. These symptoms usually fluctuated in severity from month to month, and even from day to day. Periods of wellness were often followed by relapses, as patients attempted to resume normal activities or strenuous exercise.

Recent studies have shown that CMV growth in blood can increase long before the onset of CFS symptoms. When researchers include CMV, EBV, and herpes simplex in their evaluations, CFS patients are found to have significantly higher viral antibody levels than do healthy controls.

CFS AND THE CYTOMEGALOVIRUS

Though not as common as the EBV, the cytomegalovirus

(CMV) is estimated to infect close to 75% of adults in Western nations, with incidences in Asia and Africa approaching 100%. In the majority of cases, primary exposure produces no clinical illness, but like all herpes viruses, CMV remains latent in the body for life. During times of immune suppression, it can reactivate and produce symptoms very similar to EBV. In fact, 10–15% of all mononucleosis cases appear to be caused by CMV, not EBV. CMV usually does produce observable illness in infected infants and immune-suppressed adults.

CMV and EBV can both infect the central nervous system in adults. A wide range of neurological symptoms can result, such as confusion, memory loss, inflammation of the brain (encephalitis), and a disorder known as Guillain-Barré syndrome. CMV also commonly infects the gastrointestinal tract. An infected gastrointestinal tract can lead to leaky gut syndrome and malabsorption. Current research suggests that the CMV may contribute to ulcers, colitis, and cancer of the colon.

CFS is chiefly an immune deficiency disease. The immune system has become compromised, allowing normally dormant viruses and other pathogens (harmful microbes) to become active. It's not surprising, then, that the majority of physicians who actively treat CFS agree that correcting immune dysfunction is the most important priority in any treatment plan.

Some of the immune disorders associated with CFS are:
- elevated levels of antibodies to various viruses.
- altered helper/suppressor T-cell ratio.
- decreased NK cells or activity.
- decreased levels of circulating immune complexes.
- low or elevated antibody levels.
- increased cytokine levels.
- increased or decreased interferon levels.
- fibromyalgia and multiple chemical sensitivities.[5]

CHRONIC VIRAL INFECTIONS AND CFS

Individuals who we suspect have chronic fatigue syndrome will have EBV and CMV blood panels drawn. This is to see if there is a virus lingering in the body that is weakening the immune system. These blood tests measure the antibodies immunoglobulin M (IgM) and immunoglobulin G (IgG). A test for IgM antibodies measures the acute (recent infection) phase of the virus. A test for IgG antibodies measures the dormant (inactive) phase of the virus. Our tests also measure Epstein-Barr nuclear antigen (EBNA) antibodies.

Due to weakened immunity, individuals with chronic fatigue have terrible problems with energy as well as reoccurring bouts with the flu, colds, sinusitis, and other immune problems.

TREATING CFS

As with so many complex chronic illnesses, CFS may be aggravated by a wide variety of environmental and physiological challenges. Food allergies, environmental sensitivities, heavy metal toxicity, yeast overgrowth, intestinal dysbiosis, parasites, and vitamin/mineral deficiencies can all contribute to CFS.

The syndrome's principal causes are a weakened immune system and a reactivated virus. These are usually treated (at our clinic) with antiviral immune boosters: prescription Valtrex and/or natural medications like thymus glandular extracts, Laktoferen, and the mushroom extracts Myoceutics and MGN-3.

YOU'RE NOT CONTAGIOUS

All of us have been exposed to mono or the Epstein-Barr virus at one time or another (usually as teenagers), but our bodies are usually strong enough to overcome it. Individuals with CFS have been exposed to the Epstein-Barr virus or mono from some other source, and it has now returned. Its return has either caused the immune system to be compromised or has taken advantage of already compromised immunity. And a weakened immune system is not contagious. So tell any nervous friends to relax. For more information, see chapter 8.

Notes
[1] Sources: *Journal of Rheumatology,* 1992 and CIBA Foundation Symposium 173
[2] Source: *Altern Med Rev,* 1997
[3] Source: Centers for Disease Control
[4] Sources: *Postgrad Med,* 1988; *Virology,* 1982; and *JAMA,* 1987
[5] We'll discuss T-cells and NK cells further in chapter 8.

For Further Reading
• *Alternative Medicine Guide to Chronic Fatigue, Fibromyalgia and Environmental Illness* by Burton Goldberg and the editors of *Alternative Medicine Digest;* 1998

3

FMS, CFS, and Your Personality Type

Most of my patients fall into one of two categories: The perfectionist (type-A) or the caregiver (type-B). Type-As "do" until they're done out. Type-Bs "give" until they're given out.

THE PERFECTIONIST

Type-As are doers. They have a demanding schedule filled with activities: a job, household duties, family responsibilities, soccer practices, PTA meetings, volunteer work, church duties, and more. They push themselves harder and harder trying to do more, be more, have more. These perfectionists can't stand to be idle. They must be busy doing something—anything. They'll be talking on the phone counseling a co-worker on job performance, while cooking dinner, emptying the dishwasher, feeding the baby, and looking over the day's mail. If they're asked to volunteer for a fundraiser at their child's school, they'll accept. If the boss calls and asks them to head an additional committee, they can't say no.

Unfortunately, type-As get so caught up in *doing* that they never take time to be human *beings*. They don't know what downtime is, and the years of constant stress finally catch up to them. They burn themselves out.

MANDY'S STORY

My parents encouraged me to be the best I could be. I graduated from college in three years with honors and immediately began my dream job as an advertising executive. I met my husband, got married, and starting having children. I worked up until delivery and took only a month off for each child.

For the first 10 years of our marriage, everything seemed to go well. I climbed the corporate ladder, had several pay increases, enjoyed volunteering, and was on the PTA board and other boards around town.

I loved being successful; who wouldn't? We had a large home we loved, two luxury cars, a lake house, three wonderful children in private school, and I was sure I'd make senior vice president at my firm in the next couple of years.

One day the bottom just sort of fell out and my life became unmanageable. My job became increasingly demanding, and my health suffered. At first it was colds that hung around and wouldn't easily go away. Then the chronic headaches started. Some days I had to drag myself through the day, living on coffee and sodas to pick me up.

I made an appointment with our family doctor, who ran a bunch of tests. She said they didn't show that anything was wrong and suggested I was depressed from the death of my mother. She recommended I take an antidepressant. I knew something must be wrong, so I started taking the medicine and thought it would get me back on track again. It didn't. I went to doctor after doctor, trying to find someone to help me. I continued to get worse with headaches, bowel problems, insomnia, sinus infections...I felt like I had the worst case of the flu—all day, every day.

I started missing several days of work each month. I saw dozens of doctors. None could help me get over this. I continued to get worse; my mind seemed to turn to mush. Even the simplest decisions became a big ordeal. I couldn't remember where I put my car keys, if I had taken my medicine, what I was supposed to pick up at the store. I began to withdraw from friends, and my social life came to a complete stop. I didn't even have the energy to walk the dog; I certainly didn't have the energy for a night out.

I was again told I was depressed. Prozac initially helped me think and feel better. Then like many of the medications I'd tried, it stopped working. I seemed to be spiraling further and further downward.

I had to take an early retirement from my job. I was losing everything I had worked for.

I read an article about Dr. Murphree and his fibromyalgia program. I had run out of options. I felt that he was my last hope, and I told him so. I started the program and faithfully did all the therapies recommended by the doctors at the clinic. The first thing that improved was my sleep. I finally began to sleep through the night or at least get five–six hours of refreshing sleep.

I think the vitamin formulas have made a huge difference. If I forget to take them for a few days, the pain and fatigue start to return. I'm not 100% better, but I'm getting my life back; I have a social life again. I'm even thinking about going back to work part-time.

JULIA'S STORY

I had always been a very active person. I played tennis and golf and was a cheerleader in college. After graduation, I married and started my career in publishing. I became pregnant the first year of our marriage. Another child followed two years later. Over the next 10 years, I worked my way up to a prominent position. I did this while raising a family and maintaining an active social life.

I remember coming down with the flu and not being able to shake it. I was prescribed antibiotics and bed rest. I stayed home and took three sick days, something I rarely do. I was exhausted, and every muscle in my body hurt. I somehow managed to go back to work. I still felt terrible and would have to go right to bed when I got home. I went back to my family doctor, and he ran dozens of tests over a period of two months. Nothing showed up on my lab work.

I was getting worse and started missing a good deal of work. My marriage was strained from the stress of almost a year of poor health. I mean, I couldn't even take the trash out to the curb without becoming totally exhausted. I was referred to a rheumatologist, who ordered dozens of tests, all of which came back normal. He then told me I had fibromyalgia. I had never heard of it. He said they weren't sure what caused it and that there was very little that could be done for it. Most of what he recommended I'd either tried or was already on.

He prescribed for me Celebrex, hydrocodone, Neurontin, Zanaflex, and physical therapy. At first I seemed to be a little better. After a couple of weeks, I started getting terrible stomach pains. The doctor said it was probably due to the Celebrex, so I stopped taking it. Then I started having more and more trouble just waking up in the morning, so no more Zanaflex. I couldn't sleep and was prescribed Ambien. This helped, and I didn't feel so groggy in the morning.

One day I was watching the news when they started talking about a local clinic that specialized in treating fibromyalgia. I went to a talk and realized everything Dr. Murphree said was true. I began the program in October, and by January, I was back at work. I still don't have the stamina I once did, but I don't pass out from exhaustion and pain at the end of the day. I know I'll always need to monitor my stress, eat right, and take the supplements Dr. Murphree recommends. If I try to do too much, I'm reminded that I have fibromyalgia. But otherwise I feel good most of the time!

THE CAREGIVER

Type-Bs might not be as busy as type-As, but they are just as taxed. They spend considerable time and energy taking care of friends and loved ones. These nurturers take care of their spouses, children, extended family, and friends. Their lives revolve around the daily challenges of those they look after. They may have an invalid living in the home or be continuously running back and forth between the hospital and nursing home. They often struggle late into the night to get everything done.

They at first like to be needed and will take on more and more of the responsibilities of caring for others. Like type-As, they can't or won't say no when asked to help do more. They take satisfaction in helping others. They feel a sense of duty that makes them continue to give more and more. They expend so much energy helping others that they leave no time for themselves. The constant emotional strain takes its toll on their marriage. They can't go out to dinner, parties (too tired), or vacation: "Who'll look after mom while we're gone?" Finally, and it's inevitable, these individuals break down.

VICKI'S STORY

About six years ago, I started getting chronic sinus infections. I was treated with cortisone shots and antibiotics. I'd have four or five infections a year and they'd hang on for weeks at a time, no matter how many shots or pills I'd take. Each time I'd take antibiotics, I'd get a raging yeast infection. I started having lots of stomach problems, bloating, gas, and pain. Two years ago, I developed pneumonia and was hospitalized. I was given more steroids and antibiotics.

My mother had recently died and then my father had a stroke. He had come to live with us and needed around-the-clock attention. I couldn't leave him but for a few hours at a time. My husband tried to get me to agree to hiring full-time sitters, but I just couldn't bring myself to do that. We were in and out of the hospital many times, but dad always managed to bounce back. My teenage daughter had a bad car accident, and she too was in and out of doctors' offices for over a year.

From that time on, I had one infection after another. I felt like I had the flu. I was totally exhausted. I'd been to dozens of different doctors, but none of them could tell me what was wrong. Instead they'd recommend more and more drugs and then refer me to another specialist. I had CAT scans, MRIs, nerve tests, tons of different blood tests. All my tests came back normal. I was beginning to think I was just crazy; I know my family already thought so. My father died, and then there was the funeral and the estate to look after. I got through this and was actually looking forward to getting my life back when my chronic sinus infections turned into pneumonia. I was never the same. I've been sick every day for over six years.

Dr. Murphree told me I had chronic fatigue syndrome. He explained how my autonomic nervous system had been overwhelmed by the years of chronic stress. My immune system had stopped working like it should. I was placed on an elimination diet, 5HTP, and the FMS/CFS formula. Each week I seem to be getting stronger, feeling better.

ABIGAIL'S STORY

I've been a nurse for over 20 years. The last seven years, I was the head nurse for the critical care unit at a large well known hospital. I was responsible for overseeing dozens of nurses, nursing aids, and medical technologists. We had the sickest of the sick patients. I enjoyed my work. It was demanding and stressful but rewarding.

Many of our patients didn't make it out of CCU, and the constant threat of death was too much for many of the nurses who rotated through my department. Sometimes we'd get close to a patient and to the family, only to watch the patient die.

Until last year, I thought I'd be happy to stay in this position for another 20 years. But now I can't seem to muster up the energy needed to sustain me through the 10–12 hour days. It seems I've lost something; I don't know what. I'm sick a lot. I feel like I've got a terrible case of the flu that just won't go away. None of the doctors I've seen can tell me what's wrong with me. I'm on several medications but don't feel any better. I wonder if I'll ever be healthy again.

Even as you learn to appreciate and value your own personality type, don't let it be the death of your health. Chronic stress, unmanaged, is the number one cause of health problems in the US today. We learn at an early age that successful people are very busy; they're doers. Our society has forgotten how to take it easy. But just remember that we're not human doings, we're human beings. No matter what your productivity level, take plenty of time to relax and just be.

4

Treating with Conventional Medicine

"Today's standard, AMA-approved medicine is roofed in treating symptoms, rather than causes. Its dependence on drugs and surgery is ruinously expensive to patients, insurance companies, and society as a whole." —Derrick Lonsdale, MD, Why I Left Orthodox Medicine

Traditional medical treatments of FMS and CFS focus on controlling the various symptoms. Physicians generally rely on several different prescription medications, including pain medications of various sorts, muscle relaxers and tranquilizers, antidepressants, and nonsteroidal anti-inflammatory medicines.

PAIN MEDICATIONS

- **Ultram (Tramadol)** is a nonaddictive pain medication. It acts on the central nervous system to reduce mild to moderate pain. It seems to work best when taken on a regular basis rather than as needed. Primary side effects include nausea, vomiting, and fatigue.

- **Oxycodone hydrochloride** is a narcotic that is present, usually along with acetaminophen, in various medications. Oxycodone is a respiratory depressant, and it affects the central nervous system. It can affect liver function and should be used with caution. It may cause sleepiness, fatigue, and poor concentration. Its most common side effects include light-headedness, dizziness, nausea, loss of appetite, and addiction. Drugs containing oxycodone hydrochloride include Percocet, Tylenol with Codeine, Lortab, Lorcet, Vicodin, Percodan (contains aspirin, oxycodone hydrochloride, and oxycodone), and OxyContin.

MUSCLE RELAXERS, TRANQUILIZERS, AND SLEEPING MEDICATIONS

- **Trazadone (desyrel)** is an antidepressant that increases serotonin levels, reduces anxiety, and promotes deep sleep. I've found this drug to be quite helpful when 5HTP or melatonin doesn't work. It can cause an early morning hangover, however.

- **Elavil (amitriptyline)** is an antidepressant now synonymous with treating FMS. It was one of the first drugs to be studied in the treatment of FMS. It can be very helpful in reducing pain, but it has several potential unwanted side effects: weight gain, early morning hangover, neurally mediated hypotension (low blood pressure), and irregular heartbeat.

- **Zanaflex (tizanidine)** is a muscle relaxer usually prescribed for uncontrollable spasms. This medication is very sedating and so is usually taken at night. It has gained some favor from various physicians who treat FMS, especially rheumatologists, because it can help with insomnia. But about one in 20 patients develop liver inflammation, and at least three people have died from liver failure, after taking Zanaflex. Needless to say, it should be avoided by those who suffer from liver dysfunction. Most CFS and FMS patients at least have a sluggish liver and should avoid the drug. I haven't seen patients do as well on this medication as others, especially since it doesn't help increase serotonin levels but only tranquilizes the nervous system. Side effects include dry mouth, sleepiness, fatigue, and weakness. It can also produce nightmares. Like all tranquilizers, Zanaflex can leave a person feeling hungover the next day.

- **Unisom (doxylamine)** is an over-the-counter antihistamine.

- **Benedryl** is an over-the-counter antihistamine.

- **Skelaxin (metaxalon)** is a nonsedating muscle relaxer. Patients and most doctors like the fact that it doesn't cause fatigue, but it might not be as effective as other, more sedating muscle relaxers.

- **Neurontin (gabapentin)** is an anticonvulsant medication originally used to control seizures. It helps improve the actions of gamma-aminobutyric acid (GABA), the major brain neurotransmitter inhibitor. This medication is now being used to block nerve-related pain. It has several side effects, including dizziness, weakness, fatigue, double vision, abnormal eyeball movement, tremors, weight gain, back pain, constipation, muscle aches, memory loss, depression, abnormal thinking, itching, twitching, and runny nose.

- **Soma (carisprodol)** is a tranquilizer that acts on the central nervous system to relax muscles. It's used as a sleep aid and muscle relaxer. The most common complaint is its sedating nature. It can be helpful, especially if there is a great deal of muscle guarding or chronic unrelenting tightness. Side effects include fatigue, rapid heartbeat, dizziness, depression, breathing difficulties, chest tightness, and trembling.

- **Flexeril (cyclobenzaprine)** is a muscle relaxer chemically similar to the antidepressant Elavil. It is sometimes used as a sleep aid. Unlike many of the prescription medications for sleep, Flexeril does allow the patient to go into deep stage four (restorative) sleep. It is quite sedating. Side effects, including gastritis and a feeling of being hungover or "out of touch," prevent most patients from remaining on this drug for very long.

- **Baclofen (lioresal)** is a muscle relaxer similar to the natural neurotransmitter GABA. Side effects include fatigue, drowsiness, low blood pressure, weakness, dizziness, nausea, headache, depression, weight gain, and insomnia.

- **Ambien (zolpidem tartate)** is a short-acting, nonbenzodiazepine sleeping medication that doesn't act as a muscle relaxer and usually lasts for four–six hours. Recommended use is for 7–10 days. If a patients take a half-dose before bed, he can take an additional half-dose if needed four–six hours later. Literature on Ambien suggests patients don't build up a tolerance. But some do build up tolerance, needing higher and higher doses until the medicine no longer works. Unlike most muscle relaxers (benzodiazepines), Ambien allows a person to go into deep stage four (restorative) sleep. It rarely produces an early morning hangover. This drug, like most drugs, is processed by the liver, so those with sluggish liver function should use this medication with caution. Most common side effects include dizziness and diarrhea. Some patients complain of loss of coordination or concentration. Ambien has caused amnesia (short-term memory loss), but this happens mostly at doses exceeding 10 mg. Patients are cautioned against abruptly stopping the medicine, since withdrawal symptoms commonly occur. Ambien may cause fatigue, headache, anxiety, difficulty sleeping, and memory loss.

- **Buspar (buspirone)** is a mild tranquilizer and antianxiety medication. Most common side effects include lightheadedness, drowsiness, fatigue, excitability, nervousness, and headaches.

- **Klonopin (klonazepam)** is an anticonvulsant/ antianxiety medication that can be used for seizure disorders. It is often prescribed to treat FMS and can be helpful for restless leg syndrome. It is, however, very sedating. Tolerance to the medication commonly occurs within three months. It is also quite addictive. Withdrawal symptoms, including severe seizures, tremors, abdominal or muscle cramps, and vomiting, are not unusual. Klonopin doesn't produce deep stage four (restorative) sleep, and I've not found it to be as effective as Ambien or Trazadone. Common side effects include poor muscle control, drowsiness, and behavioral changes.

- **Xanax (alprazolam)** is a benzodiazepine tranquilizer usually used to treat anxiety, but it can provide four to five hours of deep sleep. A relative of Valium, this tranquilizer is relatively short-acting. It can be addictive, and patients may build up a tolerance so that it eventually loses it effectiveness as a sleep aid. Common side effects include drowsiness, weakness, fatigue, and mental confusion. Depression, headache, low blood pressure, insomnia, and fluid retention are less common side effects.

- **Sonata (zaleplon)** is a good choice for those who wake up in the middle of the night and can't get back to sleep. It is designed to last for only four hours, and this helps prevent early morning hangover. I've not found it to be very effective with my patients, since most of them have trouble getting to sleep as well as waking up during the night. But it can be helpful for those FMS/CFS patients who take a natural remedy like 5HTP that works for only a few hours.

ANTIDEPRESSANTS

Selective Serotonin Re-Uptake Inhibitors (SSRIs)

SSRIs work by increasing the brain's use of the neurotransmitter serotonin. Serotonin deficiency is linked to depression, lowered pain tolerance, poor sleep, and mental fatigue.

All SSRIs are partially or wholly broken down in the liver. This can create liver dysfunction in some patients. Patients with a sluggish liver should be cautious in taking these medications. Milk thistle and other natural liver supplements should be used by anyone taking these medications.

Most common side effects include headache, anxiety, nervousness, sleeplessness, drowsiness, weakness, changes in sex drive, tremors, dry mouth, irritated stomach, loss of appetite, dizziness, nausea, rash, and itching.

Examples of SSRIs include: Zoloft (sertraline), Paxil (paroxetine HCL), Celexa (citalopram), Prozac (fluoxetine), Luvox (fluvoxamine), Desyrel (trazadone), Wellbutrin (bupropion HCL), and Effexor (venlafaxine).

- **Desyrel (trazadone)** is chemically different from other antidepressants. It is an older drug that doesn't receive the kind of attention that surrounds the newer SSRIs. It works just as well, though, and without as many side effects as other antidepressant medications. I've seen it be very effective in FMS patients. It can be extremely helpful in promoting deep stage four (restorative) sleep. Most common side effects include upset stomach, constipation, bad taste in the mouth, heartburn, diarrhea, rash, rapid heartbeat, mental confusion, hostility, swelling in the arms or legs, dizziness, nightmares, drowsiness, and fatigue.

- **Wellbutrin (bupropion HCL)** is usually reserved for major depression. It increases the neurotransmitters serotonin, epinephrine, and dopamine. Some of the more common side effects include seizures, dry mouth, rapid heartbeat, headache (including migraines), sleeplessness, loss of concentration, and fatigue.

- **Effexor (venlafaxine)** is chemically different from other antidepressants. It helps the brain hold onto serotonin, epinephrine, and dopamine. Most common side effects include blurred vision, fatigue, dry mouth, sleeplessness, nervousness, tremors, weakness, nausea, constipation, loss of appetite, and vomiting.

Tricyclic Antidepressants

Tricyclic antidepressants block the stimulate hormones serotonin and norepinephrine. This produces a sedative effect. They also reduce the effects of the hormone acetylcholine.

Like other antidepressant medications, these drugs are processed by the liver and can cause liver toxicity. Most common side effects include sedation (they are usually used at night and for insomnia), confusion, blurred vision, muscle spasms or tremors, dry mouth, convulsions, constipation, difficulty in urinating, and sensitivity to light. Examples of tricyclic antidepressants include Pamelor (nortriptyline) and Elavil (amitriptyline).

- **Elavil (amitriptyline)** is used to treat insomnia related to depression. It can also be useful for individuals who have insomnia associated with FMS/CFS. Elavil is very sedating and typically produces a deep stage four (restorative) sleep. Unfortunately, it can cause severe fatigue.

For information on natural tranquilizers, see chapter 13 and our Brain Function Profile on page 257.

NONSTEROIDAL ANTI-INFLAMMATORY DRUGS

- **Relafen (Nambumetone)** can cause gastrointestinal (GI) bleeding, ulcers, and stomach perforation.

- **Celebrex (Celecoxib)** is a new breed of NSAID, designed to prevent the side effects associated with older COX-2 inhibitors. Unfortunately many patients taking Celebrex report GI problems. This medication is processed by the liver. One in 250,000 patients taking Celebrex develops serious stomach and intestinal problems. Stomach perforation, GI bleeding, and ulcers are some side effects.

- **Vioxx (Rofecoxib)** is another COX-2 inhibitor. Common side effects include respiratory infection, GI bleeding, ulcers, diarrhea, and nausea. Research in laboratory animals indicates that COX-2 inhibitors may be dangerous for those with heart disease. Studies have shown Vioxx users to have twice the number of heart attacks as those taking Naproxen. These new drugs may promote excessive blood clot formation by narrowing the blood vessels.

- **Naproxen and naproxen sodium** work by blocking the body's production of a hormone called prostaglandin, as well as COX-2 and COX-1 (Naproxen primarily blocks COX-1). Unfortunately, they block the good and bad prostaglandins. They can also cause stomach perforation, GI bleeding, and ulcers. Examples include Aleve, Anaprox, and Naprosyn. Mobic (meloxican) is an NSAID that acts much like these medicines.

LIMITATIONS OF DRUG TREATMENT

Prescription medications can be invaluable for those with acute and chronic illnesses. Unfortunately most drugs have unwanted side effects. So sometimes the cure can be worse than the disease. Studies now show that complications from prescription medications kill over 100,000 people a year. These complications are the fourth leading cause of death in the United States! Only heart disease, cancer, and accidents claim more lives each year.

Drugs can be helpful, but long-term use by those with chronic illnesses can lead to dependence and further complications. Short-term use to mask unwanted symptoms is certainly justified and appreciated by both the patient and the doctor. But FMS and CFS don't develop from a deficiency of pain medicine; they are caused by a body's inability to maintain homeostasis (a healthy balance). This cause must be addressed, not merely cloaked by chemicals.

In addition, many of the side effects of these drugs are similar or identical to the symptoms of FMS and CFS. These similarities can cause confusion when trying to determine the effectiveness of treatment. Look back over the drug descriptions above. Do some of the side effects sound familiar? They might be the very symptoms from which you suffer! So how will you be able to know whether or not the drugs are working? Figuring it out can be quite frustrating.

I believe prescription medications serve a valuable role in today's health care. I also feel that those with chronic illnesses including FMS and CFS can and do benefit from taking prescription medications. The medical doctors at Advanced Family Medicine do use prescription medications when needed. Not everyone can be drug free, and most of our patients are on at least one prescription medication. However, I also feel it's best to use drugs judiciously. Drug therapy in and of itself will not correct all the symptoms of FMS and CFS. If it did, everyone would get well, and there would be no reason to be reading this book.

Conventional medicine is at its best when treating life-threatening illnesses. Its technology never ceases to amaze me: CAT scans, MRIs, SPECT scans, laser surgery, and medications that save the lives of millions. However, conventional medicine has overstepped its bounds, attempting to find a "magic bullet" for every illness that arises. There are antidepressant medicines for the depressed, tranquilizers for the anxious, sleeping pills for the insomniac. Unfortunately, drugs don't correct the root causes of depression, anxiety, and insomnia. The same is true for numerous other illnesses.

Prozac, for instance, is helpful as it increases the brain's ability to effectively use serotonin. But what originally caused the brain to suffer serotonin deficiency? Most likely, it was years of unchecked stress and a poor (including low-fat) diet. So let's address those problems first. Also, ask the question, how is serotonin made? It's produced from the amino acid tryptophan, in combination with certain synergistic nutrients. So why not try increasing a person's tryptophan intake? It's a natural solution that's risk- and side effect-free. Are you getting the picture?

A study conducted by the Mayo Foundation for Medical Education and Research demonstrates the need for FMS and CFS treatment beyond drug therapy. Thirty-nine patients with FMS were interviewed about their symptoms. Twenty-nine were interviewed again 10 years later. Of these 29 (mean age 55 at second interview), all had persistence of the same FMS symptoms. Moderate to severe pain or stiffness was reported in 55% of patients, moderate to a great deal of sleep difficulty was noted in 48%, and moderate to extreme fatigue was noted in 59%. These symptoms showed little change from earlier surveys. The surprising finding was that 79% of the patients were still taking medications to control symptoms. We can conclude that the medications weren't making a significant impact.[1]

NUTRITIONAL AND HERBAL MEDICINE

Natural medicine uses naturally occurring foods, vitamins, minerals, amino acids, essential fatty acids, and herbal supplements to augment the nutritional status and therefore the health of the body.

Herbs have always been integral to the practice of medicine. The word "drug" comes from the Old Dutch word *drogge,* meaning "to dry," because pharmacists, physicians, and ancient healers often dried plants for use as medicines. Today approximately 25% of all prescription medications are derived from trees, shrubs, or herbs.

The World Health Organization notes that of the 119 plant-derived pharmaceutical medicines, about 74% are used in modern medicine in ways that correlate directly to their traditional uses by native cultures. Yet for the most part, modern medicine has ignored the potential benefits of using pure herbs in treating disease. The simple reason? Money. Herbs are naturally available, and their use can't be patented by drug companies. Without exclusive patents, these companies can't reap profits over the millions of dollars it takes to bring a product to market. The cost of proving a new treatment safe is over 200 million dollars. What drug company would fund such research when the results could make their synthetic drugs obsolete?

Consequently, Americans have been conditioned to rely on synthetic, commercial drugs to provide quick relief, regardless of the potential side effects. This paradigm seems to be changing as our country is starting to mirror the European model of treatment with herbals and natural therapeutics. In Germany, the Ministry of Health has a separate commission that deals exclusively with herbal medicine. German doctors study herbal medicine in medical school, and since 1993, all physicians in Germany must pass a section on these medicines in their board exams before becoming licensed. European physicians, health professionals, and researchers have formed the European Scientific Cooperative for Phytotherapy (ESCOP). This organization publishes monographs on individual herbs used in clinical medicine. These monographs, representing the culmination of all the scientific information known on each herb, are published in the *European Pharmacopoeia*.

In general, herbal medicines are somewhat slower acting than today's rapid, intense conventional drugs. But they work in much the same way: via their chemical makeup. Herbs contain a large number of naturally occurring chemicals that have biological activity. In the past 150 years, chemists and pharmacists have been isolating and purifying the active compounds from plants in an attempt to produce reliable pharmaceutical drugs. Examples include digoxin, from foxglove (digitalis purpurea), resperine from Indian snakeroot, and morphine from the opium poppy.

The common assumption that herbs are slow to act and therefore free of potential side effects, is not true. Herbal medicines should be prescribed by a professional who is familiar with the actions and interactions of herbals and prescription medications. It should be noted that even with the potential for side effects, herbals have an extremely large window of safety, especially when compared to synthetic prescription drugs.

Most US medical schools are still woefully deficient in training physicians in nutrition. This is beginning to change as more and more physicians begin to take and prescribe nutritional supplements. It's estimated that over 80% of the population takes at least one nutritional supplement a day. Sales of nutritional supplements have contributed to the 27 billion dollar natural health industry. With this much money involved, it is no wonder many of the large pharmaceutical companies that were opposed to nutritional supplements have started marketing their own line of vitamins, minerals, and herbals.

Notes
[1]Source: www.lef.org
[2]Source: *Bulletin of the World Health Organization,* 1985

For Further Reading
- *Herbal Prescriptions for Health and Healing: Your Everyday Guide to Using Herbs Safely and Effectively* by Don Brown; 2000
- *Why I Left Orthodox Medicine: Healing for the 21st Century* by Derrick Lonsdale, MD; 1994
- *The Pill Book,* 10th edition by Harold M. Silverman; 2002
- *Professional's Handbook of Complementary and Alternative Medicines* by Charles W. Fetrow and Juan R. Avila; 2001
- *Essential Guide to Psychiatric Drugs* by Jack M.Gorman, MD; 1998

5

The Bucket and the Onion: What Causes FMS/CFS

There is no one cause of fibromyalgia or chronic fatigue syndrome. Myriad causes combine to create a toxic environment where a healthy body slowly degenerates into illness.

AN OVERFLOWING BUCKET

A colleague of mine uses the analogy of everyone being born with a bucket. The size of your bucket is determined by whom you picked as parents (genetics). As you go through life, you're constantly dumping toxins into your bucket: too much work, not enough sleep, trauma, car accidents, poor diet, weight gain, yo-yo diets, junk food, pesticides, allergies, chronic infections, overdependence on prescription medication, alcohol, caffeine, nicotine, emotional distress, pollution. I'm sure you can think of other stressful things that have gone into your bucket: the death of a loved one, divorce, too many antibiotics, unhappy work situation, financial troubles. The bucket keeps filling up until one day, it overflows and spills all over your life.

Many of our patients can remember the day when their bucket overflowed. It might have been after an illness, a trauma, surgery, or an emotional crisis. Patients report that they were never the same again. Try as they might, they can't get well. When they *do* get enough rest or the bucket stops over-flowing, they often attempt to do something as mundane as sweep the kitchen floor, only to be wiped out once again. (Forget about grocery shopping; that could put them in bed for weeks.) There just isn't any room left in the bucket.

Sound hopeless? It's not. There is a way to get your life back, a way to reduce or even eliminate most of the toxins you've stored up for years. But cleaning out the bucket takes time. A handful of pills won't do it. Neither will any one therapy by itself.

FMS and CFS are results of internal biochemical (hormonal, enzymatic, neuronal, and chemical) imbalances that manifest themselves as physical symptoms (pain, weakness, and mental impairment). In order to correct the homeostatic (self-regulating) system you must correct the underlying biochemical problems. How do you do this? Just like with an onion, you peel away one layer at a time until you get to the core. We must start with the most significant symptom first—this is usually sleep dysfunction. Then we'll peel the other layers away, one at a time.

All people are born with the ability to heal themselves. When operating at peak performance, their homeostatic mechanism corrects any and all imbalances. So our ultimate goal is to get the body's own innate healing ability to return to normal.

THE LAYERS OF THE ONION

Your symptoms might be the result of one or many related causes. These might include but aren't limited to:
   • emotional, physical, and/or mental stress

   • dysautonomia

   • dysfunction of the hypothalamus gland

   • dehydration

   • low human growth hormone and DHEA

   • decreased cortisol

   • low ovarian or testicular function

   • hypothyroidism

   • intestinal permeability (leaky gut syndrome)

- malabsorption syndrome
- environmental toxins
- nutritional deficiencies
- parasites
- food allergies and hypersensitivity
- yeast overgrowth
- trauma
- depression
- chronic viral or bacterial infections
- inadequate sleep
- liver dysfunction
- adrenal dysfunction
- serotonin deficiencies

In addition, FMS and CFS seem to run in some families, but no genetic component has yet been identified.

EMOTIONAL, PHYSICAL, AND MENTAL STRESS

German physician Dr. Hans Seyle demonstrated that under normal conditions, the body is able to use its homeostatic mechanisms (internal regulatory system) to counter and cope with various stresses. However, these same mechanisms can be overwhelmed by too much stress. A person can then develop various symptoms associated with burnout. Burnout doesn't have to result from a major catastrophe. Many minor stresses—each too small to trigger an alarm reaction within the body—can lead to debilitating illness when combined or sustained.

Stress is not itself a negative thing. It is a person's response to mental, biochemical, emotional, and physical challenges that determines whether the results of the stress are positive or negative. We wouldn't get very far without some amount of stress. For instance, without the stress (fear) of losing a job or of being thrown out of school, some people wouldn't get out of bed in the morning. But some individuals handle stress better than others. Some type-As are walking time bombs for burnout. Other people seem to thrive on the adrenaline rush of constant stress. For those suffering from FMS and CFS, any additional stress makes their symptoms worse. So limiting and managing stress is one of the most important steps toward overcoming these syndromes.

DYSAUTONOMIA

Dysautonomia is a malfunction in the body's autonomic nervous system, which sustains homeostasis (balance) in the body. The autonomic nervous system controls such involuntary and subconscious reactions as breathing, endocrine hormone release, blood flow, smooth muscle tone, immune response, heartbeat, detoxification, and elimination. We don't have to think about breathing; we just do it. We don't concentrate on pumping blood through the heart and into the muscles; it is initiated and monitored by the autonomic nervous system, which controls millions of bodily functions.

Normally all the systems in the body coordinate with one another. It's as if they all speak the same language. But when the autonomic nervous system becomes dysfunctional, the immune system starts to speak in Spanish, the endocrine system in German, the musculoskeletal system in Greek, the digestive system in French. And there are no translators to set it all straight! Since the systems are all supposed to work together, a malfunction in one sets off a chain reaction, and they all become, to some degree, dysfunctional.

The autonomic nervous system is controlled by the hypothalamus gland. This gland helps maintain water balance, sugar and fat metabolism, body temperature, and various hormones. Improper functioning of the hypothalamus can cause a variety of problems, including neurally mediated hypotension (NMH), which causes blood pressure to drop suddenly upon standing. This drop in pressure can result in dizziness and weakness.

To check for NMH, your doctor might suggest a tilt-table test. This procedure is painless but expensive. You can easily check for the condition this way: have someone check your blood pressure while you are calm and lying down. Then stand up. After 30 seconds, take your blood pressure again. Normally the systolic (top number) pressure will go up 10 or more points. A decrease in the systolic number indicates adrenal dysfunction and dysautonomia. If a person has mitral valve prolapse, NMH, and a positive adrenal dysfunction test, dysautonomia is probably the cause.

DYSFUNCTION OF THE HYPOTHALAMUS

The hypothalamus gland controls the activity of most other glands in the body. Though small, it coordinates a phenomenal portion of the body's activity. Because of its broad sphere of influence, the hypothalamus could be considered the homeostatic regulating center. It regulates appetite and monitors blood sugar, blood volume (fluid level within the circulatory system), and metabolism. It's the coordinating center for much of the autonomic nervous system.

The hypothalamus also releases several different chemicals, including the stress-related hormones epinephrine, norepinephrine, and corticosteroids. The hypothalamus also has immunologic functions, and any dysfunction of this gland may interfere with immunity.

Dr. Leon Chaitow writes about how the hypothalamus, pituitary, and adrenal glands are connected, and discusses a chemical known as substance P, a neurotransmitter that increases and enhances pain receptors. Chaitow contends that an imbalance in the glands can result in an increase in substance P, leading to more feelings of pain.[1]

Substance P is normally kept in check by the neurotransmitter serotonin, but FMS patients have little if any serotonin to spare.

Chaitow also notes that imbalances in the glands above can lead to fatigue and to decreased production of growth hormone, so that muscle fibers don't receive proper repair.

DEHYDRATION

Poor hypothalamic function can result in a low level of the hormone vasopressin, which is an antidiuretic. Low levels can cause a decreased ability to hold on to fluid. This can result in frequent urination and increased thirst. Dehydration then occurs, despite increased water intake. I've heard it truly remarked, "How do you tell who has the worst case of FMS or CFS? By the size of her water bottle."

Dehydration can cause many of the chronic symptoms seen in FMS and CFS, including NMH, depression, excess body weight, high blood pressure, fatigue, low back and neck pain, and headache. Dehydration also depletes the neurotransmitter tryptophan. A reduction in tryptophan is associated with insomnia, increased pain, and depression.

According to Dr. Batmanghelidj, 75% of the human body—85% of the brain—is made up of water. Every bodily function is dependent on an adequate supply of water. Water helps transport various elements including nutrients, neurotransmitters, hormones, and other essential chemicals to their destination organs. Any deficiency of water, no matter how small, results in a disruption of essential bodily processes, so symptoms associated with disease states may respond quickly to increased water intake.[2]

LOW HUMAN GROWTH HORMONE AND DHEA

When hypothalamic function suffers, human growth hormone (HGH) levels begin to drop. This also causes low levels of dehydroepiandrosterone (DHEA), a hormone produced by the adrenal glands. DHEA is used by the body to make other hormones, including estrogen and testosterone. DHEA is important in creating appropriate energy levels and maintaining feelings of well-being. HGH helps increase energy, repair damaged muscles, stimulate immune function, reduce body fat, improve sleep, and enhance mental acuity (especially short-term memory).

> "Long-term studies show GH [HGH] deficiency to be consistently associated with extreme impairment of psychological well being. Patients in these studies typically exhibit similar symptoms, including lack of energy, optimism, and "zest for life"....They report difficulty with memory, concentration, and motivation." —*Growth Hormone: The Methuselah Factor* by James Jamieson and Dr. L.E. Dorman, with Valerie Marriott

The best way to increase HGH levels is to get eight hours of deep sleep each night. Other options are HGH replacement injections (available by prescription) and exercise. There are also over-the-counter supplements that can help boost HGH levels. To order HGH supplements, see page 274.

DECREASED CORTISOL

Adrenal exhaustion depletes cortisol, an adrenal stress hormone. Low levels of cortisol can cause immune dysfunction, increased inflammation, hypoglycemia (low blood sugar), hypotension (low blood pressure), and fatigue.

LOW OVARIAN OR TESTICULAR FUNCTION

Low estrogen can contribute to decreased blood flow to specific areas in the brain. This may explain some fibro fog. Low testosterone, both in males and females, can cause immune dysfunction. Research is now showing that males who have low testosterone have an increased risk of heart disease.

HYPOTHYROIDISM

The symptoms of FMS and CFS are consistent with those associated with low thyroid function: low body temperature, cold hands and feet, tingling in the extremities, fatigue, depression, and decreased mental acuity. Recent studies show that over 43% of FMS patients have low thyroid function. It's estimated that those with FMS are 10 to 250,000 times more likely to suffer from thyroid dysfunction. For more information, see chapter 19.

INTESTINAL PERMEABILITY (LEAKY GUT SYNDROME)

Most of the individuals I evaluate are plagued by poor digestion and detoxification systems. Intestinal permeability occurs when the lining of the small intestine becomes irritated and leaks undigested proteins across the cellular membrane. This is like turning on your garden hose and watching helplessly as water leaks from small holes placed along the length of the hose. The leaked proteins are potentially hazardous and can trigger allergic reactions. These allergic irritants initiate an immune reaction associated with chronic inflammation.

MALABSORPTION SYNDROME

With this syndrome, many of the nutrients needed to make the body work in an optimal manner are simply not absorbed. Deficiency of these vital nutrients leads to depression, insomnia, fatigue, pain, decreased immunity, poor memory, and other ill effects.

ENVIRONMENTAL TOXINS

The body eliminates toxins either by directly neutralizing them or by excreting them in the urine, feces, lungs (breathing), and skin (sweat). The liver, intestines, and kidneys are the primary organs of detoxification. Detoxification of harmful substances is a never-ending process.

The ability to detoxify and eliminate toxins largely determines an individual's level of health. Toxins that the body is unable to eliminate build up in tissue, especially fat cells. A number of toxins, including heavy metals, pesticides, solvents, and microbial toxins are known to cause significant health problems. Most individuals with FMS/CFS suffer from an overburden of toxins. For more information, see chapter 18.

NUTRITIONAL DEFICIENCIES

Some "health experts" have stated, "If you eat a balanced diet you'll get all the nutrients you need." Individuals who continue to cling to this draconian idea haven't read the research over the past 20 years. The standard American diet (even if you eat fruits and vegetables every day) is loaded with toxic chemicals, and modern processing removes 25–75% of original nutrients.

An FDA study analyzing more than 230 foods over a two-year period found the average American diet to have less than 80% of the RDA of one or more of the following: calcium, magnesium, iron, zinc, copper, and manganese.

> Other studies have demonstrated magnesium deficiency in well over 50% of the population. A magnesium deficiency can contribute to arteriolosclerosis, fatigue, tight muscles, leg cramps, insomnia, constipation, cardiac arrhythmia, and heart disease.

One important nutrient that can cause big problems is vitamin B6. Vitamin B6 deficiency is more damaging to immune function than a deficiency of any other B vitamin. This is because a deficiency of B6 results in the loss of cell mediated immunity. This leads to a reduction in the size and weight of the thymus gland, an important part of the immune system. When it shrinks or is compromised, the total number of lymphocytes (white blood cells) decreases.

Vitamin B6 deficiencies are common in women of childbearing age. The female hormones, estrogen and progesterone, tend to consume vitamin B6 during its metabolism in the liver. Women who have had multiple pregnancies or long-term use of birth control pills are at higher risk of developing a B6 deficiency. PMS has been attributed to a B6 deficiency. Vitamin B6 is also a cofactor in producing the neurotransmitter serotonin, so restoring and utilizing optimal levels of serotonin are dependent on adequate quantities of vitamin B6.

It's been found through clinical trials that individuals who do not dream have low levels of B6. It's not necessary to remember what your dreams were, only that you did, in fact, dream the night before to know whether you are deficient in B6. Increasing vitamin B6 (along with 5HTP) usually restores normal circadian rhythm. Some individuals can't adequately break down regular vitamin B6 and will need to take a special form of it known as pyridoxal-5-phosphate (P5P).

Low-fat Diets Can Be Disastrous

Well intentioned health professionals have been recommending low-fat, high-carbohydrate diets for the past 10–15 years. This has been disastrous to our nation's health. Americans are now the most overweight country in the world. While on this so-called healthy diet, the average American has gained over ten pounds. And incidents of heart disease, cancer, and other chronic conditions, including type-2 diabetes, have actually increased.

Why the disastrous results? Because low-fat usually means low-protein, too. And protein deficiency contributes to depression, fatigue, poor concentration, poor detoxification, and many other illnesses. Our bodies simply must have the essential amino acids that comprise a protein. These amino acids regulate our neurotransmitters (brain chemicals), sex hormones, immune system, glucose-insulin levels, wound healing, and thousands of essential bodily functions. High carbohydrate diets are now being implicated as the cause of high cholesterol, heart disease, diabetes, and obesity.

PARASITES

Based on medical records and disease patterns, health experts now claim that 60% of Americans will experience parasitic infections in their lifetime. Over one million Americans are infected with *Ascaris lumbricoides,* also known as roundworms. Twenty to thirty million Americans are infected with *Enterobiusvermicularis,* also known as pinworms. And *Giardia lamblia* infects eight to 10 million Americans. The parasites *Giardia lamblia, Entameba histolytica,* and *Ascaris lumbricoides* are all associated with CFS.

FOOD ALLERGIES AND HYPERSENSITIVITY

Albert Rowe, MD, one of the foremost allergists of this century, described a syndrome known as allergic toxemia, which included the symptoms of fatigue, muscle and joint pain, drowsiness, difficulty in concentrating, nervousness, and depression. This syndrome was known as the allergic tension-fatigue syndrome in the 1950s, but it sounds an awful lot like CFS/FMS.[3]

Hypersensitivity to environmental chemicals is a growing public concern that afflicts an estimated 15% of the US public. Patients with CFS often complain of a heightened sensitivity to environmental chemicals, including odors from cosmetics, perfumes, new carpet, paint, smog, cigarettes, newsprint, copier machines, fabrics, vinyl, household cleaners, and other man-made products.

YEAST OVERGROWTH

Unchecked yeast growth can lead to Candida yeast syndrome. Fatigue, allergies, decreased immunity, chemical sensitivities, depression, poor memory, and digestive complaints are some of the symptoms associated with this illness.

TRAUMA

Recent findings report that people with neck injuries or flexion extension (whiplash) are 13 times more likely to develop fibromyalgia than those with other injuries. Only 21% of those who have experienced whiplash had fibromyalgia within 3.2 months of the accident.

DEPRESSION

Some physicians would lead us to believe that FMS is nothing more than depression. Studies show FMS is not caused by depression, but that FMS does cause reactive depression (depression due to circumstances). Who wouldn't be depressed with such an illness? Individuals with FMS have lost their lives to an illness they can't control and largely don't understand.

CHRONIC VIRAL OR BACTERIAL INFECTIONS

Although infections are more often associated with CFS, remember FMS and CFS are two sides of the same coin. Viral infections, most notably the Epstein-Barr virus, have received most of the attention. However, bacterial, fungal and mycoplasma infections are common in the FMS and CFS patients I treat.

INADEQUATE SLEEP

Non-restorative sleep reduces the production of serotonin and human growth hormone, lowers the pain threshold (more pain is felt), and causes fatigue and mental decline.

LIVER DYSFUNCTION

The liver is the main player in the detoxification of our bodies, protecting us from environmental impurities. But when the liver isn't functioning correctly, we don't rid ourselves of toxic substances that can deplete needed nutrients and leave us vulnerable to illness: FMS, CFS, arthritis, allergies, or other syndromes or diseases. Measuring and uncovering functional weaknesses in the detoxification system can help explain any number of chronic symptoms, including:
- intolerance to certain foods, drinks, smells, or drugs, and to caffeine.
- why you can't drink alcohol or tolerate much if you do.
- why the smell of perfumes, colognes, cigarette smoke, and other environmental chemicals can make you ill.

- why you can't take certain vitamins, especially a multi-vitamin, without feeling nauseated.

- why you can't tolerate most medications (a little goes a long way).

- why some drugs have the opposite effect on you. Sleep medications make you wired.

ADRENAL DYSFUNCTION

The adrenal glands secrete certain hormones that help us manage stress. Chronic stress can lead to adrenal dysfunction, a condition characterized by fatigue, lowered immunity, poor memory, pain, and depression.

SEROTONIN DEFICIENCIES

This neurotransmitter (brain chemical) regulates sleep, mood, mental clarity, and pain perception. A deficiency can lead to insomnia, fatigue, increased pain, depression, and poor mental function.

Notes
[1]Source: *Fibromyalgia and Muscle Pain,* 2001
[2]Source: *Your Body's Many Cries for Water,* 1995
[3]Source: *Food Allergy: Its manifestations and control and the elimination diets: A compendium,* 1972

For Further Reading
- *Textbook of Natural Medicine* by Joseph E. Pizzorno, ND, (ed.) and Michael T. Murray (ed.); 1999
- *Total Wellness: Improve Your Health by Understanding the Body's Healing Systems* by Joseph E. Pizzorno, ND; 1996

6

Sweet Dreams at Last!

"Our cells pulse in a rhythm whose timekeeper is the universe as a whole. The flow of intelligence that regulates mind and body in us attends to its own cycles and functions best when these cycles are closely heeded." —Deepak Chopra, MD[1]

The first question I ask new patients is "How are you sleeping at night?" If you don't get a good night's sleep, you're not going to get well. It really is that simple. Most people with FMS/CFS haven't slept well in years. Many of our patients take tranquilizers, muscle relaxers, or over-the-counter sleep aides to get them to sleep. But most of them never go into deep restorative sleep. It is in this deep delta-wave sleep that the body repairs itself. It does this by making human growth hormone (HGH) and other hormones that help repair damaged muscles, tissues, and organs. Deep sleep also builds and rejuvenates the immune system.

Years of poor sleep, on the other hand, create an imbalance within a person's sleep regulatory system known as the circadian rhythm. The longer someone's sleep cycle has been compromised, the longer it usually takes for her to experience lasting symptom relief. But just a few nights of consistent deep sleep will provide a tremendous amount of improvement for most patients. Unfortunately, many sleep medicines are not useful long-term, because they lose their effectiveness over time. It's not uncommon to hear stories like the one below.

Margaret's Story

I'd taken every sleep medicine there is. My doctor said I couldn't sleep because I was depressed. I didn't know why I wasn't sleeping, but I knew I was exhausted. So, even though I didn't think that all of my problems were due to depression, I was willing to try Prozac. It seemed to help for a while. Then after about six months, I was worse than when I started the medicine. I then started Celexa, but it wore off after about three and a half months. I used Elavil for a while. It helped me get to sleep, but I usually felt hungover the next day. I was in a downward spiral that I couldn't escape.

I consulted a rheumatologist for my pain, and he diagnosed me with fibromyalgia. He prescribed Ambien for my insomnia and Zanaflex for my pain. I felt better for a while—maybe a couple of weeks. But the medicines made me feel drugged out.

The Ambien worked for several months, but then I started needing a higher and higher dose. Finally it also stopped working. I then tried Sonata, but it would only work for four hours. I'd wake up at 3:00 in the morning—wide awake—and wouldn't be able to go back to sleep.

I walked around for four years totally exhausted and in so much pain. I was losing all hope until I tried 5HTP. It, along with the other supplements Dr. Murphree recommended, allowed me to consistently fall asleep and wake feeling rested.

After about a month, I noticed my constant pain was getting better. It was less of an issue. I actually had energy to go shopping and fix dinner. I used to have so much anxiety about going to sleep. The closer it got to bedtime the more worried I got that I wouldn't be able to get to sleep. Now I simply take my 5HTP and in 30 minutes, I'm sound asleep.

A GOOD NIGHT'S SLEEP

We've all heard that we need eight hours of restful sleep each night. The amount of sleep an individual actually needs will vary from person to person. A five-year-old might need 11–12 hours of sleep; an adult, 7–9 hours of sleep. But why is a good night's sleep so important? Poor sleep has been linked to various health problems including depression, fatigue, CFS, FMS, and headaches. This is not news to those who suffer from FMS and CFS. They already know that their symptoms get worse when they don't get a good night's sleep.

One study showed that college students who were prevented from going into deep (REM) sleep for a week developed the same symptoms associated with FMS and CFS: diffuse pain, fatigue, depression, anxiety, irritability, stomach disturbances, and headache.

Another study, conducted by the University of Connecticut School of Medicine, compared the sleep patterns and associated symptoms of fifty women with FMS. The study showed that a poor night's sleep was followed by an increase in the subjects' symptoms, including body pain. Sadly, the study also showed that a poor night's sleep, followed by an increase in symptoms, then went on to prevent the person from getting a good night's sleep the next night, even though the subject was exhausted. This cycle continues and creates a pattern of declining health.[2]

SLEEP CYCLES

There are two types of sleep: REM (rapid eye movement) sleep and non-REM sleep. During REM sleep, the eyes—still closed—rapidly move back and forth as dreaming takes place.

Non-REM sleep is divided into four stages; stage four is the deepest and is crucial for overall well-being. Stages one and two, while important in maintaining the correct sleep cycle, don't provide the restorative powers of three and four.

The non-REM sleep cycle begins when we start to fall asleep. The first two stages of non-REM have a faster brainwave pattern—as measured with an electroencephalogram (EEG)—than the second two, and they are considered lighter. As brain activity begins to slow down, we enter into stages three and four of non-REM. This usually occurs one and a half hours after falling asleep. The non-REM cycle is then interrupted by ten minutes of REM sleep. REM sleep then elicits a flurry of brain activity. These cycles occur five to six times a night. The time spent in REM continues to grow and may last up to an hour in the last cycle of sleep.

If you're not dreaming, you're not going into deep sleep. Many of our patients have been on brain-numbing medications that render them brain-dead for eight hours. Most of these powerful sedatives (tranquilizers) don't allow a person to go into deep restorative sleep. So the patients have their eyes closed while they're knocked out for eight hours, but they don't receive the health benefits of deep restorative sleep.

WHAT IS SEROTONIN AND WHY DON'T I HAVE ENOUGH?

Serotonin is the neurotransmitter (brain chemical) responsible for regulating your sleep, raising your pain threshold (decreasing your pain) and elevating your moods.

Poor dietary habits, especially low-fat (often low-protein) diets, is one of the main reasons people suffer from low serotonin. A healthy diet that combines complex carbohydrates, adequate protein, and fatty acids provides the nutrients needed to produce serotonin.

Low-protein diets rob the body of the essential amino acids needed to make serotonin. Low-fat diets deprive your body of essential fatty acids, such as omega 3, 6, and 9. These essential fatty acids allow brain cells to communicate with one another. Low-fat diets also deprive the body of cholesterol. Contrary to popular medical fiction, cholesterol is an important part of overall health and doesn't cause (in and of itself) arteriosclerosis. Cholesterol is essential in maintaining proper hormone production. Testosterone, dehydroepiandrosterone (DHEA), progesterone, estradiol, and cortisol are all made from cholesterol. Cholesterol also plays a major role in brain cell function. Low cholesterol has been linked to certain mood disorders, including depression and anxiety, as well as increased risk for heart attack.

Vitamins and minerals are essential, too, of course. A deficiency of any of the synergistic nutrients magnesium, calcium, and vitamins B_6, B_{12}, B_1, and B_3 will prevent the production of serotonin.

THE INSULIN CONNECTION

The amino acid tryptophan competes for brain absorption along with other, larger amino-acid molecules. Tryptophan is like the little MG Midget sports car competing with the SUVs to enter onto a crowded highway; usually size wins over style. Tryptophan needs a little bit of the hormone insulin (released when we eat carbohydrates) in the bloodstream to help carry it past the blood-brain barrier. Once past this barrier, tryptophan enters the brain and turns into serotonin. This is why so many individuals with low serotonin crave sugar. After eating carbohydrates, especially starches, the body secretes insulin to counter the rise in blood-sugar levels. Insulin then helps pull tryptophan into the brain. This is also why individuals will often eat starches when they're under stress. These starches don't provide the long-term reserves needed to maintain adequate levels of serotonin, but they are very important as part of a healthy diet. So diets too low in calories or carbohydrates—or skipping meals—can cause low serotonin.

STRESS, STIMULANTS, AND SEROTONIN

Stress is another reason people become deficient in serotonin. Emotionally stressful situations cause the body to release adrenaline, cortisol, and insulin. These stress hormones stimulate the brain to secrete serotonin. That's fine, as long as the stress is handled in a timely manner. Long-term stress can deplete the body's serotonin stores. Stress can also deplete the body of magnesium (a common occurrence in FMS and CFS patients) and B6. Vitamin B5 (pantothenic acid) can counter the effects of stress and may help spare magnesium and B6.

Stimulates like caffeine, chocolate, diet pills, refined sugar, and nicotine cause a rapid rise in blood insulin levels. This is then followed by the brain releasing serotonin. Serotonin helps the person feel better and think clearer, yes, but this is only temporary. A stimulate high is always followed by an unpleasant low. This then leads to further use of stimulates to keep your serotonin levels high, and addictions are created. People become dependent on stimulates to help them raise their serotonin levels, and the addiction causes further depletion of serotonin.

WHY NOT JUST TAKE AN ANTIDEPRESSANT?

Antidepressant drugs have been used with varying degrees of success in treating the sleeplessness of FMS and CFS. Many of our patients are on SSRIs. SSRIs are supposed to help a patient hang on to and use his naturally occurring stores of serotonin. This is like using a gasoline additive to help increase the efficiency of your car's fuel. But most of the patients I see are running on fumes! A gasoline additive won't help. Using 5HTP is like pouring gasoline straight into your tank; you fill your brain with serotonin. There's no need for an additive when you can simply replace your serotonin stores any time you get low.

Are you convinced yet that getting your serotonin stores back up to optimal levels is important in getting a good night's sleep? It absolutely is! Replacing and building optimal serotonin stores is the first thing that must be done. Once this has occurred, and again it may take months, your body starts to normalize its homeostatic systems. But you don't necessarily need prescription drugs to get you to this point. And drugs might actually make the problem worse. Let's look at some natural sleep aids that are free of risks and side-effects.

5-HYDROXYTRYPTOPHAN (5HTP)

Most of our patients are prescribed 5HTP, a natural supplement. This is a derivative of the amino acid tryptophan and, when taken correctly, turns right into serotonin.

One European study showed that the combination of MAOIs, such as Nardil or Parnate, with 5HTP significantly improved FMS symptoms, whereas other antidepressant treatments were not effective.

> The doctors who conducted this study stated that a natural analgesic effect occurred when serotonin levels and norepinephrine receptors were enhanced in the brain. More norepinephrine means more energy and improved mood. Tests in Europe show tryptophan to be just as effective in treating depression as the prescription drugs Elavil and Tofranil, which have side effects.

Some of our patients say they can't take 5HTP or melatonin, because they cause them to have strange or disturbing dreams. These dreams usually go away over time and are a by-product of finally going into deep sleep for the first time in years. (On a side note: if you're not dreaming at night, you're probably deficient in vitamin B6. Vitamin B6 helps convert tryptophan to 5HTP and then into serotonin.)

> 5HTP should be taken on an empty stomach,
> 30 minutes before bed, with four ounces of juice.

This allows it to get past the blood-brain barrier and be absorbed directly into the brain. It can take several nights before 5HTP works, so patients should try a lower dose for two–three nights before increasing it. If 100 mg. doesn't get you to sleep within an hour, increase first to 150 mg. and then to 200 mg., if needed. I don't recommend going above 300 mg. If you feel hungover the next day (very few do), then decrease your dose. If after two weeks, you're still not falling asleep within an hour, discontinue the 5HTP and try melatonin instead.

Once you are falling asleep, it still might take months, even years, before you can get your circadian rhythm corrected. Until then, stay on 5HTP. If you do need to stay on 5HTP for more than three months (most do), take an amino acid supplement like the one in our CFS/Fibromyalgia formula. This will help balance your other neurotransmitters.

5HTP can be found at health-food stores. But remember that the supplement industry is not regulated at this time. Unlike the German nutritional industry, supplements in the United States receive little if any scrutiny. I always encourage patients to avoid inexpensive and overly advertised products. It's best to consult a health care professional who is familiar with supplements. If a patient is counting on 5HTP to get her to sleep, I want her to use the very best product out there. Otherwise, as has happened in the past, patients can try an inferior brand and, after not getting the desired results, give up on the recommendation. They falsely assume that the supplement won't work.

There has been some recent bad press about 5HTP and the contaminant known as "peak X." The 5HTP I recommend has been thoroughly tested and is guaranteed to contain no "peak X" or other contaminants. To order 5HTP, see page 274.

5HTP and Chronic Fatigue Syndrome

CFS patients are more likely than FMS patients to have trouble taking 5HTP. One theory is that those with CFS have too much serotonin and that this is why they are so tired. Additional serotonin, then, can't be tolerated. This may be true; I don't know. However, increasing serotonin levels is the number one priority for 95% of the patients I see. There are patients—usually at the far end of the CFS scale—who have serotonin sensitivity. And excessively high serotonin levels can cause insomnia, hyperactivity, headache, and increased heart rate. But I suspect that most patients who have a serotonin sensitivity reaction do so because of a sluggish liver. These are usually the same patients who have trouble taking most medications. They get depressed from taking an antidepressant and hyperactive from sleeping pills. They usually can't take the normal dose of medicine and instead need a smaller dose.

If you are having trouble sleeping and suspect that you have a high sensitivity to serotonin, try 5HTP for one–two nights. If you have a hypersensitive reaction, simply discontinue the 5HTP and begin taking melatonin instead.

Anyone taking a prescription antidepressant such
as Prozac or Celexa should consult a health care
professional before beginning 5HTP therapy.

MELATONIN

The pineal gland, located at the base of the brain, was considered by the ancient Greeks to be the seat of the soul. This might not have been far off, since the pineal gland is responsible for releasing the hormone melatonin.

Melatonin, the primary hormone of the pineal gland, acts to regulate the body's circadian rhythm, especially the sleep-wake cycle. Its release corresponds to sleeping periods. The highest blood concentration is at night and the lowest is during the day. So if you aren't getting enough deep, restorative sleep, you aren't releasing enough melatonin. And if you don't have enough melatonin, you won't get deep, restorative sleep.

Serotonin, mentioned earlier, helps produce melatonin. If you are deficient in serotonin, you'll be deficient in melatonin.

Over the past two decades, scientists have learned a great deal about melatonin. Once a curiosity, it is now known to slow down or perhaps even reverse the effects of aging. Melatonin is also a powerful antioxidant that, unlike other antioxidants, is able to cross the blood-brain barrier and attack any free radicals floating around in the brain. Melatonin also protects the cells' nuclei and DNA blueprint. This is a major reason why melatonin is able to fend off the adverse affects of cancer.

Dr. Joan Larson discusses how melatonin and the immune system are connected: "Melatonin rejuvenates the thymus gland to protect our immunity...Melatonin will 'reset' your immune system when it has been under siege from infections, cancer, stress, and so on. Such attacks disrupt its rhythms and diminish its effectiveness. Any disruption in our immune system's twenty-four-hour rhythm lowers our immunity, leaving us prone to more illness."[3]

It's easy to put two and two together; if you're deficient in melatonin, you can't get to sleep at night. If you don't sleep, you won't make melatonin. It's a vicious cycle. A deficiency of restorative sleep leads to accelerated aging, lowered immune function, and susceptibility to cancer and brain oxidation. Chronic insomnia leads to a gradual disconnection to our own biorhythms. Once we become out of tune with our sleep-wake circadian rhythm, we begin to lose the ability to right ourselves through homeostasis. This in turn leads to further chemical, physical, and emotional stress. When this stress is at its worst, we lose the ability to sense anything our body is trying to tell us. We begin to lose the very essence of who we are. Therefore, restoring circadian rhythm must be the first priority in overcoming FMS and CFS.

Melatonin Supplementation

When administered in pharmacological doses (1–3 mg. before bed), melatonin acts as a powerful sleep-regulating agent that controls the circadian rhythm. A low dose of melatonin has also been shown to be effective in treating insomnia and jet lag. In a recent study, volunteers were either given a .3 mg. or a 1 mg. dose of melatonin or a placebo. Both levels of melatonin were effective at decreasing the time needed to fall asleep.

Seasonal Affective Disorder

Melatonin production is affected by a person's exposure to light. Melatonin levels start to rise as the sun goes down and drop off as the sun comes up. The retinas of the eyes are extremely sensitive to changes in light, and an increase in light striking the retina triggers a decrease in melatonin production—this is nature's wake-up call. Conversely, limited exposure to light increases melatonin production—nature's lullaby. This explains why some individuals suffer from seasonal affective disorder (SAD). This disorder is triggered by the onset of winter and the reduction of sunlight. As melatonin levels increase and serotonin levels decrease, depression sets in. One in 10 people, including children, suffer from SAD. Symptoms associated with SAD include depression, fatigue, lethargy, anxiety, and carbohydrate cravings.

One to two hours of exposure to bright, ultraviolet light will usually decrease melatonin levels to a normal level. Special ultraviolet (full spectrum) bright lights are found in various stores and catalogs. Individuals with SAD should use these lights every day during the winter months. Those suffering from insomnia should avoid bright lights two to three hours before bed.

Other Effects on Melatonin Production

Melatonin production can also be decreased by exposure to electric and magnetic fields, stress, and the aging process. Exposure to both static and pulsed magnetic fields has been shown to significantly decrease melatonin production in the pineal gland of experimental animals.

TRYPTOPHAN (L-TRYPTOPHAN)

One of the most important amino acids for FMS and CFS patients is tryptophan. It produces the neurotransmitter serotonin. Serotonin is involved in regulating proper sleep, reducing pain, and avoiding depression. Tryptophan is now available by prescription. If combined with either a tricyclic antidepressant or an SSRI, the dosage must be reduced in accordance with your doctor's recommendation. Most physicians discourage using tryptophan with SSRIs.

Showa Denko, the Japanese company that once supplied most US tryptophan, tried to bypass a critical step in its processing. This caused some people taking tryptophan to contract eosinophilic myalgia syndrome, and a few died as a result. Despite this tragedy, tryptophan is a very safe supplement and an essential amino acid. Many foods contain tryptophan as an additive, including baby formulas.

The Food and Drug Administration (FDA) overreacted, took tryptophan off the market, and labeled it a prescription drug in 1989. They effectively discouraged the use of a naturally occurring supplement by millions of Americans suffering from depression, insomnia, and other illnesses. At the same time, they advocated the use of potentially harmful antidepressants. (Is it a coincidence that tryptophan was banned shortly before Prozac and other antidepressants began to be marketed to patients and doctors?)

EXERCISE

Walking has been shown to increase the efficient use of serotonin in the brain. From Dr. Batmanghelidj comes this quote: "There is a direct relationship between walking and the buildup of the brain's Tryptophan reserves. There are several amino acids that compete for crossing the naturally designed barrier system into the brain....These competitors to tryptophan are grouped under the title of branched-chain amino acids (BC amino acids). During exercise, these BC amino acids, along with fats, are used as fuel in the larger muscles. The muscles begin to pick up these amino acids from the circulating blood. As a result, the odds are changed in favor of Tryptophan for its passage across the blood-brain barrier."

Dr. Batmanghelidj goes on to write about tryptophan's importance: "The brain Tryptophan content, and its dependent neurotransmitter systems, are responsible for maintenance of the 'homeostatic balance of the body.' Normal levels of Tryptophan in the brain maintain a well-regulated balance in all functions of the body—what is meant by homeostasis. With a decrease in Tryptophan supply to the brain, there is a proportionate decrease in the efficiency of all functions in the body."[4]

MAGNESIUM

Magnesium is a natural muscle relaxer and helps regulate neurotransmitters, including serotonin. FMS and CFS patients are usually low in magnesium. I recommend a minimum of 500 mg. of magnesium daily. An additional 100–150mg. at bedtime may also be helpful. It's best to use a chelated form of magnesium: magnesium citrate, taurate, or aspartate.

Gamma-aminobutyric Acid (GABA)

This amino acid complex can mimic the effects of such prescription tranquilizers as Valium and Xanax, without the side effects. It is not sedating by nature but can help to filter out all the "mind chatter" that can prevent falling asleep. The usual dose is 500–1,000 mg. on an empty stomach before bed.

Valerian Root

A perennial herb native to Eurasia and naturalized worldwide, valerian root inhibits and facilitates the release of GABA. Studies have shown this herb to induce a mild-sedating effect. These studies are debatable, however, and the US Pharmacopeia Expert Advisory Panel has determined that there is insufficient evidence to support the use of valerian root for the treatment of insomnia. I don't usually recommend this herb, but I've seen some patients who have done quite well on it. It also acts as a mild but effective antispasmodic for gastrointestinal ailments. It's contraindicated in those with any type of liver dysfunction.

Passion Flower

Though it's used as a sedative and approved in Germany as an antianxiety medication, there is no clinical data to support the use of this herbal medicine. I've seen it used in combination with other sleep-enhancing herbals. It alone doesn't seem to be effective for FMS-related sleep disorders.

Chamomile

Chamomile is an herbal remedy sometimes used in children's formulas to treat restlessness. It also has an anti-inflammatory and antispasmodic effect in the GI tract. Some people have found chamomile tea (which is caffeine-free) to be an effective way of relaxing before bed.

YOUR EVENING RITUAL

Our bodies are designed to wake up when light hits our eyes and to get sleepy when darkness falls. Our ancestors before the invention of electricity were usually in bed soon after the sun went down and up with the morning sunrise.

Modern man can now have bright light 24 hours a day. But I recommend you use the off switch! Before bed, turn off the TV, and find a quiet room (not your bedroom) where you can use a soft, low-voltage (75-watt) lamp by which to read. After 30–60 minutes, take your bedtime supplement or medication, and move to your bedroom. Keep the lights on low, and avoid any stimulation, including the TV. (Take the TV out of your bedroom, tonight!)

You might want to try a warm Epsom-salt bath before bed. Simply pour one cup of Epsom salts (magnesium sulfate) into a warm bath. Soak 20–30 minutes. Again, use low light and no stimulants. The herb lavender is also calming. It can be used in bath gel, lotion, or soap, or you can sprinkle it along with the Epsom salts directly into your bath water.

Notes

[1]from *Creating Health Beyond Prevention, Toward Perfection;* 1987
[2]from *Textbook of Natural Medicine* by Joseph E. Pizzorno, ND, (ed.) and Michael T. Murray (ed.); 1999
[3]from *Seven Weeks to Emotional Healing;* 1999
[4]from *Your Body's Many Cries for Water;* 1995

Resources

- Dr. Murphree's Essential Therapeutics line of supplements, including GABA and 5HTP, is available online at www.drrodger.com or by calling (205) 879-2383.
- Valerian root, magnesium citrate, and passion flower are available at many health food stores.

7

Those Invaluable Adrenals

The proper function of our adrenal glands is second only to a good night's sleep in winning the battle against fibromyalgia and chronic fatigue syndrome.

Our adrenals are pea-sized glands located atop each kidney. In the inner region of each adrenal gland is what's known as the medulla. This adrenal medulla produces norepinepherine and epinephrine (adrenaline). Norepinepherine increases both systolic and diastolic blood pressure. Epinephrine increases systolic blood pressure, pulse rate, and cardiac function. It is released during times of stress, and its main function is to increase the rate and depth of respiration to allow more oxygen to reach the bloodstream. It regulates circulatory, nervous, muscular, and respiratory systems when needed. It also inhibits the muscle tone of the stomach, so you may feel a "knot" in your stomach during times of stress.

Your adrenal glands might be small, but they're tough. Like personal bodyguards, they protect the body from harm by fighting off its enemies. If yours fail, it's like opening the door of your being to whatever shady characters (viruses and bacteria) happen to be passing by. And I believe that insufficient or failed adrenal glands (hypoadrenia) contribute significantly to nearly all cases of FMS and CFS. Hypoadrenia is already known to cause many of the same problems associated with CFS and FMS: hypoglycemia, hypotension, NMH, low energy, decreased mental acuity, low body temperature, decreased metabolism, a compromised immune system, and a decreased sense of well-being. Therefore, restoring proper adrenal function is a crucial step in peeling away the layers of dysfunction associated with FMS and CFS.

NOT ENOUGH CORTISOL

According to research, the adrenal glands of about two-thirds of CFS patients appear to not produce enough cortisol, a steroid essential for well-being. Since its discovery some 50 years ago, it has gained increasing prominence in the treatment of autoimmune diseases, allergies, asthma, and athletic injuries. Over the years, researchers have developed powerful synthetic forms of cortisol with stronger anti-inflammatory effects. When first introduced, these corticosteroids were hailed as wonder drugs. But in continued high doses, they can cause adverse side effects: depression, fluid retention, hypertension, bone loss, gastrointestinal ulcers, cataracts, breathing disorders.

One reason for cortisol deficiency might be that the hypothalamus does not make enough corticotrophin-releasing hormone (CRH), which is the brain's way of telling the adrenals that more cortisol is needed. Dysautonomia, discussed earlier, can also contribute to CRH deficiency.

I suspect that many people also have low cortisol levels because of adrenal burn-out. In today's society, we process more information in one day than our great-great-grandfathers processed in three months. People often experience stress reactions every few minutes when bombarded by stimulus coming from our radios, driving in traffic, cell phones, pagers, and from electromagnetic pollution. CFS, which may go on for years, puts relentless stress and strain on the adrenal glands. Persistent, unrelenting stress will ultimately lead to adrenal burnout, and this burnout renders a person defenseless against the continuous chemical, emotional, and physical damage that occurs with chronic stress.

More severe than simple adrenal lows is Addison's disease. This is severe adrenal insufficiency resulting from the actual destruction of adrenal glands. This major disease is usually permanent and occurs when cancer or an infection, such as tuberculosis, invades and destroys the glands. A relatively simple blood test can quickly diagnose Addison's disease.

But the adrenal weakness that accompanies chronic stress (and FMS and CFS) results in a marginal and temporary insufficiency much more difficult to diagnose. The "stressed-out" adrenal gland might enlarge a bit, but otherwise it appears structurally sound and usually produces normal blood levels of cortisol. However, a saliva test, as performed by Great Smokies Diagnostic Laboratory (see page 275) can accurately uncover most adrenal weaknesses.

In *Safe Uses of Cortisol,*[1] Dr. William Jefferies concludes that weak adrenal glands *can* supply adequate cortisol when the body suffers little stress. Therefore, single determinations of blood cortisol in a person with marginal adrenal insufficiency are usually normal. However, expose the same person to a major stressor event, and the adrenals might flunk the challenge due to their low reserves. Poor health quickly follows.

Not Enough DHEA

The adrenal cortex, when healthy, produces adequate levels of dehydroepiandrosterone (DHEA). DHEA boosts our energy, sex drive, resistance to stress, self-defense mechanisms (immune system), and general well-being. It raises cortisol levels, restores adrenal function, improves mood, and increases cellular energy, mental acuity, strength, and stamina. Unfortunately, DHEA is notoriously low in FMS and CFS patients. Chronic stress initially causes the adrenals to release extra cortisol and DHEA, and eventually they can't produce enough DHEA. The result is an elevated cortisol-to-DHEA ratio.

Aging makes holding on to DHEA even tougher. The hormone pregnenolone acts as a ready defender in our bodies, changing into DHEA or progesterone when needed. As we age, we begin to loose the ability to make pregnenolone. Naturally, this increases the likelihood of a DHEA deficiency. Even in healthy individuals, DHEA levels begin to drop after the age of 30. By age 70, they are at about 20% of their peak levels.

An important note for those with CFS:
DHEA increases the activity of a potent antioxidant
known as superoxide dismutase (SOD), which can
counter the free-radical damage found in the brain
tissue of some CFS patients.

GENERAL ADAPTATION SYNDROME

General adaptation syndrome (GAS) is a group of processes
that the body reverts to in times of stress. The syndrome is
divided into three phases: fight-or-flight response, resistance
reaction, and exhaustion.

PHASE ONE: FIGHT OR FLIGHT RESPONSE

This response is an alarm reaction triggered by messages
in the brain that cause the pituitary gland to release adreno-
corticotropic hormone (ACTH). This hormone then causes
the adrenal glands to secrete adrenaline, cortisol, and other
stress hormones. The fight-or-flight response encourages the
body to go on "red alert" and be ready for physical and mental
activity. The heart beats faster to provide blood to the muscles
and brain. The breath rate increases to supply extra oxygen to
the muscles, heart, and brain. Digestion and other functions
not essential for maintaining the alarm reaction are halted.
The liver rids itself of stored glycogen and releases glucose
into the bloodstream. The body is now ready for any real or
imagined danger.

PHASE TWO: RESISTANCE REACTION

While the fight-or-flight response is usually short-lived, the
resistance reaction can last for quite some time. In this phase,
cortisol and DHEA are secreted by the adrenal glands. These
hormones increase sodium retention and therefore increase
blood pressure (one sign of adrenal fatigue is hypotension).
They also help to regulate blood sugar. DHEA, along with
other adrenal hormones, converts fatty acids, carbohydrates,
and protein into energy. Cortisol helps increase cellular energy and acts as a potent anti-inflammatory. It can be a lifesaver
when used in allergic reactions (anaphylactic shock).

The resistance reaction allows the body to endure ongoing stress—pain, fatigue, injury—for long periods of time. However, long-term stress can generate a host of health problems, including hypertension, anxiety, fatigue, headaches, hypoglycemia, decreased immune function, thyroid dysfunction, diabetes, and adrenal exhaustion.

PHASE THREE: EXHAUSTION

In the third stage of general adaptation syndrome, chronic oversecretion of cortisol and DHEA leads to adrenal exhaustion. Adrenal exhaustion accelerates the downward spiral towards chronic poor health. Chronic headaches, nausea, allergies, nagging injuries, fatigue, dizziness, hypotension, low body temperature, depression, low sex drive, chronic infections, and cold hands and feet are just some of the symptoms that occur with adrenal exhaustion.

The majority of patients I see for chronic illnesses, including FMS and CFS, are suffering from adrenal exhaustion. They have literally burned their stress-monitoring organ out. Amid years of poor sleep, unrelenting fatigue, chronic pain, excessive stimulants, poor diet, and relying on a plethora of prescription medications, the adrenal glands and the hormones they release have been used up.

Once adrenal exhaustion sets in, it's not long before the body begins to break down. Getting "stressed out" and staying "stressed out" is the beginning of chronic illness for most, if not all of, the FMS and CFS patients I evaluate.

SECRETORY IgA, IMMUNE FUNCTION, AND STRESS

Antibodies, or immunoglobulins (Ig), offer protection against viruses and bacterial pathogens such as *Haemophilus influenzae, streptococci,* and *staphylococci.* Secretory immunoglobulin A (secretory IgA) is found in saliva, tears, colostrum, and respiratory and gastrointestinal tracts. It provides antiviral and antibacterial defense and is the single most important aspect of immunity in mucous secretions of the digestive system, mouth, lungs, and urinary tract.

The lining of the digestive tract is populated by mucosal cells. These cells adhere to any unwanted foreign substances, including bacteria, that enter our stomach and digestive system. The antibodies in the digestive tract must be able to recognize the good substances from the bad. This is not an easy task, since our intestinal tract is populated by trillions of mostly good bacteria that help digest food and manufacture certain nutrients. Secretory IgA orchestrates a delicate balance of destroying the foreign invaders that arrive along with the foods we eat, while ignoring the friendly bacteria (micro flora) that inhabit the digestive tract. When the secretory IgA defenses are compromised or overwhelmed by chronic exposure to foreign invaders, they fail, and poor health is inevitable. Any decline in the levels of secretory IgA decreases a body's resistance to unwanted bacterial and viral agents. This is one reason that FMS and CFS patients are so prone to illness and take so long to recover.

So what can overwhelm the secretory IgA and short-circuit our stay-well system? Certain drugs, such as aspirin and NSAIDs; pollutants; pesticides; heavy metals; parasites; yeast overgrowth; and food sensitivities and allergies.

The ability to even produce secretory IgA also appears to be influenced by stress. Daily problems, lack of a sense of humor, and negative emotions can decrease secretory IgA levels. Even a single five-minute experience of anger can produce a significant decrease in secretory IgA levels, and the decrease can still be measured up to five hours after the emotional experience.

To examine the impact of stress on the intestinal tract's micro flora, researchers investigated people who were preparing for space flight—an understandably stressful process. During this time, there was a distinct decrease in the numbers of diphidobactrum and lactobacilli (good bacteria) and a corresponding increase in the numbers of E. coli and enterobacteria (bad bacteria) in the potential space travelers.

Billie Jay Sahley, PhD, writes "oversecretions of the stress hormones [cortisone, cortisol, and corticosterone], caused by long-term mental or physical effort, could lead to cancer, arthritis, and susceptibility to infections. Many psychosomatic disorders are transmitted from the brain to the skeletal muscle system. Anxiety, stress, anger, or any other psychic state can greatly change the amount of nervous stimulation to the skeletal muscles throughout the body, and either increase or decrease the skeletal muscular tension."[2]

These same stimulatory responses that affect the muscles also cause changes in various bodily organs: abnormal heartbeats, peptic ulcers (too much stomach acid), hypertension, spastic colon, and irregular menstrual periods. This is why you can't separate emotional stress from physical stress. As I'll discuss in later chapters, our emotional state plays a major role in determining our level of overall health.

Says Dr. David Walther, "Hypoadrenia displays itself in a variety of ways, such as severe depression, suicidal tendencies, asthma, chronic upper respiratory infections, hay fever, skin rashes, colitis, gastric duodenal ulcers, rheumatoid arthritis, insomnia, headaches, fatigue, fainting spells, obesity, heart palpitations, edema in the extremities, learning difficulties—the list goes on and on....The tragedy is that thousands of persons today are suffering from some manifestation of hypoadrenia. They may have sought help for their problems, and been given tranquilizers and psychotherapy for the emotional depression; analgesics for rheumatoid arthritic pain; sedatives for insomnia; amphetamines and diuretics for obesity; anticholinergic and a bland diet for colitis; antihistamines and bronchial dilators for asthma....They may have had extensive examination, with no pathology found. Therefore, these victims of hypoadrenia are given treatment to diminish the symptoms rather than eliminate the cause."[3]

Testing for Hypoadrenia
We routinely use saliva adrenal hormone profiles to test for adrenal and DHEA deficiencies. However, these tests might take two–three weeks before they're returned to us. A quick blood pressure test that monitors lying and standing systolic numbers can help us begin a trial treatment of adrenal boosting supplements.

Ragland's sign is an abnormal drop in systolic blood pressure (the top number) when a person arises from a lying to a standing position. There should be a rise of 8–10 mm. in the systolic number. A *drop* indicates adrenal insufficiency.

Another way to test for adrenal dysfunction is the pupil dilation exam. To perform this on yourself, you'll need a flashlight and a mirror. Face the mirror, and shine the light in one eye. If after 30 seconds the pupil (black center) starts to dilate (enlarge), adrenal deficiency should be suspected.

Why does this happen? During adrenal insufficiency, there is a deficiency of sodium and an abundance of potassium, and this imbalance causes an inhibition of the sphincter muscles of the eye. These muscles normally initiate pupil constriction in the presence of bright light. However, in adrenal insufficiency, the pupils actually dilate when exposed to light.

Rogoff's sign is a definite tenderness in the lower thoracic (mid-back) spine where the ribs attach.

Muscle testing involves a measurement of strength under stress. With your arm raised beside you, have someone test your strength by pushing down on your arm while you resist. Then retest after placing a small amount of table sugar or honey on your tongue. In individuals with adrenal insufficiency, any additional stress, including sugar, will cause a momentary weakening of a strong muscle group. Refined carbohydrates are poison to the weakened adrenal glands. Most individuals with adrenal insufficiency suffer from hypoglycemia, and simple sugars should be avoided while attempting to repair deficient adrenal hormones.

CORRECTING HYPOADRENIA

- **Test yourself for hypoadrenia,** or have someone test you, using the pupil dilation or blood pressure test. Consider having an adrenal cortex saliva profile test (Ask your doctor, and see pg. 275).

- **Take adrenal cortical extracts.** These extracts are used to replenish and eventually normalize adrenal function. They have an advantage over cortisol hormone replacement in that they can be instantly discontinued once they have done their job of repairing adrenal function. Adrenal extracts have been successfully used to treat many conditions related to hypoadrenia, including many symptoms of FMS and CFS. They can increase energy and speed recovery from illness. Adrenal extracts are not a new treatment. In the 1930s, they were very popular, used by tens of thousands of physicians. They were still being produced by leading drug companies as recently as 1968. Today, these extracts are available without a prescription. Dosage is usually listed as four–eight capsules daily. Some patients need more.

- **Take DHEA if needed.** It's best to be tested before taking DHEA supplements. As a general rule, females may need 25–50 mg. daily and males 50–100 mg.daily. I've found sublingual (dissolving under the tongue) to be the best form of DHEA.

- **Increase sodium (salt) consumption.** Yes, it's OK to eat salt. Your body needs plenty in order to work properly, and adding salt is an important step in helping those with FMS/CFS feel better.

  First, salt is a natural antihistamine, and histamine, along with its regulators, prostaglandins and kinins, can cause pain. (Salt's antihistamine effects are one reason why saline nasal rinses help with sinus congestion.)

  Salt is also needed for healthy blood sugar levels. In order for glucose (blood sugar) to be absorbed in the small intestine, two minerals must be present: sodium and potassium. But in the case of hypoadrenia, there's an increased loss of sodium and an increased retention of potassium. The result is hypoglycemia, fatigue, and a general sense of illness.

  Too little salt can cause the kidneys to reabsorb less water than is needed by the body. Swelling may occur in the hands and feet, and blood pressure may drop, leading to fatigue. Adequate blood pressure allows nutrients, including oxygen, to travel to muscles, organs, and other cells throughout the body. It also allows blood to be pumped back up the veins of the leg and into the heart. Just like a garden hose with not enough water pressure, the fluid you need won't reach all the places in your garden.

  Inadequate reabsorption of salt can also cause spillage of bicarbonate ions in the urine, resulting in acidosis. The major effect of acidosis is depression of the central nervous system. This then causes an increased rate and depth of respiration.

  If you suffer from high blood pressure, obviously, increasing your salt intake may pose a problem. I recommend you monitor your blood pressure a few times a day. You can purchase a sphygmanometer (blood pressure cuff) at most pharmacies. If your blood pressure rises while adding salt to your diet, simply reduce your salt intake once again.

- **Drink plenty of water.** I recommend you drink half your weight in ounces of water each day. (So if you weigh 120 lb., consume at least 60 ounces—seven and a half cups—per day.) Sodas, tea, coffee, and other drinks don't count—only pure water. You can add a lemon or lime wedge.

- **Supplement with vitamin C.** Vitamin C is perhaps the most important nutrient in facilitating adrenal function and repair. In fact, before we were able to measure a patient's adrenal function, we measured the amount of vitamin C in his blood to determine how well his adrenal glands were doing. I recommend a minimum of 1,000 mg. daily, but much larger amounts will be needed to actually help restore the adrenal glands. Begin with 2,000 mg. daily, and increase by an additional 1,000—2,000 mg. each day. The maximum dosage should be 10,000 mg. in a day. If you have a loose bowel movement while taking vitamin C, reduce your dose by 1,000 mg. Keep reducing by 500–1,000 mg. each day until you are no longer having loose stools. This is your ideal supplement dose of vitamin C. For more information on vitamin C, see chapter 11.

- **Take a quality, comprehensive multivitamin and mineral formula.** Our Essential Therapeutics CFS/Fibromyalgia Support Pack contains extra B5, C, and other energy-boosting and stress-busting nutrients.

- **Supplement with vitamin B5 (pantothenic acid).** Vitamin B5 helps recycle adrenal hormones, and a deficiency of it can cause adrenal atrophy and lead to fatigue, headache, sleep disturbance, nausea, and abdominal discomfort. It is converted to the enzyme acetyl CoA, which converts glucose into cellular energy. Individuals with low adrenal function should take between 1,000–1,500 mg. daily

- **Try licorice root extract.** It has been used for over 5,000 years and is one of China's most popular herbal medicines. It acts like the adrenal hormone aldosterone, which is involved in salt and water metabolism. Glycyrrhizin, a component of licorice, is structurally similar to cortisol and appears to possibly act to increase cortisol levels. It weakly mimics the role of natural steroid hormones and can spare cortisol, essentially extending its half-life. Components of glycyrrhizin can also counteract adverse immunosuppressant effects.

Large amounts of licorice root can cause side effects, such as water retention, potassium deficiency, and elevated blood pressure. However, most individuals with adrenal insufficiency have low blood pressure, increased potassium, and low blood volume. So raising blood pressure and lowering potassium levels can have dramatic positive effects on them; many times their nausea, dizziness, and fatigue will simply disappear. For this reason, the side effects don't strongly concern me when treating FMS and CFS patients. If blood pressure becomes elevated or the patient starts to retain unwanted water, I simply reduce or eliminate the treatment. My patients are usually taking the CFS/FMS Support Pack, which contains potassium. A trial of licorice root with or without adrenal glandulars may be needed for those patients suffering from extremely low blood pressure. Typically, side effects appear with a dose of 10–14 grams of crude plant extract. Some sensitive individuals could have adverse reactions from as little as one–two grams. However, some individuals have been known to take as much as 30g. before side effects occurred. I recommend a maximum of 900 mg. per day. If adverse symptoms arise, discontinue use.

· **Supplement with magnesium.** It plays a role in over 300 bodily functions, including creating cellular energy, especially in the adrenal glands.

Magnesium is the most important mineral (and perhaps the most important supplement) in the battle against FMS and CFS.

· **Get plenty of rest.** You won't get well until you're getting a minimum of eight hours of deep, restorative sleep. If possible, periodically sleep late. This allows the adrenal glands an opportunity to rest and regenerate. Midday naps of 15–20 minutes are also helpful.

• **Reduce your stress.** Don't overdo it. Once patients start to feel better, they have a tendency to try to do too much. Don't try to be the Tasmanian devil, only to be wiped out for the next few days. It may take months for your energy reserves to build back up. Pace yourself, and enjoy the newfound energy. See chapter 25, "Feeding the Spirit."

• **Always eat breakfast, and never skip meals.** Individuals with low adrenal function are usually not hungry when they wake up. They instead rely on chemical stimulants (coffee, sodas, cigarettes, etc.) to get them going. Your morning cortisol level is at its highest around 8:00 a.m., so you won't feel very hungry then. Eat anyway! A small snack (avoid simple sugars) is all you need until you get hungry, usually a couple of hours later. Then eat another balanced snack to tie you over until lunch. Then, don't skip lunch! It's best to eat little meals throughout the day. Don't let your blood sugar drop too low. Avoid simple sugars. As any "sugarholic" can attest, a soda, doughnut, or pastry can provide a quick energy fix. But this rapid rise in blood sugar is followed by a equally rapid nosedive. And low blood sugar produces all the unwanted symptoms associated with low adrenal function: fatigue, irritability, fibro fog, depression, nausea, and more.

• **Eliminate—or at least limit—all caffeine, nicotine, and alcohol.** I know this can be tough. But if you want to get well, this is really not an option. At the very least, drastically reduce your consumption of these adrenal hormone robbers.

HYPOGLYCEMIA PROTOCOL

Hypoglycemia is a complex set of symptoms caused by faulty carbohydrate metabolism. It's also synonymous with low blood sugar. Normally, the body maintains blood sugar levels within a narrow range through the coordinated effort of several glands and their hormones. If these hormones, especially glucagon (from glucose) and insulin (produced in the pancreas), are thrown out of balance, hypoglycemia or type-2 diabetes can result.

Hypoglycemia (in people not taking insulin) is usually the result of consuming too many simple carbohydrates (sugars). "Syndrome X" describes a cluster of abnormalities that owe their existence largely to a high intake of refined carbohydrates leading to the development of hypoglycemia, excessive insulin secretion, and glucose intolerance. This condition is followed by decreased insulin sensitivity, elevated cholesterol levels, obesity, high blood pressure, and type-2 diabetes.

Numerous studies have demonstrated that depressed individuals have faulty glucose/insulin regulatory mechanisms. Other studies have clearly shown the relationship between low blood sugar and decreased mental acuity. Hypoglycemia has also been implicated as a major trigger for migraine headaches.

The following foods are not recommended for anyone with hypoglycemia or hypoadrenia tendencies: table sugar, maltose, honey, sucrose (fruit sugar), bananas, raisins, dates, fruit juices, apricots, beets, white flour, white potatoes, white rice, cooked corn, corn flakes, and cereals.

It's best to combine protein, fat, and carbohydrate in each snack or meal. Avoiding simple sugars and consuming a balanced diet help stabilize blood sugar levels. (For a complete list of simple sugars to avoid, see chapter 15). Eating healthy snacks throughout the day can also help keep your blood sugar levels stable. One simple snack that combines protein, fat, and carbohydrate is a handful of nuts (such as cashews, almonds, walnuts, or pecans) along with an apple, pear, or whole wheat crackers.

Supplements to Combat Hypoglycemia

- **Chromium** is a trace mineral that helps reduce glucose-induced insulin secretion. Chromium works with insulin to facilitate the uptake of glucose into the cells. Glucose levels remain elevated in the absence of chromium. A normal dose is 200 mcg. taken 30 minutes before or after meals, two–three times daily.

- **Vitamin B₃ (niacin)** helps regulate blood sugar levels and may help alleviate the symptoms of hypoglycemia.

- **Magnesium** levels must be sufficient in order to avoid hypoglycemic reactions.

- **Zinc** levels must be sufficient in order to avoid hypoglycemic reactions.

- **L-glutamine,** an amino acid, helps regulate blood sugar levels. I've found it to be very effective in eliminating sugar cravings and hypoglycemic episodes. A normal dose is 500–1000 mg. once or twice daily on an empty stomach.

- **Gymnema sylvester** is a climbing plant found in Asia and Africa. It's used in Ayruvedic medicine, an indigenous healing practice from India, for the treatment of type-2 diabetes. Scientific studies have shown this herb to be a valuable addition in preventing the symptoms of hypoglycemia. It's also routinely used to reduce sugar cravings.

All of the above vitamins and minerals (excluding gymnema sylvester) are included in our CFS/Fibromyalgia formula.

Notes
[1]1996
[2]From *The Anxiety Epidemic,* 1994
[3]From *Applied Kinesiology: The Advanced Approach in Chiropractic*

Resources
- Dr. Murphree's CFS/Fibromyalgia formula, sublingual DHEA, and adrenal cortical supplements are available online at www.drrodger.com or by calling (205) 879-2383.
- Licorice root, L-glutamine, and gymnema sylvester are available at many health food stores.

For Further Reading
- *Boosting Immunity: Creating Wellness Naturally* by Len Saputo, MD and Nancy Faass MSW MPH; 2002
- *Adrenal Fatigue: The 21st-Century Stress Syndrome* by James L. Wilson; 2002
- *Merck Manual Diagnosis and Therapy* by Mark H. Beers (ed.) et al; 1999
- *Toxic Success: How to Stop Striving and Start Thriving* by Paul Pearsall; 2002
- *Functional Assessment Resource Manual,* Great Smokies Diagnostic Laboratory; 1999
- *Boost Your Energy* by Sandra Cabot, MD; 1997

8

The Immune System

The strength of our immune system determines the state of our health. When it is compromised, we are susceptible to all sorts of illnesses. When it is strong, we gravitate towards wellness.

The human immune system is nothing short of amazing. It's so complex and sophisticated that we only now understand a small fraction of it, maybe 1–2%.

We do know that the immune system has special cells known as white blood cells that patrol the body for invading organisms. Proteins in the form of antibodies help us identify and resist repeated infections. In addition to the circulatory system that regulates our blood flow, we also have a separate circulatory system for the immune cells, known as the lymph system. This system is made up of water, dissolved proteins, and waste toxins that leak through the capillaries into the spaces between the body tissues. This fluid, called lymph, is collected and rerouted through the body's lymph nodes. The lymph nodes are pea-sized structures containing large numbers of immune cells. They can be found in the armpits, the groin, and the area behind the ears, as well as in the thorax, abdomen, and other places. Lymph nodes may become enlarged when our bodies are fighting off an infection, and those of people with CFS may be chronically inflamed and enlarged. This condition can be detected by feeling in the armpits or along the throat just below the chin.

Pathogens (disease-producing microorganisms) are ever-present in our environment. They are in the air we breathe, the food we eat, and the surfaces to which we are exposed. In fact, if our skin, throat, or other mucous membranes were cultured, most all of us would be found to contain one type of pathogen or another. At any given time, 5–40% of us have *pneumococcus* bacteria in our nose and throat, yet we rarely develop pneumonia, because our immune system keeps these pathogens under control.

So why does one person comes down with the flu but her co-worker or family member doesn't? There are many factors that affect who gets sick and who doesn't, but the strength of our immune system ultimately determines our fate. To put it figuratively, it's not the planted seed that determines who gets sick, but the state of the soil it's planted in.

TWO TYPES OF IMMUNITY

When a foreign invader enters the body or a cell becomes cancerous, the immune system handles it with two types of defenses: non-specific and specific.

- **Non-specific defenses are called cell-mediated immunity.** Cell-mediated immunity involves special white blood cells—typically T-cell lymphocytes and neutrophils—that immediately organize an attack against the invading pathogen. Cell-mediated immunity attempts to either prevent the invader from entering the body or quickly destroy it once it does. It's best suited to helping the body resist infection by yeast, fungi, parasites, and viruses, including those associated with CFS: herpes simplex, Epstein-Barr, and cytomegalovirus. Cell-mediated immunity is commonly involved in allergic reactions and is also critical in protecting against the development of cancer.

- **Specific defenses are known as humoral immunity.** Humoral immunity relies on special molecules, including white blood cells and antibodies, present in body fluids. The humoral immunity forms antibodies to match the surface cells of foreign invaders. It may take several days before these antibodies can be produced and delivered to the offending microorganisms.

THE THYMUS GLAND

Immune cells originate in the bone marrow, and about half of them are then transported to the thymus gland. The thymus gland, about the size of a walnut, is located at the base of the neck, right below the thyroid and above the heart.

> The thymus gland is the master gland of the immune system but is especially susceptible to free radicals, stress, infection, chronic illness, and radiation. When overly stressed, it becomes smaller.

It is in charge of cell-mediated immunity and is the source of powerful hormones that transform newly formed immune cells into mature T-cells.

T-CELLS

T-cells make up the majority of the cell-mediated immune system. These specialized cells patrol every part of the body for foreign invaders and help prevent cancer by destroying abnormal cells before they can proliferate.

> T-cells also help fight against bacteria, fungi, parasites, and yeast. The production of T-cells creates resistance to many viruses, including herpes simplex, Epstein-Barr, and the viruses associated with hepatitis.

There are many different kinds of T-cells. The most important ones are helper T-cells, which enhance the action of the other T-cells (they sound the alarm); killer T-cells, which destroy invaders, including viral and cancerous cells (they answer the call to battle); and suppressor T-cells, which dampen or turn down the immune system (they signal "all clear").

B-CELLS

The other type of blood cell that plays a major role in the immune response is the B-cell. The B-cell is an agent of the fast-acting humoral immune system. It helps manufacture antibodies and releases them into the blood steam where they are carried to the specific site of infection. These antibodies can perform in various ways. Some neutralize the poisons produced from bacteria. Others coat the bacteria and allow phagocytes (scavenger cells) to engulf and digest it.

NATURAL KILLER CELLS

Null cells are neither T- nor B-cells. One of the most important of these is the natural killer cell (NK cell).

> NK cells are especially important for those with
> CFS, because boosting NK cell function helps
> contain and eliminate the viruses associated with
> the syndrome. This is because NK cells seek out
> and destroy virally infected cells. Those with CFS
> tend to have lower NK cell levels than others.

HOW ALL THE PARTS WORK TOGETHER

The first line of defense is the surfaces of the body that work to prevent pathogens from entering. This line of defense is composed of three parts: mucous, antibodies, and the cells themselves. Mucous is a sticky substance that's found in many places within the body, including the respiratory tract. It traps pathogens and moves them off the membranes (for instance, out of the nose or into the intestines where they can be destroyed by the stomach acid). Secretory IgA, an important immunoglobulin in the body, releases chemicals that bind to the pathogens and block the penetration of the mucous membranes. Finally, the mucous membranes themselves form physical barriers to the invader.

But if a pathogen gets past the surface defenses, it invades the tissues, begins to spread, and damages cells. When this happens, the cells secrete a wide range of special chemicals including histamine, bradykinins, and serotonin. These chemicals alert the immune system that the body is under attack and trigger an increase in blood supply to the area (this is why someone who's sick gets inflammation and has a fever).

Now the non-specific response, the cell-mediated immunity, is activated. Various classes of white blood cells migrate to the area and attack the invaders. As a pathogen is damaged by the white cells, parts of it leak out of the cell.

These foreign parts (antigens) activate the specific response, the humoral immunity team. The antigens come in contact with special white cells called B-lymphocytes, which then produce specific antibodies. These antibodies directly attack the invaders and make them more recognizable to the macrophages, which are white blood cells that roam the body destroying pathogens. Then like Pac-Men, the macrophages gobble up the leftovers.

IMMUNE ZAPPERS

This list, borrowed partly from Dr. Joseph Pizzorno,[1] gives an idea of the many elements that can suppress the work of your immune system and short circuit your body's defenses.

- **Sugar in any form**—table sugar, honey, or fruit juice—lowers immunity. Just one tablespoon of simple sugar results in a 50% reduction in white blood cell activity for up to five hours.

- **Alcohol and other simply carbohydrates** can reduce the activity of certain white blood cells.

- **Food allergies** can cause a 50% reduction in white blood cell count. When the allergic food is eaten daily, the allergy can cause intestinal inflammation and destruction of white blood cells. Food allergies can also lead to leaky gut symptoms and autoimmune reactions. For more on leaky gut, see chapter 17, "The Digestive System: Our Fragile Ally."

- **Hypothyroidism** can lower metabolism and reduce enzyme activities associated with initiating proper immune functions.

- **Adrenal dysfunction** causes an inability to cope with acute or chronic stress. This leads to a taxed immune system that is always on "red alert."

- **Pesticides** and other environmental toxins, including heavy metals, can overwhelm the immune system.

- **Drugs,** both prescription and over-the-counter, decrease antibody production.

- **Poor sleep** results in suppressed NK cell activity.

- **Candida overgrowth** can cause a host of unwanted immune reactions.

What You Can Do: Immune Boosters

- **A healthy diet and plenty of rest** can go a long way toward fixing a sluggish immune system. Avoid simple sugars, eat balanced meals, exercise regularly, and allow yourself plenty of time for rest.

- **Thymus extracts**[2] have proven to be one of the best immune-boosting agents for treating CFS. A recent study published in the *Journal of Nutritional and Environmental Medicine* showed that patients taking ProBoost, a patented thymus extract, obtained dramatic improvements in their CFS symptoms. The increase in their immune function, as demonstrated by blood tests, resulted in myriad benefits: a 47% improvement in sleep quality, a 43% reduction in food sensitivities, a 53% reduction in chemical sensitivities, a 47% improvement in short-term memory, a 79% improvement in depression symptoms, and a 100% improvement in panic disorder symptoms. A substantial amount of clinical data now supports the effectiveness of using thymus extracts. They may well provide the answer to chronic viral infections and low immune function. Double-blind studies reveal not only that orally administered thymus extracts are able to effectively eliminate infection, but also that treatment over the course of a year significantly reduced the number of respiratory infections and significantly improved numerous immune parameters.

  Thymus glandular extracts are able to raise T-cell numbers when needed but will lower T-cell numbers when an autoimmune disease is present. This balancing act is the big advantage that glandular extracts and many natural herbs have over prescription, synthetic drugs.

- **Zinc** is an important cofactor in the manufacture, secretion, and function of thymus hormones. When zinc levels are low, T-cell numbers drop. This might explain why zinc lozenges, when used at the first sign of a cold, can reduce the number of sick days.

- **A good multivitamin/mineral formula** can provide antioxidants that will help protect the thymus gland from free-radical damage. Vitamins A, C, and E and the minerals zinc and selenium play a vital role in reducing the damage associated with free-radical toxicity.

- *Astragalus membranaceus,* a Chinese herbal, is used to treat a wide variety of viral infections. Clinical studies in China have even shown it to be effective (with ongoing use) against the common cold. Research in animals has revealed that it apparently works by stimulating NK cells and T-cells. *Astragalus* appears particularly useful in cases where the immune system has been damaged by chemicals or radiation.

- **Selenium** boosts the "killer instinct" of your blood cells. One study, using 200 mcg. daily in individuals with normal blood selenium levels, resulted in a 118% increase in the ability of their white blood cells to kill tumor cells, and an 82.3% increase in NK cell activity.

- **Echinacea** (purple coneflower) is one of the most popular herbal medicines in the United States and Europe. In 1994, German physicians prescribed echinacea more than 2.5 million times. There are over 200 journal articles written about echinacea. This herb, from the sunflower family, can be grown in your garden and is thought to stimulate the immune system by increasing the production of and activity of white blood cells, especially NK cells. Persons with autoimmune illnesses such as multiple sclerosis, lupus, or tuberculosis should not take echinacea. A typical dose is up to 900 mg. three times daily. Some physicians suggest discontinuing use after two–three weeks, then restarting as needed after one week.

- **Goldenseal** *(Hydrastis Canadensis)* is a perennial herb native to eastern North America, and it has shown itself to be a potent immune stimulator. It increases the blood flow to the spleen and the number and activity of macrophages. A typical dose is 250–500 mg. one–three times daily.

- **MGN-3** is a nutritional supplement with special patented chemicals, especially those derived from the immune-boosting Chinese Shiitake mushroom. Research has shown that MGN-3 triples the amount of natural killer cells. I've had good results with this product in CFS patients, but it is costly: $60–$70 for 50 capsules. A usual dose is two–four capsules a day. I am confident that it does in fact raise NK cell levels, which are notoriously low in CFS patients.

- **Essential Therapeutics CFS/Fibromyalgia Support Pack** is nearly always recommended for an FMS/CFS patient in our office. It contains zinc, selenium, and other potent immune-boosting vitamins.

- **Nature's Way Stay Well Formula** is an extremely comprehensive product, and I've been impressed with our patients' response to it. It contains over 33 nutrients designed to boost the circulatory, systemic, cellular, digestive, respiratory, lymphatic, and epidermal (skin) systems. Stay Well contains vitamins A, C, and D and the minerals selenium and zinc. The herbal extracts include garlic, echinacea, astragulas, olive leaf, shiitake mushroom, goldenseal, and many more. For $36–$40, this is an incredible product.

- **Cold water bath therapy** promotes increased health. The Thrombosis Research Institute found dramatic value in carefully graduated cold baths taken daily for six months. The institute gathered 5,000 volunteers, many of them suffering from CFS. The results of their first study showed that cold water baths, when properly applied, resulted in a boost to sex hormone production (which helps regulate potency in men and fertility in women), renewed energy in many CFS sufferers, rapidly improved circulation, increased levels of specific enzymes that aid in circulation, improved immune function (through an increase in white blood cell levels), reduced risk of heart attack and stroke (due to improved blood clotting abilities), and a reduction in unpleasant menopause symptoms. The key to experiencing these inexpensive, dramatic benefits is consistency. Follow these steps. (Important: cold water bath therapy is not recommended for people with heart disease, high blood pressure, or chronic disease, except under a doctor's supervision.)

Step one: For the first one–four weeks, simply stand daily in 55–60°F bath water for one–five minutes. Use a non-slip bath mat.

Step two: Once fully used to this temperature, take time to walk in place while standing in the bathtub. Do this for two full weeks. The internal thermostat is now stimulated and at the ideal level for the next step.

Step three: After standing in the cold water, sit down in it for another one–five minutes. Do this for four–six weeks, until you feel used to it.

Step four: Over the next four–six weeks, build up to being fully immersed in cold water for 10–20 minutes daily. You may need to start off at one–two minutes. This is the most important part of the program. After bathing in cold water, exit the tub and towel dry. Then move around for a few minutes to warm up.

Notes
[1]See *Total Wellness: Improve Your Health by Understanding the Body's Healing Systems* by Joseph E. Pizzorno, ND, 1996.
[2]To order supplements, see page 274.

Resources
• Dr. Murphree's CFS/Fibromyalgia formula and thymus extracts are available online at www.drrodger.com or by calling (205) 879-2383.
• Other supplements mentioned in this chapter are available at many health food stores.

For Further Reading
• *Beyond Antibiotics: 50 (Or So) Ways to Boost Immunity and Avoid Antibiotics* by Michael A. Schmidt, et al; 1994
• *Healer Within: The New Medicine of Mind and Body* by Steven Locke, MD; 1986
• *Dr. Braly's Food Allergy and Nutrition Revolution* by James Braly and Laura Torbet; 1992
• *Dr. Whitaker's Guide to Natural Healing* by Julian M. Whitaker; 1996

9

Food Allergies

Food allergies are known as the great masqueraders for their ability to cause or contribute to virtually any disease. So it's crucial to discover and eliminate all allergic reactions.

An allergy is a hypersensitive state acquired through exposure to a particular allergen (the substance that you are allergic to). A subsequent exposure to the same allergen then triggers an inappropriate immune response called an allergic reaction. If you have an allergy to hickory pollen, then you sneeze (allergic reaction) when you breath in the pollen (allergen). Allergens are usually some sort of protein molecules.

Food allergies are considered rare or inconsequential by many traditional doctors. But research and better diagnostic testing procedures are validating what many health care experts have known for quite some time: food allergies play a major role in our health. Conservative estimates are showing that 20% of young children in industrialized countries have food allergies.

I've found over the years that individuals with FMS/CFS have several food sensitivities or food allergies that contribute to their fatigue, depression, joint pain, muscle pain, and digestive problems.

ARCHAIC TESTING MISSES ALLERGIES

One problem is that many doctors (the same ones who would tell you "it's all in your head") use outdated testing and theories: specifically, the Reagin theory of allergic reactions. Around 1925, scientists in Europe discovered a substance they called Reagin. This substance appeared to be involved with allergic reactions involving the skin. Consequently, skin testing has become the primary means for determining allergies. Myopic thinking has prevented modern allergists from acknowledging that there might be another response that validates allergies, other than skin sensitivity.

Reagin was actually what we now know as immunoglobulin E (IgE), an antibody measurable through a skin prick test and the radioallergosorbent test (RAST). Both of these tests can detect acute or immediate allergic responses, but they're best for airborne allergens. They can't measure delayed sensitivity responses to food. 95% of all food allergies occur one hour to three days after eating allergic foods. These delayed reactions must be measured using a different antibody, immunoglobulin G1-4 (IgG1-4). Many of my patients come to me having already been tested and told they had allergies. Unfortunately they were only tested for IgE antibodies. Their airborne allergies were detected, but many of their food allergies were not.

Two tests that measure immediate IgE and delayed IgG1-4 reactions are the Enzyme-linked Immuno-absorbent Assay (ELISA) test and the Food Immune Complex Assay (FICA) test. Both offer the convenience and accuracy of measuring both types of antibodies, while costing hundreds less than RAST and skin prick tests.

SYMPTOMS OF FOOD ALLERGIES

Food allergies can cause headache, eczema, psoriasis, diarrhea, colitis, asthma, hyperactivity, rheumatoid arthritis, gout, chronic pain syndromes, edema, ear infections, anxiety, depression, and many other maladies too numerous to list.

CAUSES OF FOOD ALLERGIES

Intestinal permeability and food allergies go hand in hand. Undigested proteins can create an allergic inflammatory response at any site within the body: muscles, heart, brain, joints, etc.

Overeating the same foods can also create food intolerances or allergies. So try to go four–five days before eating the same food. Eat a varied but balanced diet.

The Elimination Diet

All allergy tests are associated with some degree of error. Even ELISA and FICA tests are no better than 85% accurate. False positives and missed allergic foods are a common occurrence on most tests, so the gold standard for uncovering allergen sensitivities is still the two-week elimination diet.

We start new patients on this diet on their first visit. It removes foods that have consistently been shown to cause allergic reactions. The elimination process creates an opportunity to uncover any hidden food allergies or intolerances, which may be contributing to the overall "toxic burden." Food allergies can cause dozens of symptoms similar to those experienced in FMS and CFS. Among them are irritable bowel syndrome, headaches, diffuse pain, depression, fatigue, irritability, sinusitis, and PMS. I've found over the years that individuals with CFS and FMS have several food intolerances and in many cases, true food allergies.

The elimination diet is an important part of our treatment plan, but following it can be a challenge. The problem most people run into is not being able to stay on the diet when they are away from home; a sudden wave of hunger comes over them, and they can't find anything in the office vending machine to eat. Don't let this happen to you. Always have plenty of snacks available at home, in the car, in your briefcase or purse, and at work. (I recommend you visit your local health-food store before beginning the diet.)

Remember, anything you can do to right your homeostatic system brings you closer to optimal health. Eliminating foods that are toxic to your body is another opportunity to feel better and lighten the toxic load zapping your homeostatic system. Don't get discouraged in the short-term! If correcting your problem was an easy thing to do, it would have already happened, right? The diet lasts two weeks.

Meredith's Story

It was so hard to stay on the diet. I craved pasta, breads, and pizza, and I didn't notice much difference in how I was feeling.

I reintroduced gluten into my diet on a Monday. I ate a bagel for breakfast, a turkey sandwich for lunch, and olive oil and lots of bread for dinner. I was so happy to be able to eat bread again! I was like a junky that had finally gotten her fix.

I immediately felt better that morning and was feeling fine until I woke up Wednesday morning barely able to get out of bed. My eyes were almost swollen shut. I had dark circles under my eyes, and I ached all over. I couldn't believe bread could have done this to me. So I waited a week and then reintroduced bread again. Once again I felt like a junky. Two days later, my symptoms returned. Not quite as bad, but they were back, and I felt awful! I've been off all wheat for a month and feel better than I've felt in years.

You Can Do It!

For the next two weeks, eliminate:

- all dairy products (except butter) including milk, cheese, yogurt, and ice cream.

- all corn and related products: corn syrup, popcorn etc.

- all gluten products, including wheat, oats, barley, kamut, spelt, and all flours.

- all soy products.

- all nightshade foods, including white potatoes, peppers, tomatoes, tobacco, and eggplant. Nightshades contain a poison similar to belladonna that may cause muscle or joint pain.

What You *Can* Eat

Lots of great vegetables (nothing fried in wheat/flour batter), including broccoli, cauliflower, squash, and spinach. All fruits, including pineapple, apples, oranges, pears, and bananas. All nuts, including pecans, walnuts, cashews, almonds, and peanuts. All meats, including chicken (not fried), beef, pork, and turkey. Fish and other seafoods (not fried). Rice, including rice pilaf, wild rice, rice cakes, rice pasta, and rice bread. Be sure to read labels and look for hidden ingredients. Some foods have wheat or soy added to them.

Yes, you can have all the eggs you want. No, it doesn't matter if you have caffeine, though I recommend you consume no more than one–two cups of coffee daily, and no sodas. Butter is fine and preferred over margarine. The diet is intended to uncover any hidden food sensitivities, not help you lose weight. However, you may experience weight loss while on this diet.

PINPOINTING THE ALLERGIC FOOD

After two weeks of totally avoiding the foods listed above, begin to challenge one food group at a time, beginning with dairy. For one day only, eat three or more servings of dairy while still avoiding the other food groups. Then immediately return to the elimination diet for three days. Remember, most food allergies are delayed reactions and can take up to three days before any symptoms are experienced. Keep a diet journal on hand to record the foods you eat and any symptoms you experience while reintroducing the eliminated foods.

After challenging dairy (and waiting three days), challenge another food group: gluten, for instance. Have oatmeal for breakfast, a sandwich for lunch, and buttered toast for a snack. Don't eat any other eliminated foods; you're only challenging gluten. Wait three more days before challenging another forbidden food group.

If you have a severe reaction, totally eliminate the offending food group for six months. Then slowly reintroduce it back into your diet: eat one small serving and wait a minimum of four days before eating another. Reactions may be avoided by slowly rotating these foods back into your diet.

In the case of a mild or moderate reaction, avoid the food group for one–three months (depending on the severity of your reaction) and then begin to reintroduce it.

Dr Coca's Pulse Test

The foods listed above are by far the most common allergic foods. However, practically any food can trigger an allergic reaction. For this reason you might want to dig a little deeper to pinpoint sensitivities to specific foods. Foods can actually be tested by merely tasting them. If a food elicits a rise in resting pulse rate, this indicates an allergic reaction. This is because the pulse is controlled by the autonomic nervous system, and stress causes this system to increase blood flow and pulse rate.

To use Dr. Coca's pulse test, you must first determine your resting pulse rate: count your pulse for a full minute while sitting still. (Sites commonly used to check the pulse are the underside of the wrist and the neck near the Adam's apple). It's best to check your pulse several times throughout the day and to notice if it changes at different times. Is it lower or higher in the morning? At night? To get the most accurate base line, take your pulse in bed before rising, before breakfast, after breakfast, in the middle of the morning, before lunch, after lunch, in the middle of the afternoon, before dinner, after dinner, in the middle of the evening, and before bed.

Keep a food diary and record your pulse rates and any symptoms. Does a pattern emerge? If there is no consistent pattern, there may be too many interfering substances undermining the process. If so, try the elimination diet for four–five days. Along with the obvious elimination foods, foods or chemicals in question should also be avoided during this time.

Your resting pulse is the pulse consistently found before eating, or an average of the lowest pulses most commonly recorded.

Testing Foods Using the Pulse Test

While sitting quietly, take your pulse. Then challenge this pulse by chewing a small amount of food or food supplement (don't swallow) for a full minute. Liquids can be held and swished around in the mouth. After one minute, take your pulse for a full minute. At the end of this time, expel the substance, and rinse out your mouth with pure water, which should also be expelled. Take your pulse again. If it returns to the resting value, you can repeat the process with another substance.

A positive-reaction food or supplement will elevate the pulse above six points. Avoid all such substances for two–three months. For someone who's been on a strict elimination diet for weeks, a rise of only one point may be significant. If other symptoms occur after testing, such as headache, sore throat, or fuzzy thinking, this is also a positive test, and the food should be avoided for three–six months. Severe-reaction foods should be avoided for at least three months.

TREATMENT OF FOOD ALLERGIES

- **Uncover any hidden food sensitivities** through elimination and pulse/blood testing. Once uncovered, these foods should be avoided for one–six months, depending on severity of reactions.

- **Begin a rotation diet** as described below to reduce the chances of developing further food allergies.

- **Supplement with vitamin C.** It's a natural antihistamine and may reduce the symptoms associated with allergic reactions. Take up to bowel tolerance (see page 120).

- **Supplement with stinging nettle root,** which helps reduce allergic rhinitis (runny nose) and hay fever symptoms. It also helps prevent the bronchial spasms associated with asthma. Take 500–1,000 mg. three times daily.

- **Supplement with quercetin,** a bioflavonoid (plant pigment) found in black tea, blue-green algae, broccoli, onions, red apples, and red wine. It inhibits the synthesis of certain enzymes responsible for triggering allergic reactions. It is chemically similar to the allergy prevention medication Cromolyn. Take 500–1,000 twice daily. It may take months before quercetin reaches its peak of effectiveness. It can interfere with the absorption of certain antibiotics, so don't take quercetin and antibiotics together.

- **Supplement with methylsulfonylmethane (MSM),** a natural organic sulfur compound found in plant and animal tissues. MSM has proven beneficial in the treatment of allergic and inflammation disorders. It provides sulfur, an essential component in detoxification. Due to its strong anti-inflammatory properties, it's included in our Essential Therapeutics Arthritis Formula. Normal dosage is 500 mg. three–four times daily.

- **Supplement with adrenal glandular extract.** See chapter 7, "Those Invaluable Adrenals."

- **Consider Cromolyn,** a prescription medication used to prevent allergic reactions. It helps reduce the number of mast cells, the major producers of histamine. It can be made into a nose spray for allergic rhinitis or into eye drops for allergic conjunctivitis. But it's associated with several unwanted side effects. I've found the natural remedies to be much more useful and without the side effects.

- **Supplement with *Boswellia serrata*** (Indian frankincense), an Indian herb with anti-inflammatory properties. It helps prevent allergic inflammation and can be used to treat allergies and arthritis. Take 200 mg. three times daily. This powerful anti-inflammatory is also in our CFS/Fibromyalgia formula.

- **Treat intestinal permeability** as I've described in chapter 17.

THE ROTATION DIET

Once someone becomes sensitive to foods, damage to the intestinal tract has most likely occurred. Repetitive exposure to the same foods may initiate allergic reactions. Left untreated, intestinal permeability and overstimulation of the immune system can create an allergy to almost any food. A rotation diet helps reduce the chances of developing further allergies.

On this diet, you eat nonallergic foods every day for four–seven days. Allergic foods (as determined by testing or elimination dieting) are slowly reintroduced into the diet over a period of months. Consult a nutritionist for help in devising a suitable rotation diet.

FOOD GROUPS

Grains
wheat, barley, oats, rice, rye, buckwheat, millet, and corn

Seeds
sesame, sunflower, and pumpkin seeds

Nuts
almonds, walnuts, pecans, pistachios, cashews, filberts, Brazil nuts, chestnuts, and coconut

Oils
safflower, sunflower, soy, cottonseed, olive, sesame, corn, and peanut oils

Sweeteners
maple sugar, beet sugar, cane sugar, corn syrup, and honey

Vegetables
olives, eggplant, tomato, potatoes, peppers, paprika, sweet potatoes, yams, broccoli, cauliflower, kale, artichokes, cabbage, Brussels sprouts, radishes, turnips, parsnips, carrots, celery, zucchini, Swiss chard, spinach, winter squash, summer squash, cucumbers, lettuces, onions, garlic, chives, and asparagus

Legumes
black-eyed peas, navy beans, pinto beans, wax beans, string beans, green beans, chick-peas, soybeans, lima beans, mung beans, peanuts, lentils, and carob

Fruit
lemons, limes, oranges, pineapples, peaches, plums, pears, apples, tangerines, grapefruit, nectarines, bananas, grapes, prunes, papayas, figs, mangoes, kiwi, cherries, apricots, cranberries, strawberries, blackberries, and raspberries

Melons
watermelons, cantaloupe, and honeydew melon

Dairy
milk, cheese, yogurt, goat's milk, cream, butter, and ice cream

Poultry
chicken, eggs, turkey, duck, pheasant, quail, and goose

Meat
beef, lamb, and pork

Seafood
fish, shrimp, oysters, clams, mussels, lobster, scallops, crayfish, and crab

Flavorings
dill, comfrey, tarragon, coriander, pepper, cinnamon, mustard, caraway, ginger, vanilla, cocoa, thyme, basil, oregano, alfalfa, rosemary, sage, peppermint, clove, and nutmeg

Fungus
mushrooms, hops, and bakers and brewers yeast

Your Rotation Diet: A Sample Menu

If you elect not to be tested by a lab, use the elimination diet and/or the pulse test method to uncover any food allergies. Then create your own rotation diet using the food groups listed above. Use a calendar with space for you to write out three meals a day plus snacks. Avoid known allergic foods for three–six months, and make sure you wait at least days before repeating a food.

Monday

Breakfast: eggs, wheat toast, orange

Snack: apple and cashews

Lunch: romaine lettuce with olive oil and vinegar; turkey breast with wheat bread, mustard, tomato, and mayo

Dinner: egg omelet with cheddar cheese, broccoli, and onions

Snack: cashews and strawberries

Tuesday

Breakfast: pork bacon or sausage with oatmeal and raisins

Snack: almonds and a pear

Lunch: chicken salad (no bread or mayo), pear, and grapes

Dinner: baked chicken, asparagus, and corn on the cob

Snack: popcorn

Wednesday

Breakfast: cream of rice topped with banana and blueberries; rice milk

Snack: tangerine and Brazil nuts

Lunch: corned beef on plain rye with sauerkraut and Swiss cheese (no mayo or mustard) and baked potato fries

Dinner: steak with okra, wild rice, and pinto beans

Snack: walnuts, blueberries, and dates

Thursday

Breakfast: honeydew melon or cantaloupe, peanut butter on millet bread

Snack: Pumpkin seeds and sunflower seeds

Lunch: Baked fish with cauliflower, squash, and zucchini

Dinner: Lobster, crab cakes, or shrimp salad and olive, artichoke, tomato, and yellow peppers

Snack: cherries and pistachios

Friday (Repeat Monday's menu)

This is an example of how to rotate your food groups, but you can create your own plan. Eating out can present a challenge, but I've found that most restaurants will accommodate your special needs once you mention food allergies.

For help, visit your local health food store. Take this book and explain your diet. These stores are especially helpful in supplying hard to find grains, seeds, snacks, and nuts.

REMOVING UNWANTED PATHOGENS

Our office uses the following tests to uncover any opportunistic infections.

- comprehensive parasitology stool test
- yeast stool profile: tests for yeast and bacterial overgrowth within the small intestine and for parasites, including *Entamoeba histolytica* and *Giardia lamblia*
- Epstein-Barr virus and cytomegalovirus profile: helps uncover active forms of these debilitating viruses

These tests usually take two–three weeks to return from the lab. This allows us time to start patients on supplements essential for correcting the homeostatic dysfunction. My experiences from treating FMS/CFS patients over the past seven years shows that building up their resistance to stress (through good nutrition and supplements) is an important step before adding prescription and/or herbal medicines to treat a viral or bacterial infection or a yeast overgrowth. FMS and CFS is usually initiated by long-term stress, and as the patient gets sicker, she's unable to tolerate even the slightest increase in stress. Physicians and patients alike must remember that all treatment modalities—drugs, supplements, physical therapy—are by nature stressful. Trying to do too much, too fast, can have negative consequences.

For Further Reading

- *Enzymes the Fountain of Life* by M. Miehlke; 1994
- *Is This Your Child?: Discovering and Treating Unrecognized Allergies in Children and Adults* by Doris J. Rapp; 1992
- *Diet and Disease* by Emanuel Cheraskin et al; 1988
- *Brain Allergies: The Psychonutrient and Magnetic Connections* by William H. Philpott, MD, et al; 2000
- *Reversing Asthma: Breathe Easier With This Revolutionary New Program* by Richard N. Firshein, DO; 1998
- *Functional Assessment Resource Manual,* Great Smokies Diagnostic Laboratory; 1999

10

Why We Recommend Supplements

Vitamins and minerals are essential ingredients for every bodily function. A deficiency in any one of these valuable nutrients will prevent you from truly winning the battle against FMS/CFS.

It is no surprise that health is declining in today's society. Many people's vitamin and mineral stores are being gradually drained, and the body processes that depend on them are suffering. Is it any wonder we have such illnesses as FMS and CFS? Frankly I'm surprised there are not more cases.

> Dr. Janet Travell, White House physician for two presidents and professor emeritus of internal medicine at George Washington University, co-wrote (with Dr. David Simons) the authoritative work on muscle pain. In one chapter alone, the doctors reference 317 studies showing that problems such as hormonal, vitamin, and mineral deficiencies contribute to muscle pain and soreness.[1]

Actually, thousands of published studies have demonstrated the benefits of taking a multivitamin and mineral on a daily basis. This healthy habit reduces the incidence of heart disease, heart attack, stroke, glaucoma, macular degeneration, type-2 diabetes, senile dementia, and various cancers. There are many causes for the nutritional deficiencies that create the need for supplements: poor eating habits, malabsorption, food allergies, inadequate detoxification, chronic use of certain medications, overuse of alcohol or caffeine, pregnancy, stress, illnesses, strenuous exercise.

Some so-called experts will tell you not to worry about taking supplements. You might hear, "Oh, you'll get all the nutrients you need by eating a balanced diet." If you ever encounter a doctor who says this, simply smile and head for the nearest exit. Such a statement is some twenty years behind in research. It demonstrates ignorance about the abundance of bleached bread, toxic meats, allergy-producing dairy products, and nutritionally-void, simple carbohydrates. How can a diet of these things (which would still be considered balanced) provide the necessary vitamins and minerals the body requires to be healthy? It's no secret that our food supply is tainted with poisonous chemicals and laden with preservatives that rob the body of needed nutrients. In addition, most of our foods are processed, and the nutrients have been leeched out of them. 70% of the population are deficient in magnesium, 65% are deficient in zinc, 48% in calcium, and 56% in vitamin C. It's clear that everyone can benefit from taking a good multivitamin. Even if you follow my recommendations and begin to incorporate healthy eating habits, you'll need to take supplements for optimum health.

THE RDA IS NOT ENOUGH

Almost as criminal as not recommending vitamin and mineral supplements is the recommendation of them based on the American recommended daily allowances (RDA). The RDA list is some fifty years out of date, and it was never intended to advance health, only to prevent diseases like scurvy and rickets. It does not take into account the depletion of our nutrient-rich top soil, environmental pollutants, chemical food processing, the addition of artificial ingredients, and the increased demands placed on an individual's homeostatic system in the twenty-first century. Taking the minimum amount of a nutrient to prevent gross deficiency diseases doesn't help those of us who want to be truly healthy.

One hundred years ago, our ancestors ate foods grown locally. Crops were harvested in mineral-rich soils free of pesticides and toxic fertilizers. Their meats contained no added hormones or antibiotics. They didn't have synthetic foods, robbed of their nutrients: bleached bread, margarine, hydrogenated oil, and junk foods loaded with preservatives and simple sugars. Their diets consisted mainly of grains, fruits, and vegetables with a little bit of dairy and organic meats. Because of this, they didn't need any supplements to shore up their diets. But following the antiquated RDA guidelines now is like traveling in a horse and buggy when you could be riding in a Cadillac. The horse and buggy may get you to the end of the road, but the luxury car makes the ride a lot smoother. And today's society calls for a car...or you'll simply get run over.

RECOMMENDED DAILY ALLOWANCE (RDA) VS. OPTIMAL DAILY ALLOWANCE (ODA)

The table below is based on clinical trials, experience, and the work of other nutritionally oriented physicians, including James Braly, MD. ("IU" represents international units.)

Nutrient	RDA	ODA
vitamin A	1,000 mcg.	5,000–7,500 IU
vitamin D	200 IU	200–400 IU
vitamin E	15 IU	200–800 IU
vitamin K	80 mcg.	80–300 mcg.
vitamin B_1	1.5 mg.	50–100 mg.
vitamin B_2	1.7 mg.	25–50 mg.
vitamin B_3	19 mg.	50–200 mg.
vitamin B_5	7 mg.	200–400 mg.
vitamin B_6	2 mg.	50–100 mg.
folic acid	200 mcg.	400–800 mcg.
vitamin C	60 mg.	1,000 mg. or more
calcium	800 mg.	500–1,200 mg.
chromium	50–200 mcg.	200–400 mcg.
copper	1.5–3.0 mg.	2 mg.
iron	10 mg.	supplement only if needed
magnesium	350 mg.	500–800 mg.

manganese	2.5–5.0 mg.	5–10 mg.
molybdenum	75–250 mcg.	same unless deficient
potassium	2,000 mg.	200–500 mg.
selenium	70 mcg.	100–200 mcg.
zinc	15 mg.	15–45 mg.

OUR ESSENTIAL THERAPEUTICS CFS/FIBROMYALGIA SUPPORT PACK

Compare Centrum or One-A-Day brand multivitamin and mineral supplements to our Essential Therapeutics CFS/Fibromyalgia formula, and you'll notice that our specially designed supplement is much more suited to optimum health. Our formulas may contain 50 times—and in some cases 100 times—the RDA of a nutrient.

Our CFS/Fibromyalgia formula contains optimal doses of vitamin C, B vitamins, and magnesium for combating FMS/CFS. Vitamin C is an antioxidant that helps repair damaged cells, boost the immune system, decrease allergies, and reduce the risk of chronic illnesses, including heart disease and type-2 diabetes. B vitamins are involved in almost every bodily function. They are needed to make serotonin and other brain chemicals that regulate our pain threshold, immune system, sleep patterns, sex hormones, and moods.

The formula also contains coenzyme Q10, which assists the work of the mitochondria (the power plants of the cells). Proper coenzyme Q10 levels help increase each cell's energy production, and a deficiency of coenzyme Q10 can lead to fatigue, muscle pain, irregular heartbeat, depression, and even premature cell death.

Essential fatty acids, such as omega 3s, 6s, and 9s, can be tough to get enough of in our diets, so they are included in our CFS/Fibromyalgia formula. These are the good fats that your body needs to be able to communicate from one cell to the next. They also can help improve mood and reduce inflammation and pain. They help reduce bad cholesterol, ease symptoms associated with attention deficit disorder, and counter certain allergic chemicals.

Our supplement also contains all of the essential free-form amino acids. These are the building blocks of each protein molecule and help with our mood, energy, immune system, metabolism, and sleep.

RHONDA JOY'S STORY

I'd say along with the adrenal supplements, the FMS formula has made the biggest difference in how well I feel. If I miss a few days of either supplement, I start to feel sluggish and run down. I've taken dozens of different supplements over the last few years, but none have seemed to help like the ones Dr. Murphree recommended.

Before, I had to carry pills around in my pockets or purse. Sometimes I'd lose them, or they would melt. And I was buying bottles of all different things. It got expensive and time-consuming. Usually I lost interest and simply gave up. Now I like the convenience of taking a pack in the morning and one in the afternoon.

Notes
[1]*Myofascial Pain and Dysfunction: The Trigger Point Manual,* 1999

Resources
• Dr. Murphree's CFS/Fibromyalgia formula is available online at www.drrodger.com or by calling (205) 879-2383.

For Further Reading
• *Total Nutrition: The Only Guide You'll Ever Need* by Victor Herbert (editor), et al; 1995

11

You Need These Vitamins

Still doubt the role of vitamins and minerals in our pursuit of good health? Read on, and I think you'll be impressed, as I am, by the critical purposes of each amazing micronutrient.

Vitamin A is a potent antioxidant with immune-enhancing abilities. A deficiency in zinc ceases vitamin A metabolism, even when the vitamin is abundant. Too much vitamin A can lead to dry lips and skin, headache, thinning hair, and bone pain, but symptoms are quickly reversed when levels are reduced. White spots on the fingernails indicate a zinc and vitamin A deficiency and suggest reduced immunity. Especially important in FMS/CFS, vitamin A helps correct intestinal permeability (leaky gut). Leaky gut is associated with such allergic reactions as migraine, asthma, rheumatoid arthritis, irritable bowel, cystitis, sinusitis, rhinitis, ear infection, dermatitis, hives, and eczema. Vitamin A's other benefits include:

- developing and maintaining the surfaces of the mucous membranes, lungs, skin, stomach, and urinary, digestive, and reproductive tracts.

- maintaining a healthy thymus gland, which controls the entire immune system.

- helping to form bones and soft tissue, including tooth enamel.
- protecting against some cancers.
- treating acne (both orally and topically).
- enabling night vision.
- usefulness in calcium metabolism.
- protecting against asthma.
- reducing allergic reactions.
- helping prevent birth defects when taken by expectant mothers (a minimum of 2,000 IUs and no more than 8,000 IUs per day).

Beta-carotene can be converted into vitamin A, and beta-carotene is relatively nontoxic, whereas too much vitamin A can be quite dangerous. Beta-carotene is a group of caratenoids, which are found in dark green, yellow, and dark orange fruits and vegetables. It is a strong antioxidant with anticancer properties—one molecule of beta-carotene can destroy 1,000 free radicals. It protects the skin from harmful ultraviolet (UV) light. Women with low levels of beta-carotene in their cervical tissues are at risk for developing cervical cancer. A nineteen-year study involving 3,000 men shows caratenoids (especially beta-carotene) may significantly reduce the incidence of lung cancer in both smokers and non-smokers. (Studies have also demonstrated a 45% reduction in lung cancer in those individuals who take vitamin supplements.) Vitamin E and selenium enhance the role of beta-carotene. The only side effect of consuming too much beta-carotene is a yellowing of the skin, and this condition disappears once the intake is reduced.

Vitamin D is produced by the body after exposure to sunlight. It helps maintain healthy nerve and muscle systems by regulating the level of circulating calcium, which is essential for proper nerve transmission and muscle function. A deficiency in vitamin D can cause degeneration of bones and possibly hearing loss, if the small bones in the ear are involved.

Vitamin E is a major antioxidant that protects cells and tissues from oxidative stress. It also protects—from free-radical damage—the pituitary and adrenal hormones, fatty acids, and myelin sheaths surrounding nerves and genetic material. A deficiency in vitamin E can lead to heart disease, muscular dystrophy, nervous system disorders, anemia, liver damage, and birth defects. Smokers need to take extra vitamin E, since research at the University of California shows that vitamin E and vitamin C levels are reduced by exposure to cigarette smoke. Studies done in Israel show vitamin E can reduce the symptoms of osteoarthritis. Its other benefits include:

- preventing abnormal blood clotting.

- increasing the efficiency of muscles—including the heart—by reducing oxygen requirements.

- effectively reducing tension in the lower extremities, which is associated with intermittent claudication and heart disease.

- relieving restless leg syndrome or "the fidgets."

- helping to slow the aging process.

- increasing and maintaining proper brain function.

- helping protect the body from the toxic effects of lead and mercury.

Many studies have uncovered the body's many uses of vitamin E. One recently conducted at Columbia University shows the ability of vitamin E to slow the effects of Alzheimer's. Researchers at Tufts University found that on a diet supplemented with 200 IUs of vitamin E, control groups had a 65% increase in immune-fighting abilities. In another study at Harvard School of Public Health, people who supplement their diets with 100 IUs of vitamin E reduced their risk of heart disease by 40 percent (100 IUs is seven times the RDA). Researchers at Duke University have demonstrated that vitamin E acts as a potent antioxidant to counter the toxic effects of air pollution. (The amount needed to combat air pollution, including ozone and nitrous oxide, is six times the RDA.)

Selenium enhances the effects of vitamin E. A zinc deficiency increases the need for vitamin E. Vitamin E may be necessary for the synthesis of Vitamin B-12. Vitamin E is relatively nontoxic, but taken in very high doses, it can cause interference with vitamin K and lead to prolonged bleeding. Vitamin

E is safe, however, even when taken in dosages several times higher than the RDA. (The body stores fat-soluble vitamins, which include vitamins A, D, E, K, and beta-carotene. Because of this, an overdose is possible when taking these vitamins. However, the side effects of vitamin toxicity are quickly eliminated once they are discontinued.)

Vitamin B1 (thiamin) is needed to metabolize carbohydrates, fats, and proteins. It is important for proper cell function, especially nerve cell function. It is involved in the production of acetylcholine, a nerve chemical directly related to memory and physical and mental energy. A deficiency of Vitamin B1 can lead to fatigue, mental confusion, emaciation, depression, irritability, upset stomach, nausea, and tingling in the extremities. Vitamin B1 has been reported to be deficient in nearly 50% of the elderly. This could possibly explain the dramatic increase in presenile dementia and Alzheimer's disease the past few decades. Diets high in simple sugars, including alcohol, will increase the chances of a vitamin B1 deficiency. The tannins in tea inhibit vitamin B1 absorption.

Vitamin B2 (riboflavin) is responsible for the metabolism of carbohydrates, fats, and proteins. Vitamin B2 is involved in producing neurotransmitters, which are brain chemicals responsible for sleeping, mental and physical energy, happiness, and mental acuity. A deficiency of vitamin B2 can cause soreness and burning of the lips, mouth, and tongue; sensitivity to light; itching and burning eyes; and cracks in the corners of the mouth. Vitamin B2 can help curb the craving for sweets and is needed for the synthesis of Vitamin B6. Vitamin B2 is needed to convert the amino acid tryptophan to Niacin (B3). Vitamin B2 is not absorbed very well, and any excess will turn the urine a bright fluorescent yellow. It is not toxic.

Vitamin B3 (niacin) plays an important role in mental health. Orthomolecular physicians have used niacin to treat schizophrenia, anxiety, and depression. It is a by-product of the metabolism of tryptophan. Some people have a genetic inability to breakdown or absorb tryptophan, and this can lead to aggressive behavior, restlessness, hyperactivity, and insomnia.

Large daily doses of niacin can decrease the bad LDL cholesterol and triglycerides while increasing the good HDL cholesterol. Niacin increases circulation, and this helps prevent blood clots and arteriosclerosis, which can lead to heart disease and stroke. A deficiency of niacin can cause weakness, dry skin, lethargy, headache, irritability, loss of memory, depression, delirium, insomnia, and disorientation. Large doses of vitamin B3 can cause a flushing of the skin, but this can be prevented by starting off with 25 mg. daily and gradually increasing the dosage over a period of days, because the flushing is due to the release of cellular histamine. Niacin acts as a wonderful sedative to calm nerves and help with sleep. Daily doses of 1,000 mg. appear to be safe, and large doses are needed to treat high cholesterol. To treat high cholesterol, use timed-release Niacin. For psychiatric disorders, including anxiety, depression, and insomnia, use a special version of vitamin B3 known as niacinamide.

Vitamin B5 (pantothenic acid) is crucial for managing stress and boosting the immune system, needed by all cells in the body, and required for normal functioning of the gastrointestinal tract. It converts carbohydrates, fats, and proteins into energy. It is needed to produce adrenal hormones, which play an important role in stress management. In fact, vitamin B5 is sometimes referred to as the "antistress" vitamin. Vitamin B5 can help reduce anxiety and may play a significant role in depression recovery. It helps convert choline into acetylcholine, which is responsible for memory. A deficiency in vitamin B5 can lead to fatigue, depression, irritability, digestive problems, upper respiratory infections, dermatitis, muscle cramps, and loss of sensation in the extremities. Vitamin B5, along with vitamin C, helps to reduce uric acid levels (increased uric acid levels are associated with gouty arthritis). Vitamin B5 helps boost endurance by manufacturing ATP, an essential chemical for cellular energy. Large doses may cause diarrhea.

Vitamin B6 (pyridoxine) may be the most important B vitamin. It is involved in more bodily functions than any other vitamin, and its benefits include:
- making neurotransmitters, including serotonin, epinephrine, and norepinephrine.
- inhibiting the formation of homocysteine, a toxic chemical associated with heart disease.

- helping to synthesize DNA and RNA.
- helping metabolize essential fatty acids.
- helping prevent the destruction caused by free radicals.
- helping produce hydrochloric acid, which is crucial for proper digestion.
- helping form hemoglobin.
- serving as a natural diuretic.
- alleviating carpal tunnel syndrome (tingling or pain in the wrists and hands).
- stimulating IgA antibodies, which help prevent tooth decay.

A vitamin B6 deficiency can cause anemia, even if normal iron levels are present. Deficiency can also lead to premenstrual syndrome, depression, insomnia, fatigue, tingling and numbness in the extremities, increased susceptibility to infections, nausea, kidney stones, anemia, irritability, tension, headache, fluid retention, and acne. Vitamin B6 may be suppressed by certain medications, including oral contraceptives and estrogen. Some asthmatics have a malfunction in the way they assimilate vitamin B6 and process tryptophan. Supplementing with 250–500 mg. of vitamin B6 a day may help with symptoms of asthma. Vitamin B6 is needed for proper magnesium levels in red blood cells. Orthomolecular physicians use megadoses of vitamin B6 to treat schizophrenia.

Vitamin B12 (cobalamin) is the only B vitamin stored by the body. A vitamin B12 deficiency occurs only in malnutrition, malabsorption, or other impediments to proper digestion. Unfortunately, these conditions still exist in American society today. We often don't even realize it.

Vitamin B12 is important in the growth of children. It is responsible for the replication of genetic material and so is essential for the development and maintenance of all the cells. Vitamin B12 helps form the myelin sheath that insulates nerve processes. This sheath allows rapid communication from one cell to another. A deficiency of B12 can cause a reduction in mental acuity, evidenced by poor memory. Alzheimer's and senile dementia, two diseases associated with memory loss, confusion, and nerve damage, might both be attributed to a deficiency of vitamin B12. B12 is only found in animal products (especially liver), so vegetarians should supplement with vitamin B12. antigout medications, anticoagulant drugs, and potassium supplements may interfere with B12 absorption, and taking antacids will block its absorption. Calcium is necessary for normal absorption of B12. High doses of folic acid can mask the symptoms of a vitamin B12 deficiency anemia.

Because vitamin B12 deficiency is routinely seen in the elderly, I believe everyone over the age of 60 should be supplementing with vitamin B12. Vitamin B12 is not toxic.

Biotin is critical to the body's fat metabolism, and it aids in the utilization of protein, folic acid, B12, and pantothenic acid. Sufficient quantities are needed for healthy hair and nails. Biotin may help prevent hair loss in some men. Biotin is also important in promoting healthy bone marrow, nervous tissue, and sweat glands. A deficiency in biotin can cause brittle nails, hair loss, and depression.

Saccharin inhibits the absorption of biotin. Raw egg whites, antibiotics, and sulfa drugs all prevent proper utilization of biotin. Due to poor absorption, infants are susceptible to a biotin deficiency. Symptoms of a deficiency include a dry, scaly scalp and/or face. This is known as seborrheic dermatitis. A biotin deficiency is considered rare, and deficiency is usually seen in hospitalized patients on intravenous feeding tubes or patients taking large dosages of antibiotics. Symptoms of a deficiency include depression, dry skin, conjunctivitis, hair loss and color, elevated cholesterol, anemia, loss of appetite, muscle pain, numbness in the hands and feet, nausea, lethargy, and enlargement of the liver. Biotin is not toxic.

Choline is essential for the health of the liver, gall bladder, kidneys, and nerves. It helps with fat and cholesterol metabolism. It prevents fat from accumulating while helping fight fat buildup in the arteries and liver. Our bodies can make choline from vitamin B12, folic acid, and the amino acid methionine. Choline is essential for brain development and proper liver function. A deficiency in choline may cause poor memory and mental fatigue. Megadoses of choline have been used to treat Alzheimer's disease, Huntington's disease, learning disabilities, and tardive dyskenesia with varying degrees of success. Choline is not toxic.

Vitamin C (ascorbic acid) produces and maintains collagen, a protein that forms the foundation for connective tissue, the most abundant tissue in the body. Benefits of vitamin C include:

- fighting bacterial infections.

- helping wounds heal.

- preventing hemorrhaging.

- reducing allergy symptoms.

- helping to prevent heart disease.

- helping prevent free-radical damage.

- acting as a natural antihistamine.

- reducing blood pressure in mild hypertension.

- preventing the progression of cataracts.

- helping regulate blood sugar levels.

- possibly improving fertility.

- lowering LDL (bad) cholesterol while raising HDL (good) cholesterol.

- increasing immune system function.

- helping the adrenal glands form important stress hormones.

- helping prevent toxicity of cadmium, a heavy metal that can increase the risk of heart disease.

- counteracting other heavy metals, including mercury and copper.

A deficiency in vitamin C can cause bleeding gums, loose teeth, dry and scaly skin, tender joints, muscle cramps, poor wound healing, lethargy, loss of appetite, depression, and swollen arms and legs. Vitamin C is important in the conversion of tryptophan to serotonin, and low serotonin levels are linked to insomnia and depression. A deficiency of vitamin C causes an increase in urinary excretion of vitamin B6 (also associated with making neurotransmitters). Aspirin, alcohol, antidepressants, anticoagulants, oral contraceptives, analgesics, and steroids can all interfere with vitamin C absorption. Ester C is absorbed four times faster than regular ascorbic acid. Most vitamin C is lost in the urine, but only one-third that amount of ester C is lost in urination. Pregnant women should not exceed 5,000 mg. in a day. Large doses of Vitamin C can cause diarrhea. I, along with many other nutritional experts, recommend gradually increasing vitamin C until you have a loose stool. Then, reduce your intake 500 mg. at a time until you no longer have diarrhea. This is your optimal dose.

Folic Acid is considered brain food. It is involved with energy production, synthesis of DNA, formation of red blood cells, metabolism of all amino acids, and production of the neurotransmitters, including serotonin. Folic acid needs vitamins B12, B3, and C to be converted into its active form. Low folic acid levels are associated with an increase in homocysteine, an amino acid linked to cardiovascular disease (vitamin B6, folic acid, and vitamin B12 all help reduce homocystesine levels). A deficiency in folic acid (one the most common vitamin deficiencies), will produce macrocytic anemia, digestive disorders, heart palpitations, weight loss, poor appetite, headache, irritability, depression, insomnia, and mood swings. A sore, red tongue may also indicate a folic acid deficiency.

When taken by pregnant women, folic acid can improve an infant's birth weight, neurological development, and chances of escaping a neural tube defect. Women trying to get pregnant and expectant mothers should take a multivitamin with at least 400 mcg. of folic acid. Large doses of folic acid can mask a vitamin B12 deficiency.

Inositol is important in the metabolism of fats and cholesterol, and in the proper function of the kidneys and liver. It is vital for hair growth and prevents hardening of the arteries. Inositol is needed for the synthesis of lecithin, which helps remove fats from the liver. Along with gamma-aminobutyric acid (GABA), inositol may help reduce anxiety. Caffeine may decrease inositol stores. There is no known deficiency or toxicity for inositol.

Para-aminobenzoic acid (PABA) is needed to form red and white blood cells, which in turn, form essential B vitamins. PABA is used in suntan lotion to help block harmful UV rays and prevent sunburn. PABA has antiviral properties and has been reported to help in treating Rocky Mountain spotted fever. PABA may help restore gray hair to its natural color.

PABA and sulfa drugs cancel each other out. Doses over 1,000 mg. can cause nausea and vomiting.

Resources
• All the vitamins discussed in this chapter are contained in Dr. Murphree's CFS/Fibromyalgia formula, available online at www.drrodger.com or by calling (205) 879-2383.

For Further Reading
• *Total Nutrition: The Only Guide You'll Ever Need* by Victor Herbert (editor), et al; 1995
• *Nutritional Influences on Illness: A Sourcebook of Clinical Research* by Melvyn R. Werbach; 1996
• *Depression: Cured at Last!* by Sherry A. Rogers; 1997
• *Orthomolecular Medicine for Physicians* by Abram Hoffer; 1997
• *Dr. Braly's Food Allergy and Nutrition Revolution* by James Braly, MD; 1992
• *Prescription for Nutritional Healing* by Phyllis A. Balch, CNC and James F. Balch, MD; 2000

12

You Need These Minerals

Magnesium, for example, is a player in over 300 bodily processes. A deficiency can trigger a chain reaction in which millions of important functions are negatively affected.

Boron is needed in trace amounts for the proper absorption of calcium. A recent study by the US Department of Agriculture showed women who consumed 3 mg. of boron a day lost 40% less calcium and one-third less magnesium in their urine. Excessive amounts of boron can cause nausea, diarrhea, skin rashes, and fatigue.

Calcium is the most abundant mineral in the body. It comprises two–three pounds of total body weight and is essential for the formation of bones and teeth. Calcium regulates heart rhythm, cellular metabolism, muscle coordination, blood clotting, and nerve transmission. Adequate intake of calcium can help lower high blood pressure and the incidence of heart disease. Calcium contributes to the release of neurotransmitters. It can also have a calming effect on the nervous system. A deficiency of calcium can result in hypertension, insomnia, osteoporosis, tetany (muscle spasm), and periodontal disease.

The ratio of calcium-to-magnesium and calcium-to-phosphorous is important. Recommended ratios are 2 to 1 (or 1.5 to 1) for calcium to magnesium and 2 to 1 (or 3 to 1) for calcium to phosphorous.

Vitamin D is needed for the absorption of calcium. Calcium absorption is decreased by high protein, fat, and phosphorous (junk food) diets. Chelated calcium (bound to a protein for easier absorption) and magnesium can help reduce aluminum and lead poisoning. Excessive calcium intake (several grams a day) can cause calcium deposits in the soft tissue, including the blood vessels (causing arteriosclerosis) and kidneys (causing stones). Oyster shell or bone meal calcium supplements often contain high levels of toxic lead. Calcium citrate or ascorbate are recommended instead.

Chromium is involved in the metabolism of blood sugar (glucose). It is essential in the synthesis of cholesterol, fats, and protein. Chromium helps stabilize blood sugar and insulin levels. Proper interaction between blood sugar and insulin insures proper protein production, reducing the chance for fat storage. A deficiency in chromium can cause type-2 diabetes, hypoglycemia, and coronary artery disease. Ninety percent of the US population is deficient in chromium! Diets high in simple sugars increase the loss of chromium, and a deficiency can cause a craving for sugar. Zinc can inhibit chromium absorption and should always be taken separately. Chromium is not toxic.

Copper maintains the myelin sheath, which wraps around nerves and facilitates nerve communication. It plays a vital role in regulating the neurotransmitters and helps maintain the cardiovascular and skeletal systems as well. It is part of the antioxidant enzyme supraoxide dismutase and may help protect cells from free-radical damage. Copper helps with the absorption of iron, and a deficiency in copper can lead to anemia, gray hair, heart disease, poor concentration, numbness and tingling in the extremities, decreased immunity, and possibly scoliosis.

Cadmium, molybdenum, and sulfate can interfere with copper absorption. A niacin deficiency can cause an elevation of copper. Zinc and copper impair the absorption of one another, so they should be taken separately. Intake of 20 mg. or more in a day can cause nausea and vomiting.

Wilson's disease is a genetic disorder characterized by excessive accumulation of copper in the tissues, as well as liver disease, mental retardation, tremors, and loss of coordination.

Iron is important in formation of hemoglobin, oxygen use, energy production, muscle function, thyroid function, and components of the immune system, protein synthesis, normal growth, and mental acuity. Excessive amounts of vitamin E and zinc interfere with iron absorption. Vitamin C helps with the absorption of iron. Vitamin B6 is needed to develop the iron-containing protein hemoglobin.

Iron should not be routinely supplemented; a blood test should first confirm an iron deficiency. The exception would be females who rigorously exercise. Studies show that only 8% of the US population is deficient in iron. However, 20% of premenopausal women and as much as 80% of women who exercise are deficient in iron. People suffering from Candida and chronic herpes infection usually have a deficiency in iron. If you suspect you have an iron deficiency, ask your health professional for a blood test.

Excessive amounts of iron are associated with an increased risk of heart disease and can lead to decreased immunity and liver, kidney, and lung disorders.

Magnesium is one of the most important minerals in the body. It is responsible for proper enzyme activity and transmission of muscle and nerve impulses, and it aids in maintaining a proper pH balance. It helps metabolize carbohydrates, proteins, and fats into energy. Magnesium helps synthesize the genetic material in cells and helps to remove toxic substances, such as aluminum and ammonia, from the body. Adequate amounts of magnesium are needed to ensure proper heart function.

Magnesium and calcium help keep the heart beating; magnesium relaxes the heart, and calcium activates it. A deficiency of magnesium may increase the risk of heart disease. Magnesium also plays a significant role in regulating the neurotransmitters. A deficiency in magnesium can cause depression, muscle cramps, high blood pressure, heart disease and arrhythmia, constipation, insomnia, hair loss, confusion, personality disorders, swollen gums, and loss of appetite. High intake of calcium may reduce magnesium absorption. Simple sugars and/or stress can deplete the body of magnesium.

Magnesium is a natural sedative and can be used to treat muscle spasm, anxiety, depression, insomnia, and constipation. It is also a potent antidepressant. It helps with intermittent claudicating, a condition caused by a restriction of blood flow to the legs. Magnesium is also effective in relieving some of the symptoms associated with PMS, and women suffering from PMS are usually deficient in magnesium—as is 80% of the general population. New studies are validating what many nutrition-oriented physicians have known for years: a magnesium deficiency can trigger migraine headaches. Magnesium helps relax constricted bronchial tubes associated with asthma. In fact, a combination of vitamin B6 and magnesium, along with avoidance of wheat and dairy products, has cured many of my young asthmatic patients.

Normal dosage is 500–800 mg. daily. Too much magnesium can cause loose bowel movements. If this occurs, reduce your dose.

Manganese aids in the development of mother's milk and is important for normal bone and tissue growth. It is involved in the production of cellular energy, metabolizes fats and proteins, and is essential in maintaining a healthy nervous system. Manganese is needed to synthesize thiamin, and it works in coordination with the other B vitamins to reduce the effects of stress.

A deficiency of manganese can cause fatigue, impaired fertility, retarded growth, birth defects, seizures, and bone malformations.

Calcium, copper, iron, manganese, and zinc all compete for absorption in the small intestine, and large doses of one of these nutrients may reduce the absorption of the others. Many of my patients who suffer from CFS/FMS are deficient in manganese. It is not toxic. Recommended dosage is 5–15 mg. daily.

Molybdenum aids in the conversion of purines to uric acid and allows the body to use nitrogen. It is important in sulfite detoxification and promotes normal cell function. Molybdenum deficiency can cause stunted growth, loss of appetite, and impotence in older males.

Excessive copper may interfere with molybdenum absorption. Molybdenum works with vitamin B2 in the conversion of food to energy.

Molybdenum can help reduce symptoms associated with sulfite sensitivities. I had a patient who broke out in a rash every time she ate foods containing the preservative sulfite. A hair analysis revealed a molybdenum deficiency. Once her molybdenum levels were normalized, she was once again tolerant of sulfites. High dosages can cause symptoms similar to gout: joint pain and swelling. Recommended dosage is 50–150 mcg. daily.

Potassium, sodium, and chloride help to regulate the nervous system and heart rhythm. These three minerals are known as electrolytes due to their electrical charge. They are responsible for maintaining a proper pH (along with calcium and magnesium).

Excess sodium can cause an elevation in blood pressure. Potassium helps lower blood pressure and can reduce the risk of stroke. Chloride helps make up the digestive enzyme hydrochloric acid. Hydrochloric acid helps digest food, destroys harmful intestinal "bugs," and synthesizes vitamin B12. Chronic diarrhea, vomiting, heat stroke, prolonged use of diuretics, and kidney disease can cause a deficiency of all three of these minerals.

A potassium deficiency manifests itself as irregular heart beats, sterility, muscle weakness, apathy, paralysis, and confusion. A chloride deficiency can lead to alkalosis, an imbalance in the body's pH system. This imbalance can cause vomiting and more diarrhea. A sodium deficiency is rare, but it can occur after long periods of sweating, fasting, and/or diarrhea.

Sodium increases urinary calcium loss, while potassium decreases urinary calcium loss. Potassium and magnesium are synergetic in lowering blood pressure and, therefore, should be taken together.

Selenium is an important antioxidant that protects the body from free-radical damage. It is a component of glutathione peroxidase, an enzyme essential for detoxification of cellular debris. Selenium, along with other antioxidants, especially vitamin E, combats free radicals that can cause heart disease. Selenium may help prevent certain forms of cancer and help

those suffering from autoimmune disorders such as rheumatoid arthritis. It is an important component of the immune
system. It helps make thyroid hormones and essential fatty
acids. A deficiency can cause birth defects, certain cancers,
and fibrocystic, heart, and liver disease. Doses above 600 mg.
can cause side effects that include tooth decay and periodontal disease. Recommended dosage is up to 200 mcg. daily.

Zinc is important in over 90 enzymatic pathways. Zinc facilitates alcohol detoxification within the liver. It plays a role in
producing and digesting proteins. Zinc is also important in
maintaining normal blood levels of vitamin A, boosting the
immune system, healing wounds, converting calories to energy, reducing low birth rates and infant mortality, controlling
blood cholesterol levels, and producing the prostaglandin hormones that regulate heart rate, blood pressure, inflammation,
and other processes. A deficiency of zinc can lead to poor taste,
anorexia nervosa, anemia, slow growth, birth defects,
impaired nerve function, sterility, glucose intolerance, mental
disorders, dermatitis, hair loss, and atherosclerosis.

Excess copper can cause a zinc deficiency, and vice versa.
Pregnant women accumulate excess copper and become zinc-
deficient. This can lead to postpartum depression. Extra zinc,
50 mg. per day, should be consumed by pregnant females to
help avoid unwanted postpartum depression. (I don't recommend prescription prenatal vitamins, because they are too low
in the needed micronutrients, especially zinc and the B
vitamins. I encourage my pregnant patients to take a high
potency vitamin with a maximum of 10,000 IUs of vitamin A.
Doses of vitamin A above 10,000 IUs should be avoided.)

Zinc lozenges have been shown to reduce the symptoms
and duration of colds by fifty percent. It is estimated that 68%
of the population is deficient in zinc. Zinc deficiency can cause
depression, since it's necessary for the production of dopamine.
Fingernails that contain white specks are indicative of a zinc
deficiency. Recommended dosage is up to 50 mg. daily.

VITAMIN AND MINERAL IV THERAPY

Clinical experience and recent research have proven intravenous vitamin and mineral therapy to be effective in treating
FMS and CFS patients. Our practice has been using vitamin

and mineral IV therapy for the past four years, and it is an important part of our program.

Nutritional deficiencies are a major reason why fibromyalgia patients can't get well. We are only as healthy as the chemicals, cells, tissues, and organs that make up our bodies. Our chronically ill patients, especially our FMS and CFS patients, are deficient in several vitamins, minerals, and other essential nutrients.

In a recently published review of 86 FMS patients on IV therapy, 74% improved, and most only needed four or fewer treatments for optimal results. Side effects leading to discontinuation of therapy occurred in 4% of the participants. Prescriptions for anti-inflammatory medications and muscle relaxants were virtually eliminated.

In our experiences at the clinic, we've found that our patients who receive vitamin and mineral IV therapy see a 200–400% faster improvement than those not receiving it. The improvement in recovery rate is because they often have problems that inhibit the digestion of nutrients: bloating, gas, indigestion, irritable bowel syndrome, malabsorption, leaky gut syndrome, and yeast overgrowth. Without essential nutrients, chronically ill patients stay chronically ill. And prescription medications often further deplete vital nutrients needed for optimal health.

Vitamin and mineral IVs act as natural muscle relaxers, enhance mood, increase energy, clear fibro fog, and help promote deep restorative sleep. We find that individuals who start off getting vitamin and mineral IVs notice a difference some time between their first and fifth treatment.

IV Vitamin C

Use of vitamin C in IV infusions originates with the work of the late Fred Klenner, MD, one of the unsung heroes in medicine. Dr. Klenner, in the small town of Reidsvill, North Carolina, discovered the efficacy and safety of IV vitamin C. He practiced and taught his technique for over 40 years and achieved tremendous success in the treatment of refractory infections and autoimmune diseases.

In our experience, intravenous vitamin C is a powerful weapon against CFS and FMS. We have seen numerous patients obtain dramatic relief from pain, fatigue, insomnia, and depression from the use of this modality.

IV Magnesium

We estimate that up to 80% of our patients with FMS/CFS are deficient in magnesium. A deficiency in this essential mineral can cause muscle pain, joint pain, headache, fatigue, insomnia, heart arrhythmias, depression, constipation, irritable bowel, and leg cramps. (Does any of this sound familiar?) Yet most physicians don't realize this connection to magnesium deficiency and therefore don't recommend supplementing with magnesium. Our vitamin and mineral IVs can deliver magnesium directly into the bloodstream.

Resources
* All the minerals discussed in this chapter are contained in Dr. Murphree's CFS/Fibromyalgia formula, available online at www.drrodger.com or by calling (205) 879-2383.

For Further Reading
* *Dr. Braly's Food Allergy and Nutrition Revolution* by James Braly, MD; 1992
* *Prescription for Nutritional Healing* by Phyllis A. Balch, CNC and James F. Balch, MD; 2000
* *Total Nutrition: The Only Guide You'll Ever Need* by Victor Herbert (editor), et al; 1995
* *Depression: Cured at Last!* by Sherry A. Rogers; 1997

13

You Need Amino Acids

Amino acids are the building blocks of life. They help regulate our thinking, energy, moods, pain, mental functions, digestion, immunity, and more. Deficiencies can cause major problems.

There are 20 amino acids. Nine are known as essential amino acids. They can't be made by the body and must be obtained from our diet. Nonessential amino acids can be manufactured from within our own cells.

Individual amino acids are joined together in sequential chains to form proteins. Protein, the body's building material, is essential to every cell and makes up our muscles, hair, bones, collagen, and connective tissue.

Essential and nonessential amino acids are involved in every bodily function. They are the raw materials for the reproduction and growth of every cell. Amino acids are in every bone, organ (including the brain), muscle, and most every hormone. Amino acids are also needed to make enzymes. Enzymes are protein molecules that coordinate thousands of chemical reactions that take place in the body. Enzymes are essential for breaking down and digesting carbohydrates, proteins, and fats.

Amino acids can occur in two forms: D-form and L-form, which are mirror images of one another. The L-form is available in the foods we eat and is the more easily absorbed. In a natural state, all amino acids are L-form. D-forms can be formed by bacteria, by tissue catabolism, or synthetically. (Most D-forms can be detrimental to normal enzyme functions; however, DL-phenylalanine is the exception. It inhibits the breakdown of endorphin- and enkephalin-limiting enzymes.) The white, crystalline free-form amino acids derived from brown rice protein are the purest supplements available. Always supplement with free-form (L-form) amino acids.

AMINO ACIDS

Essential		Nonessential	
isoleucine	leucine	glycine	glutamic acid
lysine	methionine	arginine	aspartic acid
phenylalanine	threonine	alanine	proline
tryptophan	valine	serine	tyrosine
histadine		cysteine	glutamine
		asparagine	

DISORDERS DUE TO AMINO ACID DEFICIENCIES

fatigue	poor immunity
anxiety	mental confusion
dermatitis	chemical sensitivities
insomnia	cardiovascular disease
osteoporosis	high blood pressure
arthritis	inflammatory disorders
depression	poor detoxification

Amino acids can be taken as a blend to shore up any underlying nutritional deficiencies. Taken individually, they act like drugs to produce specific reactions. It's best to take single amino acids on an empty stomach: 30 minutes before or one hour after eating. Individuals with malabsorption syndrome, irritable bowel, leaky gut, and chronic illnesses are wise to take an amino acid blend in addition to any single amino acids. The Essential Therapeutics CFS/Fibromyalgia formula contains all of the essential amino acids. Here are some of the amino acids and how they are used in nutritional medicine:

Carnitine increases energy. It is produced by combining two other amino acids, methionine and lysine. It helps transport fats into the cells for the mitochondria to use as energy. The mitochondria burn fatty acids during physical activity, which makes carnitine a valuable tool for reducing weight and the risk of fat buildup in heart muscle. Its efficient use of fats helps the body lower cholesterol, triglycerides, and possibly the risk of heart attack. The consumption of alcohol can cause a buildup of fat in the liver, but carnitine inhibits this buildup. It also helps boost cellular energy and is helpful in reducing fatigue associated with CFS.

Cysteine helps detoxify the body. It is formed from the amino acid methionine and plays an important role in detoxifying the body. Cysteine is the precursor to the most abundant and important amino acid in the body, glutathione. Glutathione is a combination of glutamine, cysteine, and glycine.

Cysteine destroys free radicals, removes heavy metals from the body, and guards cells—including heart and liver cells—from toxic chemicals like alcohol, xenobiotics, and other damaging substances. Glutathione and cysteine are effective in reducing or eliminating skin conditions such as psoriasis, acne, liver spots, and eczema. Those with respiratory problems, asthma, bronchitis, and allergies may benefit from taking a specialized form of cysteine known as N-acetylcysteine.

I prescribe cysteine and methionine, usually in a combination formula, to my patients with aluminum toxicity and poor liver function. By itself, cysteine should be taken on an empty stomach at 500–1000 mg. daily.

Gamma-aminobutyric acid (GABA) treats anxiety. It can be formed from the amino acid glutamine and has a calming effect on the brain similar to Valium and other tranquilizers, but without the side effects. GABA, used in combination with the B vitamins niacinamide (a form of vitamin B3) and inositol, can alleviate anxiety and panic attacks. Many of my patients are surprised by the effectiveness of GABA in treating their anxiety and panic attacks.

To treat anxiety, start with 500 mg. two–three times daily (or as needed) on an empty stomach. Some individuals may need up to 1,000 mg. two–three times daily.

Glutamine helps heal intestinal permeability. It is converted to glutamic acid in the brain. Glutamic acid increases neuronal activity, detoxifies ammonia (an abundant waste product in the body) from cells, and like glucose, is used to feed the brain. Glutamine plays an important role in intestinal maintenance and repair and is the major energy source of the intestines. It is one of the most important nutrients for the cells that line the colon.

Individuals with intestinal problems, including Crohn's disease, colitis, irritable bowel syndrome, intestinal permeability, yeast overgrowth, and food allergies, especially need glutamine supplementation. Studies in Britain and Canada show that when individuals with inflammatory bowel disease (IBD) were given glutamine, their symptoms, including abdominal pain and diarrhea, improved dramatically. In another study, children who took glutamine supplements showed increased mental abilities and tested higher on IQ tests. It also helps reduce sugar cravings and acts as an appetite suppressant.

Glutamine is one of the three amino acids that form glutathione. Glutathione is a powerful antioxidant and plays an important role in the detoxification system of the body. It helps clear unwanted toxins through the kidneys and liver.

Glutamine is the precursor to two very important neurotransmitters: glutamic acid (glutamate) and GABA (gamma-aminobutyric acid). Glutamate is excitatory while GABA is an inhibitory (relaxing) neurotransmitter.

Usual glutamine dose is 500–1,000 mg. twice daily on an empty stomach. Higher doses are necessary to repair leaky gut syndrome.

Glycine helps detoxify the body. It is another inhibitory amino acid. It can be used to reduce the symptoms of bipolar depression, epilepsy, and nervous tics. It is also important in neutralizing toxic chemicals (especially alcohol). It helps synthesize glutathione and has been used in the treatment of depression and in the inhibition of epilepsy. It is usually taken in a combination formula.

Histidine improves digestion. A histidine imbalance can cause anxiety, schizophrenia, nausea (particularly in pregnant women), lethargy, fatigue, and anger. Histidine improves digestion by increasing the production of stomach acid.

Histidine is the precursor of histamine, which is known to play a role in allergic reactions. But histamine also acts as an inhibitory neurotransmitter by increasing alpha-wave activity within the brain. Alpha waves are associated with relaxation and when activated, help increase a person's resistance to stress and tension. Histidine is usually taken in a combination formula.

Lysine treats viral outbreaks. As the essential component of all proteins, it plays a major role in soft-tissue formation and repair. A lysine deficiency can cause a person to bruise easily and have a difficult time healing wounds. It is used for treating cold sores and is one of the most important and cost-efficient supplements I prescribe in treating herpes.

Lysine is also one of the most effective therapies for shingles. Cortisone reduces the itching but does nothing to rid the body of the skin lesions. In addition, steroids (such as cortisone) weaken the immune system and can cause further outbreaks. To treat shingles, use the natural antibiotic, antiviral herb echinacea along with 1,000 mg. of lysine and 25,000 IU of vitamin A, daily for two weeks or until the lesions disappear.

Methionine helps detoxify the body. An essential amino acids, methionine allows the body to digest fats, combat toxins, produce choline, and deal with allergic reactions. It's the precursor of cysteine, glutathione, and taurine and contributes to the production and regulation of insulin. Methionine is an excellent chelator, meaning it attaches itself to heavy metals (such as aluminum and lead) and escorts them out of the body.

I prescribe methionine to my patients with faulty detoxification systems. People with chronic fatigue, fibromyalgia, liver problems, and heavy metal or xenobiotic overload need extra methionine. The recommended dose is 500–1,000 mg. daily on an empty stomach. It may also be taken in a combination formula.

Methionine is the main component of s-adenosyl-methionine (SAM). SAM is involved in synthesizing neurotransmitters, and its deficiency can contribute to depression. For more information on SAM and depression, see chapter 22.

Studies involving FMS patients and SAM have shown dramatic improvements in pain reduction. One study showed that patients taking SAM for a period of six weeks had an improvement of 40% in pain reduction and 35% in depression. Recommended dose for SAM is 400–800 mg. daily

DL-phenylalanine assists pain control. This is a combination of the D- and L-form of phenylalanine, which acts as a natural pain reliever. It blocks the enzymes responsible for the breakdown of endorphins and enkephlins, which are substances within the body that help relieve pain. Endorphins are similar in chemical structure and far more powerful than the drug known as morphine. They are produced in small cells located throughout the nervous system.

DL-phenylalanine acts as an appetite suppressant and mild stimulant. It has also shown to be effective in helping patients afflicted with Parkinson's disease.

DL-phenylalanine is an effective supplement in treating musculoskeletal pains, including those associated with FMS. Many of my fibromyalgia and chronic pain patients have benefited from taking DL-phenylalanine. A clinical study shows subjects taking DL-phenylalanine saw a remarkable improvement in their condition: improvements were seen in 73% of lower-back pain sufferers, 67% of those with migraines, 81% with osteoarthritis, and 81% with rheumatoid arthritis.

For pain control or as an antidepressant, take 1,000–4,000 mg. twice daily on an empty stomach. Phenylalanine can elevate blood pressure, and very high doses cause rapid heart beat. Start with a low dose and increase to higher doses only as needed and only if no side effects are noticed.

L-phenylalanine fights depression. It is an important amino acid that is involved in the production of the neurotransmitter catecholamines. Catecholamines stimulate mental arousal, positive mood, and the fight-or-flight response to stress. It creates the following neurotransmitters: adrenaline, epinephrine, norepinephrine, and dopamine. These help to elevate mood and reduce depression, pain, fatigue, and lethargy. Phenylalanine also curbs the appetite by stimulating a hormone known as cholecystokinin (CCK), which tells the brain when you've eaten enough.

Phenylalanine is converted to the nonessential amino acid tyrosine. Individuals with a rare but life-threatening illness known as phenylketonuria (PKU) can't make this conversion. The thyroid hormone thyroxin is made from tyrosine (see below). So supplementing with phenylalanine and tyrosine helps increase the thyroid gland and rate of metabolism. This in turn helps mobilize and burn fat.

As an antidepressant, use 1,000–4,000 mg. twice daily on an empty stomach. Phenylalanine can elevate blood pressure, and very high doses cause rapid heart beat. Start with a low dose and increase to higher doses only as needed and only if no side effects are noticed.

Tyrosine boosts thyroid function. Because of this, it can be a lifesaver for those suffering from depression that has been resistant to all other medications. It elevates mood, drive, and ambition by stimulating the neurotransmitters norepinephrine, epinephrine, and dopamine. Tyrosine also helps those suffering from fatigue and asthma.

Tyrosine, which can be produced from phenylalanine, aids in the production of the adrenal, thyroid, and pituitary hormones. Many of my patients with low thyroid function have benefited from taking a special supplement that contains L-tyrosine. Low energy, brittle nails, and cold hands and feet can mean a person is suffering from adrenal hormone insufficiency. These people may benefit from taking tyrosine along with an adrenal extract supplement.

Tyrosine can also raise blood pressure, so use with caution. To treat low thyroid, supplement with 1,000 mg. twice daily on an empty stomach. For depression and fatigue, use phenylalanine (see above).

Tryptophan is discussed in chapter 6.

Resources
- All the amino acids discussed in this chapter are contained in Dr. Murphree's CFS/Fibromyalgia formula, available online at www.drrodger.com or by calling (205) 879-2383.
- SAM is available at many health food stores.

For Further Reading
- *Orthomolecular Medicine for Physicians* by Abram Hoffer; 1997
- *Total Nutrition: The Only Guide You'll Ever Need* by Victor Herbert (editor), et al; 1995
- *Depression: Cured at Last!* by Sherry A. Rogers; 1997
- *The Amino Revolution* by Robert Erdmann; 1989
- *Healing the Mind the Natural Way* by Pat Lazarus; 1995
- *Anxiety Epidemic* by Billie J. Sahley; 1994

14

Great News About Fats and Fatty Acids

Fat provides energy, produces certain hormones, insulates us from the cold, and makes up cellular membranes. It is the primary source of fuel for the muscles, including the heart.

Fats have gotten a bad rap in our society. Low-fat diets have been the rage for years, promising weight loss and improved health. But this line of thinking has contributed to yo-yo dieting, heart disease, and type-2 diabetes. In fact, researchers at the National Institute of Health have recently shown that while our consumption of fat and cholesterol have drastically declined over the last several years, we've actually gained an average of ten pounds per person. Statistics show that during the years between 1960 and 1980, one-quarter of the population was overweight. But that number has grown to 60% of the population. Researchers and health officials are still scratching their heads over these statistics. It is now estimated that by the year 2010, over 80% of the US population will be overweight. The "fat-free" mantra has proven to be the most misguided medical blunder since bloodletting.

The fear of fat and its derivative, cholesterol, has spawned a multibillion-dollar industry of low-fat foods, but it's not turning the tide. We trust medical intervention, but drugs that lower fats and cholesterol have been shown to increase the risk of certain cancers. Dieters dutifully avoid fat, but hidden sugars in our processed foods are being turned into fat right under our noses (and our belts!).

> The truth is that fat is in all natural foods. It is an essential nutrient that plays a vital role in our overall health. We can't live without fat in our diet.

Fat provides over twice the amount of energy of carbohydrates and 70% of the energy needed just to keep the body warm. Fats make up 70% of the brain. The fat insulates the brain cells and allows the neurotransmitters to communicate with one another.

Cholesterol and fats make up each and every cell. Cholesterol helps keep cell membranes permeable, and this permeability allows good nutrients in and toxic waste products out. Over 8% of the brain's solid matter is made up of cholesterol, and cholesterol is essential for proper brain function and normalized neurotransmitters such as serotonin. A deficiency in cholesterol can result in mood disorders including depression, anxiety, irritability, and fibro fog. Cholesterol is also involved in the production of such essential hormones as DHEA, testosterone, estradiol, progesterone, and cortisol.

Because it is essential to our very survival, cholesterol is manufactured by the body on a daily basis. Eliminating cholesterol from our diet only triggers the body to make more! But a diet deficient in EFAs and high in trans-fatty acids provides the ammunition for cardiovascular disease and poor health.

THE SKINNY ON FATS

Fats are lipids, meaning they can't be dissolved in water. Lipids include fats, oils, phospholipids (lecithin), and other substances made by the body. The brain, nerves, reproductive organs, liver, and heart all need particular lipids for optimal function.

Fat is made up of fatty acids, and there are three main types of these: saturated, unsaturated, and polyunsaturated.

- **Saturated fatty acids** (SFAs) are found in butter, shortening, coconut oil, eggs, meat, and cheese. They consist of long, straight chains of molecules packed tightly together, and they are solid at room temperature. A diet too high in SFAs may contribute to atherosclerosis, heart disease, and stroke. However, even saturated fats are part of a balanced diet.

- **Monounsaturated fatty acids** (MUFAs) are found in almond oil, avocados, canola oil, oats, peanut oil, and olive oil. Monounsaturated oils are usually liquid at room temperature but may become cloudy or hardened in the refrigerator. MUFAs have one kink or bend in their structure, so they are more flexible than SFAs.

- **Polyunsaturated fatty acids** (PUFAs) are found in corn oil, primrose oil, flaxseed oil, borage oil, certain fish, and sesame, sunflower, safflower, and wheat germ oil. PUFAs are liquid at room temperature. They have many bends in their chains and are quite flexible. Although a person needs all types of fat, PUFAs are generally considered the healthiest type.

ESSENTIAL FATTY ACIDS (EFAs)

Essential fatty acids are, as their name implies, essential for our existence. They make up the outer membranes of each cell. These membranes determine which nutrients get into and out of the cells. The membranes of healthy cells can resist entry by viruses and other pathogenic agents and, at the same time, facilitate the entry of nutrients. But when EFAs are deficient, cell membranes are weakened in their abilities, and the wrong substances are allowed into the cell. A deficiency in EFAs can cause some of the very symptoms associated with FMS and CFS: fatigue, depression, malabsorption, muscle pain, insomnia, poor mental function, and lowered immunity. It's estimated that at least 25% of the population suffers from some amount of EFA deficiency.

Essential fatty acids cannot be manufactured by the body and must be obtained from food. But getting enough EFAs can be tricky, as we'll explore later in the chapter.

EFAs are divided into two families: omega-6 and omega-3.

- **Omega-6** fatty acids are in pure vegetable oils, including sunflower, safflower, and corn oil.

- **Omega-3** fatty acids are found in flax seed, soybean, walnut, and chestnut oils, as well as some dark green leafy vegetables. Eicosapentaenoic acid (EPA) and DHA (docosahexanoic acid) are omega-3 derivatives found in most cold water fish such as salmon, tuna, and mackerel. Omega-3 fats regulate and normalize the proper functioning of cholesterol and omega-6 fats.

THE CAUSES OF EFA DEFICIENCIES

Certain groups of people have inherited a need for more EFAs and especially GLA (gamma-linolenic acid) in their diet. These include individuals of Irish, Scottish, Welch, Scandinavian, Danish, British Columbian, and Eskimo decent. But even for those without special EFA needs, obtaining enough EFA can be challenging.

Dramatic changes in our agricultural, food processing, and food preparation methods in the past several decades have helped deplete the soil and our foods of valuable nutrients. For instance, changes in flour milling technology have resulted in the elimination of essential fatty acids from most machine-processed grains. Even our meat is less nutritious. One hundred years ago, our ancestors ate real butter, unprocessed grains, flax seed oil (a rich source of EFAs), and free-range cattle and chickens. Today's farmer, in most cases, keeps cattle and chickens caged and feeds them processed grains devoid of EFAs. Consequently, the meat is significantly less nutritious to humans. Free-range cattle, chicken, and dairy products can have over five times the omega-3 and omega-6 fats in their tissues as industrially raised animals.

Trans-fats have replaced healthy EFAs in many of our processed foods, so these foods are not only devoid of life-giving, health-building EFAs, but they also prevent what EFAs are present from being absorbed and effectively utilized.

Alcohol and caffeine can also block the conversion of EFAs to anti-inflammatory prostaglandin hormones (see below for more about prostaglandins).

Increased ingestion of toxins in our food, water, and air depletes our EFAs.

Lack of breastfeeding can create EFA deficiencies, as omega-3 fats and DHA (docosahexanoic acid) are not present in most infant formulas or in commercial cow's milk.

Excessive consumption of omega-6 fats (too many grains) may interfere with the absorption of omega-3 fats.

RESULTS OF EFA DEFICIENCIES

EFA deficiency can contribute to a number of health problems, such as eczema, acne, psoriasis, PMS, Sjogren's syndrome (dry eyes and mouth), cancer, arthritis, heart disease, and asthma.

If you are pregnant, consider EFA supplements, since intelligence and mental acuity in children have been linked to EFA intake in the womb. In children, diaper rash, eczema, and cradle cap are all associated with a deficiency in EFAs.

Blocked Prostaglandins

Prostaglandins are made from essential fatty acids. These biochemicals are similar to hormones and affect almost every bodily function. They can stimulate or relax uterine muscles, reduce swollen nasal passageways, and help regulate the happy hormones, blood pressure, air passageways, allergic reactions, and fat metabolism. They are intimately involved in the functions of the immune system. They can help stimulate steroid production, reduce appetite, and cause or reduce inflammation.

Many FMS patients have been on NSAIDs for years by the time we see them in our clinic. These medications, which include aspirin, Aleve, Vioxx, Advil, Tylenol, and Motrin, block the prostaglandins that cause inflammation, but they also block those that *stop* inflammation. A safer way to reduce inflammation is to increase EFA, especially omega-3, consumption.

Food Allergies and Sensitivities

Allergies can be caused by leaky cell membranes or intestinal permeability (leaky gut syndrome). But omega-3 fatty acids and gamma-linolenic acid (GLA) help normalize allergic and inflammatory reactions. Anti-inflammatory prostaglandin hormones (PGE1 and PGE2) are derived from omega-6 fatty acids in the gastrointestinal tract, and a deficiency in these hormones reduces mucous secretions, increases gastric acid, and causes too much inflammatory histamine to be released.

Primrose and flax seed oil taken with meals often
bring about marked improvements in food allergies
as well as allergies in general.

Lowered Immunity

Essential fatty acids are the major components of all cellular
membranes in the body, and the integrity of these membranes
is the key to preventing infection. Our bodies, including our
skin, digestive tract, mouth, sinuses, lungs, and throat are cov-
ered with trillions of bacteria, virus, parasites, and yeasts. So
a membrane's capacity to recognize what is beneficial and to
keep out what is harmful is vital for the immune system. But
without enough EFAs, these membranes are compromised.

New evidence reveals that EFAs have direct
antiviral effects and are lethal at surprisingly low
concentrations to many viruses.

Specifically, EFAs play a crucial role in the body's production
and utilization of the hormone interferon. Interferon is a
chemical our immune system produces to kill viruses; it is
dependent on EFAs and compromised in their absence. (The
antiviral activity of human mother's milk seems to be largely
attributable to its EFA content.)

This helps explain why some people get sick and others
don't when exposed to the same virus. In the case of the
Epstein-Barr virus, for example, a good 90% of the US population carries this virus, yet only a fraction become ill from it.
One theory is that those who actually develop symptoms have
below-normal levels of EFAs and their derivatives. A study
investigating sufferers of the EBV particularly confirms this:
Both eight and 12 months into the study, subjects who had
recovered from the virus showed normal or near normal EFA
blood levels. In contrast, those who were still clinically ill from
the EBV showed persistently low EFA levels.

Fatigue

Insufficient EFAs in the bloodstream can lead to fatigue.
Consider one Scottish trial, in which patients with CFS were
given EFA supplements with great success. Placebo-controlled

trials were held for 70 patients with persistent CFS, giving them linolenic acid (flax seed oil) and eicosapentaenoic acid (fish oil). After six months, 84% of the patients in the supplemented group rated themselves as "better" or "much better." Only 22% of those in the placebo group reported such improvement. In another study of 63 adults with CFS, 74% of the patients taking EFA supplements, and 23% of those on placebo, assessed themselves as improved after one month.

Depression

Omega-3 fats work to keep us mentally and emotionally strong in three ways: They act as precursors for the body's production of preprostaglandins and neurotransmitters; they provide the substrate for B vitamins and coenzymes to produce compounds that regulate many vital functions, and they nourish our nerve and brain cells. A deficiency in omega-3s is one of the main causes of depression and other mental disorders.

Eczema

One of the best uses for flax seed oil and GLA is in the treatment of eczema. A malfunction of essential fatty acid metabolism has been solidly established to be a major, if not the principle, cause of eczema. Many people report substantial improvement in eczema when they eliminate refined and processed oils and use flax seed oil and sometimes GLA in the form of primrose oil.

TIME FOR AN OIL CHANGE

Paying attention to the types of fats we consume is the first place to start. Try to avoid processed or overly refined oils, which yield trans-fatty acids.

Refined Oils

Refined oils have undergone deodorization, bleaching, and/or hydrogenation. These processes remove lecithin, beta-carotene, EFAs, and vitamin E. Hydrogenation is the process of adding hydrogen atoms to oils for the purpose of creating solid fats like margarine. In order to make a hydrogenated oil, natural oils are heated under pressure for six to eight hours at 248–410°F and reacted with hydrogen gas by the use of a metal such as nickel or copper. (Both of these heavy metals have been linked, incidentally, to depression and fatigue.)

When oils are processed in this manner, their molecular bonds change, and poisonous trans-fats are created. These trans-fats prevent the omega-6 EFAs from attaching to their receptors on cell membranes. The membranes then becomes impermeable. Then, because nutrients can't get in and toxins can't get out, the cells begin to die. Neurotransmitters (serotonin and others) are also blocked from attaching themselves to the cell, and this can lead to depression, insomnia, anxiety, fatigue, and ADD.

In addition, trans-fatty acids also increase the amount of LDL—bad cholesterol—in the blood and decrease the amount of HDL—good cholesterol. Trans-fatty acids are now being linked to cancer and free-radical proliferation. By blocking the EFAs from adhering to cell membranes, they are also inviting a host of other illnesses: arthritis, eczema, psoriasis, PMS, depression, fatigue, FMS, and CFS.

Natural Oils

Natural oils are derived from pressing seeds and nuts. Sunflower, cotton, corn, olive, canola, and almond oils are natural oils. They are primarily polyunsaturated oils containing omega-6.

So all vegetable oils are natural, right? Well, yes and no. Vegetable oils contain a mixture of saturated fats, monounsaturated fats, and essential fatty acids. They rarely contain the essential fatty acid derivatives (GLA), but the body is usually able to manufacture the derivatives it needs. The problem is that vegetable oils turn into trans-fats at relatively low heat. So we could be creating trans-fats in our kitchens as we cook!

The American public has been misled into believing that all vegetable oils are good for them. The American Heart Association, which unbelievably advocates the use of margarine, has promoted this line of thinking, and margarine is made up of 15–50% trans-fats! Processed vegetable oils devoid of healthy essential fatty acids are primarily toxic trans-fats in a bottle.

In addition, cottonseed oil is laden with toxic ingredients, as cotton is one of the most heavily sprayed agricultural crops. Soy oil is difficult to extract. The soybeans are subjected to extremely high temperatures, which damages the oil.

Instead, choose cold processed, nonhydrogenated, polyunsaturated oils. These oils are usually organic and haven't been heated to the high temperatures that create trans-fatty acids. Cook with cold-pressed extra-virgin olive oil or organic canola oil. They are able to withstand higher temperatures without producing trans-fatty acids. Choose organic when possible to avoid pesticide residue that can cause health problems. Individuals with chronic illnesses like FMS and CFS should supplement with primrose, borage, flax, or fish oil.

Avoid lard, coconut oil, and palm oils. Also remember that most vegetable oils, including sunflower, corn, and safflower, have been processed and are loaded with trans-fats. Peanut oil contains high levels of arachidonic acid, which causes tissue inflammation. Margarine should never be used unless made from cold-pressed organic vegetable oil.

For additional healthy fats, snack on nuts and seeds, such as almonds, walnuts, cashews, pecans, and pumpkin seeds—but not peanuts. Also enjoy guacamole, olives and olive oil, lean (preferably free-range) meats, cold-water fish, tofu, and fruits and vegetables. All these contain poly- and monounsaturated fats. Use real butter—organic, if possible.

Consult your nutritionally oriented physician about supplementing omega-3 and 6 fatty acids, flax seed oil, and primrose oil. Most individuals who need to supplement need a higher ratio of omega-3 to omega-6, at least initially. This is because most people get omega-6s through grains on a daily basis. I recommend starting with an EFA blend containing two–four times as much omega-3 as omega-6. Our Essential Therapeutics CFS/Fibromyalgia formula contains an essential fatty acid blend and is a good start for most patients.

Resources
- All the essential fatty acids are contained in Dr. Murphree's CFS/Fibromyalgia formula, available online at www.drrodger.com or by calling (205) 879-2383.

For Further Reading
- *The Schwarzbein Principle* by Diana Schwarzbein, MD and Nancy Deville; 1999
- *Sugar Busters! Cut Sugar to Trim Fat* by H. Leighton Steward et al; 1998
- *Food & Mood* by Elizabeth Somer, MA, RD; 1999
- *Essential Fatty Acids in Health and Disease* by Edward N. Siguel; 1995
- *The Facts About Fats* by John Finnegan; 1993

15

What You Should Know About Carbohydrates

There is a big difference between man-made, preservative-rich, simple carbohydrates and naturally occurring complex carbohydrates. We were designed to thrive on the latter.

Carbohydrates are made up of sugar molecules connected together. They're found in both plant and animal products. There are two types of carbohydrates.

- Simple carbohydrates (sugars) have one or two connected sugar molecules. These include fructose (found in fruits), galactose (in dairy products), maltose (in starches and grains), levulose (in cane sugar), and glucose (in corn and other syrups)

- Complex carbohydrates are made up of chains of three or more sugar molecules. Complex carbohydrates are found in most vegetables, unprocessed grains, and legumes.

Most importantly, carbohydrates are loaded with nutrients! They contain essential vitamins and minerals and phytochemicals (nutrients found in plants) that help us combat and prevent disease. For instance:

- **Cruciferous vegetables,** like cauliflower and broccoli, contain powerful antioxidants, including beta-carotene, glutathione, vitamin C, and quercetin. Eggplant contains glycoalkaloids. These substances are used as a topical cream to treat skin cancer.

- **Figs** contain an antitumor chemical called benzaldehyde.

- **Cranberries** are used to treat urinary tract infections. Chemicals in cranberry juice act as antibacterial agents and prevent bacteria from adhering to the cellular wall of the bladder.

- **Red grapes** contain the potent antioxidants quercetin and pycnogenol. They also have antibacterial and antiviral properties.

- **Most nuts,** including almonds, brazil nuts, and walnuts, are high in selenium, vitamin E, and omega-3 oils, and they help lower high cholesterol.

- **Onions and garlic** have strong antibacterial, antiviral, and anticancer chemicals. Both are potent antioxidants and help boost the immune system.

- **Soybeans** contain anticancer protease inhibitors. They're also loaded with natural estrogen, making them effective in the treatment of benign prostate hypertrophy, PMS, and menopause.

BRAIN FUEL

Just as importantly, carbohydrates feed the brain. They provide glucose (blood sugar), or the building blocks for it, and the brain depends on glucose for function. If the brain doesn't get sufficient glucose from food, it will pull it out of muscle and then fat tissue. (This is what can happen on high-protein, low-carbohydrate, or low-calorie diets). This process is known as gluconeogenesis, and it compromises the muscle tissue. This explains why people on extended low-calorie or high-protein diets can actually lose muscle mass.

Each day, the brain consumes two-thirds of available glucose. Low blood sugar (hypoglycemia) can trigger bouts of fatigue, irritability, anger, anxiety, depression, and mental lethargy. Keeping the body fueled with adequate amounts of glucose is a challenge, since the liver, which stores glycogen (the breakdown of glucose), can only accommodate the equivalent of two cups of pasta. And this must be replaced every five hours. However, eating excessive amounts of carbohydrates, especially simple carbohydrates, causes the body to store the excess as *fat*.

COMPLEX VERSES SIMPLE CARBOHYDRATES

All carbohydrates are turned by the body into glucose. Glucose levels in the blood are then monitored and adjusted by the release of two hormones: insulin and glucagon.

Insulin is released into the bloodstream by the pancreas. It keeps the glucose moving into the cells, so it doesn't all build up in the bloodstream and so the cells don't starve.

Glucagon is also secreted by the pancreas. Its job is to prevent the blood sugar from becoming too low. It releases stored glucose (glycogen) from the liver if needed and can also cause the protein in muscles to be converted to glucose if no other source is available (such as during periods of fasting, exercising, or carbohydrate-deficient dieting).

The consumption of simple carbohydrates (also called simple sugars) is extremely difficult on the pancreas. And processed foods are our greatest source of simple sugar (many processed starches are no better for us than table sugar.) Processed foods are, for the most part, devoid of fiber, and low fiber intake is directly related to high cholesterol, digestive problems, and colon cancer. Without fiber, the sugars in processed foods have little to slow down their transformation into glucose, and the body processes them too quickly—faster than it can respond to the rise in blood sugar.

Complex carbohydrates, in comparison, take a considerable amount of time to be broken down and utilized by the body. This prevents unhealthy blood-sugar highs and lows, and provides long-lasting energy.

THE EPIDEMIC OF INSULIN RESISTANCE

The relationship between glucose, glucagon, and insulin is a self-regulating system that serves us well—until our metabolism starts to slow down. Years of eating excess carbohydrates, especially simple ones, and the effects of metabolic aging begin to take their toll in our mid-thirties and forties. By this time in our lives, most of us have used up the sugar-storage space in our cells, and there is simply no more room. The body attempts to remedy this problem by reducing a cell's insulin receptors. This sends a message to the pancreas to release even more insulin, and this results in hyperinsulinemia (insulin resistance): more insulin is produced than is required.

How do we get so much sugar in our bodies? According to one very reasonable theory, it all starts with an overconsumption of processed foods. The high simple-carbohydrate content of these foods causes the healthy pancreas to overreact.

For example, you eat a candy bar. The sugar in the bar enters the small intestine, is rapidly broken down, and is dumped into the bloodstream. The pancreas, in response to a large wave of sugar being released so fast, oversecretes insulin. The excess insulin lowers blood sugar too quickly, and the person enters a hypoglycemic state. Since the brain must have glucose to work properly, lack of glucose sends it into a panic! Symptoms might include fatigue, irritability, depression, headache, sugar cravings, nausea, and dizziness. When it wants carbs, the brain doesn't care whether or not it's a complex carbohydrate; it just needs a glucose fix. So to satisfy these strong cravings for sugar, a person will eat whatever is convenient—usually a simple sugar. (Many people have gotten into a bad habit of skipping meals. Then, when they do eat, they are in a hypoglycemic state and it's too late to make good food choices.)

As a result of all these highs and lows, the cells are jam-packed with sugar, and the body becomes resistant to its own insulin. This state can cause many of the same symptoms experienced by those with FMS and CFS: fatigue, depression, irritability, weight gain, decreased immunity, anxiety, poor concentration, and insomnia.

In addition to insulin resistance, increased insulin levels, decreased insulin cell receptors, and cells stuffed full of fat prevent sugar from reaching its intended destination. Instead, it remains in the bloodstream where it can cause damage to the arterial walls, high blood pressure, arteriosclerosis, high blood lipid levels, heart disease, and type-2 diabetes.

As we age, we also tend to produce less and less of the pancreatic digestive enzymes. This leads to malabsorption conditions and more unwanted weight gain, as well as fatigue, bloating, and constipation—even depression.

EAT HEALTHY, LOSE WEIGHT, AND FEEL BETTER

Insulin is a very efficient hormone; it does its job beautifully. Centuries ago, before people were agriculturally inclined, insulin was our best friend. A person's very survival depended on bodily reserves of fat, as our diet consisted of wild animals, berries, nuts, and fruits. Often, the people were being hunted more than the animals; and people would go days—sometimes weeks—without eating. During these lean times, glucose stored in fat tissue served as bodily fuel. In today's fast-food, megamarket, eat-'till-you-flop world, insulin's efficiency is underappreciated, leading to unwanted weight gain. Consequently, Americans are obsessed with losing weight. Unfortunately, 90% of all dieters fail in their efforts. Many experience a yo-yo effect, losing weight and then gaining it back—and then some.

Starving the body on a too-low calorie diet doesn't work; it just reduces the body's ability to burn fat. Realistically, you can only lose a pound or two of fat a week; anything more is water or muscle loss. So starvation diets are extremely hard on the body. Some dieters start to lose their hair and muscle tone, and their skin starts to sag. So we know that starving the body is a sure way to cause unwanted health problems.

For the past two decades, some well-meaning nutritionists have been telling us to avoid fats and increase our carbohydrate consumption. Fat has become a nasty three-letter word, something to be avoided at all costs. But fat-free potato chips are really nothing but a man-made simple sugar, and we know what simple sugars can do...make us fat!

I don't believe in counting calories, and if you eat properly, as I explain in the next couple of chapters, you won't need to. However, eating junk calories to excess, regardless of fat content, only causes unwanted weight gain.

Remember: our ancestors didn't eat 150 pounds of sugar a year as does today's average American. They didn't eat processed breads and pastas designed to stay on store shelves for weeks at a time. A simple diet of lean meat (killed that day) and gathered fruit, nuts, and berries supported our ancient fathers and mothers. Genetically, we haven't changed in thousands of years; we are still pretty much designed as God intended. But our environment, lifestyles, and habits have certainly changed—in some ways, for the worse.

The increase in weight as experienced in this country is due to several factors, including sedentary lifestyles and stress. But the readiness of processed foods and lack of nutritional wisdom play a large part.

THE GLYCEMIC INDEX FOR BLOOD SUGAR BALANCE

The glycemic index (GI) is a measurement of how quickly a carbohydrate elevates the glucose levels of the circulating blood. It has nothing to do with the amount of carbohydrates in a food but the rate at which the carbohydrates are digested. The lower the GI number, the slower the rate of absorption.

Below is a list of foods grouped by high, moderate, and low GI levels. It should offer enough guidance to significantly improve your diet. For a more specific numerical listing, talk to your nutritionist or nutritionally-oriented physician.

High GI Foods

- bleached (white) breads
- white potatoes
- rice cakes
- most breakfast cereals, including corn flakes, GRAPE-NUTS, Corn Chex, Rice Krispies, Whole Grain Total, Cheerios, Cream of Wheat, puffed rice, puffed corn, puffed millet.
- cheese pizza
- muffins
- croissants
- waffles
- most simple sugars
- white rice
- oats and oat bran
- corn and cornmeal
- taco shells
- corn chips

- some pasta, including gnocchi, rice pasta, macaroni and cheese, couscous
- Wheat Thins
- low-fat ice cream
- ripe bananas
- raisins
- apricots
- papaya
- pineapple
- mango
- watermelon
- most syrups, including maple syrup and corn syrup
- honey
- most cookies, cakes, and sweets

Moderate GI Foods
- spaghetti
- sourdough rye bread
- wild rice
- brown rice
- non-instant oatmeal
- some cereals, including Special K and no-sugar-added muesli
- whole-grain pumpernickel
- pita bread
- oranges and orange juice
- peas
- many legumes, including pinto beans, garbanzo beans, baked beans, navy beans and canned lentils
- lactose (milk sugar)

Low GI Foods

- slow-cooking oatmeal
- barley
- rye grain
- most fruits (not fruit juice), including apples, grapes, peaches, pears, cherries, grapefruit, plums, nectarines, tangerines, oranges, limes, dates, lemons, berries, kiwis, and cantaloupe
- many legumes, including soybeans, lima beans, lentils, black beans, kidney beans, butter beans, pinto beans, and black-eyed peas
- tomato soup
- regular ice cream
- yogurt
- all meat (watch out for breading)
- fish and shellfish
- butter
- eggs
- cream
- cheese
- nuts
- seeds
- most vegetables, including squash, zucchini, mushrooms, asparagus, artichokes, okra (nonbreaded), lettuces, spinach, turnip greens, cabbage, celery, cucumber, dill pickles, radishes, bell peppers, cauliflower, broccoli, Brussels sprouts, eggplant, and onions

LOSING WEIGHT THE HEALTHY WAY

To lose weight, avoid high glycemic foods, go easy on the moderate ones, and follow a diet of approximately 40% complex carbohydrates, 30% fat (focus on the good fats), and 30% protein.

I know this diet doesn't sit well with many of you who have believed that all fat is bad, but remember, we need the good fats and their essential fatty acids. And fat helps delay the release of insulin, slowing down the rate at which carbohydrates are released into the bloodstream. Fat also stimulates the hormone cholecystokinin. Cholecystokinin sends a message to the brain that you are full. This is why you can only eat so much fat before quickly becoming full. Think about it. Most people can eat a whole bag of fat-free chips at one sitting. However, try eating a stick of butter...you won't get far!

To help you avoid sugar, use a plant-based sweetener like Stevia or fructoligosaccharide (FOS). Both are available at health food stores. Saccharine is preferable to aspartame.

ARE YOU ALLERGIC TO CARBOHYDRATES?

Many people are carbohydrate intolerant. Their cells have become full of stored carbohydrates (turned into fat) and can't effectively metabolize large amounts of carbohydrates. Intolerance to carbohydrates may cause fatigue, mental lethargy, confusion, depression, headache, bloating, indigestion, and weight gain. A two-week trial on a low-carbohydrate diet is an easy way to see if you are carbohydrate intolerant.

Individuals with low serotonin levels should be careful not to reduce their carbohydrate intake too quickly. Carbohydrates stimulate the release of insulin. Insulin allows the amino acid tryptophan to cross the blood-brain barrier, where it then turns into serotonin.

For Further Reading
- *Sugar Busters! Cut Sugar to Trim Fat* by H. Leighton Steward et al; 1998
- *Food & Mood* by Elizabeth Somer, MA, RD; 1999
- *Diet and Disease* by Emanuel Cheraskin et al; 1988
- *The Zone: A Dietary Road Map* by Barry Sears; 1995
- *The Schwarzbein Principle* by Diana Schwarzbein, MD and Nancy Deville; 1999

16

The Meat of the Matter: Protein

Protein is the main structural component of cells, of enzymes responsible for bodily functions, of antibodies (which help fight off infection), and of many of our hormones, including insulin.

Protein molecules are the key building blocks of all forms of life. They make up over one-half of the body's dry weight and are second only to water molecules in abundance within the body. Muscles, skin, hair, the brain, blood vessels, connective tissue, and nails are all made from protein.

Low-protein diets (often the result of low-fat or low-calorie diets) are a recipe for disaster. They can cause a host of health problems including depression, ADD, low thyroid function, immune deficiency, poor wound healing, and fatigue.

Proteins are basically long chains of amino acids, and without amino acids, our bodies simply can't work properly. Amino acids are needed for making neurotransmitters such as serotonin, dopamine, and norepinephrine.

Protein—along with fat—actually buffers the effects of insulin and allows the body to use glucose at a slower rate. So protein and fat consumption within reasonable levels will actually aid in weight loss.

WHAT ABOUT HIGH-PROTEIN DIETS?

Written by cardiologist Robert Atkins and published in 1972, *Dr. Atkins's New Diet Revolution* has had a profound affect on the way Americans eat. For over thirty years, Dr. Atkins and his legion of fans have advocated a low-carbohydrate approach to improved health and weight loss.

This controversial diet is now gaining a foothold in mainstream medicine. The National Institute of Health is about to begin a study based on Dr. Atkins's work. Recent studies have shown positive—even dramatic—results. One study compared low-fat dieters to low-carbohydrate dieters. Over a six-month period, individuals on the two diets lost 20 pounds and 31 pounds, respectively. Low-fat dieters had a 22% reduction in their triglycerides (blood fat levels), while those on the Atkins diet decreased their triglyceride levels by a whopping 49%.

The Atkins diet is based on consuming 10% of calories from carbohydrates, 60% from fat, and 30% from protein. In the induction phase, however, dieters consume no more than 20 grams of carbohydrates a day—equal to one medium-sized apple. This extreme beginning phase is then transitioned into a diet that allows for increasingly more carbohydrates as long as desired weight loss is maintained.

The majority of people who have stayed on this diet have successfully lost weight. But in our carb-heavy culture, the Atkins diet can seem very limiting; fruits and starches are just too tough to forgo. The diet does allows most vegetables, but many people don't cook at home much. Eating out, you find only a limited variety of vegetables. And people need to eat live foods, as we are now learning of the far-reaching health benefits of plant-based flavonoids (nutrient chemicals).

SO WHAT IS THE BEST DIET?

To begin the road to better health, I recommend a *form* of the Atkins diet that I call the "two-week low-carbohydrate challenge" (described below). It's excellent for jumpstarting a person's metabolism, and it can also jumpstart her willpower. Losing a quick five–six pounds can be a big psychological boost! However, I don't recommend this diet long-term, and I don't agree with the toxic food choices Dr. Atkins recommends. No one should live off of fried pork skins, hunks of processed cheese, and excessive amounts of hormone-fed livestock!

For long-term health after the duration of the two-week challenge diet, I recommend the following diet parameters:

- 40% (mostly complex) carbohydrates

- 30% protein

- 30% (mostly unsaturated) fat

You don't need the burden of counting calories or carbohydrate grams, so do your best without adding to your stress load. And don't forget to avoid the foods we now know sabotage your hopes of losing weight: simple sugars!

THE TWO-WEEK LOW-CARBOHYDRATE CHALLENGE

Do not begin this or any other diet (except the elimination diet) before correcting any sleeping disorders and normalizing the adrenal glands. Consult your nutrition-oriented physician.

For two weeks, eliminate all breads, pastas, cereals, milk, fruit juices, simple carbohydrate snacks, potatoes, cake, cookies, and other sweets. Stick to low glycemic-index foods, and try to keep total carbohydrate intake at or below 20 grams a day. If after two weeks on this diet you feel a whole lot better, then you are most likely carbohydrate intolerant and this is the right diet for you. If you are feeling good and have lost some weight, stay on this regimen for another two–four weeks.

Most individuals will do well on this test diet. Others with extremely low serotonin levels may bottom out and feel miserable. Sugar-withdrawal symptoms are not uncommon, but over time, this diet helps curb sugar cravings. Long-term use, though, can cause unwanted side effects. Here's why:

The main fuel of the brain is glucose, which is most easily derived from carbohydrates. A low-carbohydrate diet works because it causes the body to use up stored carbohydrates (glycogen). Once the glycogen stores are depleted, the body starts to turn protein into glucose (this is known as gluconeogenesis). But when the body starts to burn up stored proteins, it must conserve the essential proteins. It does this by producing a substitute fuel from the breakdown of fatty acids, and this yields a by-product known as ketones (and creates a state known as ketosis). The kidneys attempt to flush out these ketones, and in so doing also rid the body of excess water (so the rapid initial weight loss experienced on a low-carb diet is due to water loss).

Continuing a low-carbohydrate diet will burn up excess fat, but it also increases the risk of ketosis. Ketosis makes the blood more acidic than it should be and can cause headache, foul breathe, dizziness, fatigue, and nausea. That's a lousy way to live, weight loss or not.

The body shouldn't be subjected to long-term ketosis. It's just not healthy. Instead, try a two-week low-carbohydrate challenge test, followed by a moderate (balanced) carbohydrate weight loss/management lifestyle diet

Lighten Up!

If you blow your diet every once in awhile (Christmas, Thanksgiving, birthdays), don't feel guilty. It's the long-term, day-in-and-day-out eating habits that matter. It's OK to eat sweets every once in awhile. Just don't make it a habit. Also, keep your diet goals simple. Don't try to count calories! Simply avoiding high glycemic carbohydrates, going easy on moderate carbohydrates, and eating balanced meals will—over time—lead to weight loss.

EAT SMALLER MEALS

Instead of three large meals only, eat healthy snacks throughout the day. Start by eating a piece of fruit or a handful of nuts a couple of hours after breakfast. Remember to combine carbohydrates, fat, and protein, even when snacking. After lunch, eat another healthy snack two–three hours before dinner. This will help you avoid overeating at dinner. By eating small meals throughout the day, you'll also avoid the pitfalls of hypoglycemia and binge eating. Smaller meals are easier to digest and allow the body more energy for other functions, like operating the immune system.

Keep healthy snacks readily available in your purse, briefcase, and car. When you feel hungry, eat a small snack. Arriving home at night ravenous and then eating a big dinner—followed by snacking in your La-Z-Boy in front of the television—just isn't going to cut it. If you're very hungry on your way home from work, then you've already blown it. If this happens, eat a small snack to tide you over until dinner.

Digesting food takes a great deal of metabolic energy, so I don't recommend eating anything one–two hours before bed. Eating at that time requires the body to digest food when it should be resting and repairing itself. (Did you know that you get a new stomach lining every five days? The cells that contact food are replaced every few minutes.)

SUPPLEMENTS TO HELP YOU LOSE WEIGHT

• **DL-phenylalanine, L-phenylalanine, and L-tyrosine** are all amino acids that act as appetite suppressants. DL-phenylalanine increases pain-relieving endorphins along with suppressing appetite. L-tyrosine has the added benefit of stimulating thyroid and human growth hormones; both of these hormones increase the body's metabolism. Even though L-tyrosine is used more rapidly than the other two aminos, I usually start my patients off with DL-phenylalanine. It has proven itself to be the most effective appetite suppressant.

These amino acids, though, can raise blood pressure or cause insomnia, headache, and irritability when taken by sensitive individuals or in excessive doses. Just as important, these supplements should not be taken along with monoamine inhibitors, a form of antidepressants.

Always take free-form amino acids on an empty stomach and start with 1,000–2,000 mg. twice daily. Gradually increase the dosage to twice that amount if necessary. Vitamin B6 is needed for these amino acids to work properly, so I recommend taking 100–250 mg. of it daily. Don't take L-tyrosine in the evening, since it has a stimulating effect that can interfere with sleep.

• **L-glutamine** can be extremely helpful in eliminating sugar cravings. Animal studies have shown L-glutamine to lower both blood glucose and insulin levels. Take 500–1,000 mg. twice daily on an empty stomach. It can be taken at the same time as DL and L-phenylalanine.

• **L-carnitine** helps the liver rid the body of unwanted waste products. It also increases the body's cellular metabolism, helping transport fatty acids to the fat-burning mitochondria. I recommend 500–1000 mg. twice daily on an empty stomach. There are no side effects.

• **5-hydroxytryptophan** (5HTP) is the precursor to the neurotransmitter serotonin. Serotonin is involved in (among many other things already discussed) regulating the appetite. A deficiency in serotonin can cause sugar cravings, but 5HTP can reduce or eliminate these cravings. It can also help prevent binge eating under stress and poor sleep due to low serotonin. (Research has shown that lack of quality sleep prevents weight loss).

The diet drug known as Fen-Phen (Fenflouramine) was once prescribed to stimulate serotonin, but it was shown to cause heart valve damage and has been recalled by the FDA.

- **Chromium** is a mineral that helps control blood sugar levels. It increases liver glycogen storage and allows for efficient uptake of glucose by muscle cells while inhibiting excessive storage of fat. I recommend 200–400 mg. of chromium with glucose tolerance factor (a patented process) daily, 30 minutes before a meal.

Nature's Way makes a product called Blood Sugar that combines chromium and an herbal extract, Gymnema Sylvestre. Gymnema Sylvestre is a plant from India used around the world to treat diabetes. It helps regulate blood sugar and reduce sugar cravings. Several studies have shown this herb to be quite effective for lowering blood sugar levels.

- **CoQ10** is similar to L-carnitine in its effect on cellular metabolism. It aids in the production of adenisinetriphosphate (ATP), the main energy compound generated from cellular mitochondria. CoQ10 should be taken by every person diagnosed with FMS/CFS. I recommend 50–200 mg. a daily.

For Further Reading
- *Sugar Busters! Cut Sugar to Trim Fat* by H. Leighton Steward et al; 1998
- *The Zone: A Dietary Road Map* by Barry Sears; 1995
- *The Schwarzbein Principle* by Diana Schwarzbein, MD and Nancy Deville; 1999
- *The Carbohydrate Addict's Diet* by Rachael F. Heller, et al; 1999

17

The Digestive System: Our Fragile Ally

The state of our health is largely determined by not only what we eat but how well we digest and absorb it. Nutrients are worthless if they can't be broken down and utilized by the body.

A typical American breakfast might include nitrate-laden bacon cooked in hydrogenated oils, sugary cereal made with bleached enriched flour, and a glass of orange juice (a simple carbohydrate). Lunch might be a fast-food hamburger loaded with saturated and trans-fatty acids, pasteurized preservative-rich cheese (containing aluminum), french fries cooked in hydrogenated oils and loaded with fat, and a Diet Coke ("I'm watching my weight").

Well, this menu does contain all the "recommended" food groups: meat, dairy, grains (bleached white flour), and fruits and vegetables (fiber-free juice and fatty french fries). Does this sound healthy to you? Of course not! Cooking in hydrogenated oils, preserving by bleaching, and adding artificial flavors and colors removes essential vitamins and minerals and adds toxins. Is it any wonder over 60% of our population (a rapidly climbing number) are overweight?

Since 50 years ago, Americans are consuming an additional 31% fat and 50% sugar while decreasing complex carbohydrate consumption by 43%. Much of our food has been processed, bleached, altered with preservatives, and tarnished with toxic pesticides. We are literally eating ourselves into the grave. Over 40 million Americans have been diagnosed with irritable bowel syndrome, and surveys have shown that as many as 73% of FMS patients have it.[1]

HOW THE DIGESTIVE SYSTEM WORKS

The digestive system includes the mouth, salivary glands, esophagus, stomach, pancreas, liver, gall bladder, small intestine, and large intestine. Digestion involves the breakdown of food, its movement through the digestive tract, the chemical breakdown of large molecules into smaller, more readily absorbed molecules, and the elimination of waste. The digestive system also functions as an important barrier against unwanted bacteria, yeasts, viruses, and parasites that may enter our bodies along with our food.

Digestion begins before you even take a bite. Just thinking about or smelling food can trigger certain chemicals, including the hormone gastrin that stimulates the stomach cells. The process of chewing also initiates chemical reactions that prepare the stomach, gallbladder, and pancreas for proper digestion. Food stuff is delivered from the mouth to the stomach by way of the esophagus, a 10-inch-long hollow organ. The esophageal sphincter works like a gate, opening to receive food and then closing to prevent stomach acid or food from returning to the throat.

Food is then pushed into the stomach where digestive enzymes and gastric juices reduce it to a liquid substance known as chyme. The digestive enzymes include trypsin, amylase, lipase, chymotrypsin, and carboxypeptidase. Amylase reduces large chains of starch polypeptides to smaller disaccharides. Lipase is the fat-digesting enzyme. These enzymes break down food stuff and allow the smaller molecules and nutrients to be absorbed into the bloodstream. They may become deficient for a variety of reasons, including advancing age, excess sugar, deficient essential fatty acids, excessive trans-fatty acids, and overeating.

The gastric juices contain hydrochloric acid and the enzyme pepsin. The hydrochloric acid breaks down the predigested food, and pepsin breaks down proteins into polypeptides (chains of amino acids). This acidic environment acts as one of the body's first lines of defense, destroying viruses, parasites, yeast, and bacteria.

After four–six hours, chyme passes through the pylorus into the small intestine, which is made up of 22 feet of hollow tubing. There are three parts to the small intestine: the duodenum, jejunum, and ileum. The small intestine needs an alkaline environment to further break down the chyme, so the pancreas releases sodium bicarbonate along with the digestive enzymes.

The Pancreas and Proteolytic Enzymes

The pancreas aids in digestion by releasing proteolytic enzymes, which help break down proteins into amino acids. Proteolytic enzymes also help regulate inflammatory reactions by reducing the amount of kinins in the body. Kinin is a tissue hormone capable of causing severe and painful inflammatory reactions. It is triggered by allergic foods or chemicals and can cause inflammation anywhere in the body, including the brain.

Proteolytic enzymes are built from amino acids. So a deficiency in amino acids means a deficiency in the inflammation- and pain-blocking proteolytic enzymes. Amino acids come from protein. So, if you're not getting enough protein (as is the case on many low-fat diets), you won't have enough amino acids to build these valuable enzymes. And if you already suffer from malabsorption, you might not be digesting the protein you take in anyway. This is why I recommend that all patients over the age of 40 or with chronic health problems take digestive enzymes, even if they're not currently suffering from a digestive illness.

Allergic or addictive food intolerances can contribute to digestive problems. When it comes to various digestive stresses, the pancreas is the first organ to suffer. The pancreas can become deficient in bicarbonate, and the proteolytic enzymes can be compromised or even destroyed. Undigested proteins are then leaked across the intestinal cellular membrane where they trigger kinin-inflammatory reactions, resulting in more gastrointestinal stress.

The Gallbladder

The gallbladder secretes bile to help break down fats. Bile is made up of bile salts, cholesterol, lecithin, and bilirubin, a breakdown of red blood cells. Digestive juices continue to break down the chyme until it is at the end of the small intestine. Then it's absorbed through the wall of the small intestine into the bloodstream. Once the nutrients enter the bloodstream, they are routed to the liver.

Could You Be Acid Deficient?

Numerous studies have shown that acid secretion declines with advancing age. It's been estimated that 50% of Americans over the age of 60 suffer from achlorhydria, a deficiency in hydrochloric acid. The resulting rise in stomach pH can cause many of the symptoms associated with FMS and CFS. For example, one study found that 34% of sufferers reported indigestion and excessive gas. Forty percent complained of fatigue.

We need gastric acid and pepsin for optimal digestion of food, absorption of nutrients, and release of pancreatic enzymes. A hydrochloric-acid deficiency triggers a chain reaction of digestive disorders, including malabsorption. Foods may be incompletely digested and subsequently absorbed into the bloodstream, where they can lead to food allergies, triggering pain and inflammation throughout the body.

Symptoms associated with achlorhydria include bloating, gas, indigestion, heartburn, distention after eating, diarrhea, constipation, hair loss in women, parasitic infections, rectal itching, malaise, multiple food allergies, nausea or nausea after taking supplements, restless legs, sore or burning tongue, and a dry mouth. Other associated signs are abnormal intestinal flora, chronic Candidiasis, chronic intestinal parasites, dilated capillaries in the cheeks and nose (in non-alcoholics), iron deficiency, post-adolescent acne, undigested food in the stool, and fingernails that are weak, peeling, and cracked.

Are Antacids the Answer?

Symptoms like these will often prompt someone to try antacids. But sometimes that's a big mistake. First, the esophageal sphincter is stimulated to close by the release of stomach acids. So when there's not enough stomach acid present—because antacids have neutralized them—the esophageal sphincter may not close properly. This allows acid to travel back up into the esophagus and cause heartburn, also called esophageal reflux or gastro-esophageal reflux disease—GERD. GERD isn't usually treated by antacids, but antacids could make the GERD worse.

Second, the stomach needs an acidic environment for hydrochloric acid to turn the enzyme pepsinogen into pepsin. No acid equals no pepsin, which is needed for digestion.

Last, an acidic environment is one of the body's first lines of defense, destroying viruses, parasites, yeast, and bacteria.

Natural Treatments for Heartburn, Reflux, GERD, and H. Pylori

If you are suffering from heartburn, try the solutions below rather than antacids. If the symptoms have just begun, try hydrochloric acid (HCL) replacement therapy. If the symptoms have been present for over six months, the esophageal sphincter may have become so irritated that adding more acid would only make things worse. In this case, use buffering agents as recommended by your doctor. Be sure to take pancreatic digestive enzymes, even if you can't take HCL.

Peppermint and DGL licorice root can be very helpful in reducing the symptoms of GERD. Have your blood tested for *helicobacter pylori,* a bacteria associated with ulcers, heartburn, and reflux. If the test comes back positive, take a prescription antibiotic (along with probiotics) or recommended herbal medicine to kill this opportunistic bacteria. Usually it can be treated with antibiotics and over-the-counter products such as Pepto-Bismol.

Supplementing With Hydrochloric Acid

Adequate protein intake and a relaxed emotional state can help increase stomach acidity, but supplementation might also be necessary. Follow the guidelines below.

Don't take HCL if you've been diagnosed with a peptic ulcer. HCL can irritate sensitive tissue and can be corrosive to teeth. Don't empty capsules into food or beverages. Take in capsule form only. I recommend that you take pancreatic enzymes along with the HCL.

1. Take one capsule containing 600–650 mg. of hydrochloric acid, along with 100–200 mg. of pepsin at the beginning of your meal. Continue taking one capsule with each meal for the next five days.

2. After five days, increase your dose to two capsules with each meal. Continue this dose for five days.

3. If you are experiencing no side effects (such as warmth, fullness, or other odd sensation in your stomach), increase your dose by one capsule each day until you do. Then reduce your dose by one capsule at your next meal.

4. Once you've established a comfortable per-meal dose (five capsules or fewer), continue at that level. As your stomach regains the ability to produce an adequate concentration of HCL, you will probably require fewer capsules. Listen to your body and reduce your dose as necessary. You may wish to reduce your number of capsules at smaller meals.

5. Be consistent. Individuals with low HCL and pepsin typically don't respond as well to botanicals and supplements, so to maximize the benefits, keep up the supplementation as directed.

Other Natural Remedies

- **Bismuth** is a natural antimicrobial that is absorbed in the stomach.

- **Citrus seed extract** is derived from grapefruit seeds. It is a potent antimicrobial that works well for intestinal bacteria and yeast overgrowth.

- **Bentonite** is clay that inhibits bacterial activity. It binds to and helps remove toxic bacterial debris.

- **Berberine** is a broad-spectrum antimicrobial. It is favored by herbalists and physicians who value its ability to discourage bacterial and yeast overgrowth.

- **Deglycyrrhizinated (DGL) licorice root** reduces irritation to the stomach lining. It also has antimicrobial effects and can be useful in treating bacterial, viral, and yeast infections. Studies have shown DGL to be an effective deterrent against *H. pylori*. I use it as an anti-inflammatory agent. To reduce the pain associated with heartburn or ulcers, try three–four chewable tablets 10–15 minutes before meals and throughout the day on an empty stomach.

- **Peppermint oil** (enteric coated) can ease the intestinal cramping and discomfort associated with irritable bowel syndrome. Take one–two capsules three–four times a day on an empty stomach.

MALABSORPTION SYNDROME (LEAKY GUT)

A yes to any of the following questions suggests you might not be completely digesting your food or absorbing its nutrients.

- Do you suffer from bloating, gas, or indigestion?
- Have you been diagnosed with irritable bowel syndrome?
- Are you constipated, have diarrhea, or alternate between the two?
- Do you eat a lot of processed foods?
- Have you taken antibiotics, nonsteroidal anti-inflammatory medicines, antacids, or cortisone for prolonged periods of time?
- Are you over the age of 40?
- Do you suffer from food allergies or food intolerances?
- Do you have a sluggish liver (have difficulty taking medications)?
- Do you have a hard time taking vitamin or mineral supplements?
- Have you had your gall bladder removed?

Malabsorption syndrome is common among those with FMS and CFS. It is usually caused by deficient digestive enzymes but can also be due to dysbiosis and intestinal permeability.

Dysbiosis

The intestinal tract contains hundreds of microorganisms that normally don't cause any health problems. However, when the intestinal tract is repetitively exposed to toxic substances, these microorganisms begin to proliferate and create an imbalance in the bowel flora. This is known as intestinal dysbiosis.

Dysbiosis causes the bowel flora to secrete toxic chemicals that can cause a myriad of health problems: Candida yeast syndrome, allergies, eczema, autoimmune diseases, chronic fatigue, irritable bowel disease, colitis, and psoriasis.

Intestinal Permeability

We can all agree that popping supplements that cannot be digested makes little sense. But that is what many of my FMS and CFS patients are unknowingly doing. In their quest to feel better—and with little or no guidance from traditional medicine—these individuals often take dozens of different supplements. But it's not helping much, because the body isn't absorbing them. That's because most of my patients have intestinal permeability or other malabsorption problems from taking nonsteroidal anti-inflammatory medications. Even a single dose of aspirin can increase the membrane permeability of intestinal cells. Other culprits include steroids, antibiotics, antihistamines, caffeine, alcohol, and a host of prescription and nonprescription drugs.

Intestinal permeability is caused by damage to the intestinal mucosa. It's also called "leaky gut." It occurs when the lining of the digestive tract becomes permeable and leaks undigested food products and toxins that may cause chronic inflammation. Studies have demonstrated the role intestinal permeability plays in such illnesses as ankylosing spondylitis, rheumatoid arthritis, food allergies, Crohn's disease, eczema, chronic fatigue, irritable bowel syndrome, cystic fibrosis, chronic hepatitis, and many others.

Intestinal permeability allows antigens to leak out of the digestive tract and into the bloodstream. This triggers an autoimmune reaction and can create pain and inflammation in any of the body's tissues. Let's say someone with intestinal permeability eats a chicken sandwich. The chicken proteins might not be properly broken down and digested. Instead they leak across the intestinal membranes and go directly, unprocessed, into the bloodstream. Well, the body is not designed to have unprocessed chicken proteins racing around in the bloodstream and it thinks it's being invaded by foreign chicken molecules. The immune system kicks in, and in accordance with an allergic reaction, releases chemicals to destroy and eliminate these renegade chicken bits. Pain and inflammation can occur anywhere these unprocessed proteins are deposited, including muscles, joints, and organs.

Testing for Intestinal Permeability and Malabsorption

Intestinal permeability can be measured by using a challenge test of the man-made sugars lactulose and mannitol. The patient drinks a lactulose-mannitol cocktail and then catches her urine for six hours. The large lactulose molecules should not be absorbed and are normally seen in the urine sample. An absence of lactulose molecules in the urine suggests intestinal permeability. The mannitol sugar is small and readily absorbable. Mannitol sugars in the urine sample suggest malabsorption. Talk to you doctor about this test; see page 275.

Treating Intestinal Permeability and Malabsorption Syndrome

Those who have (or suspect) malabsorption syndrome, intestinal permeability, or irritable bowel syndrome should take the following steps:

- **Start supplementing digestive enzymes,** including hydrochloric acid.

- **Treat and eliminate** any parasite or yeast overgrowth.

- **Immediately begin the elimination diet** to pinpoint any food allergies. See page 98 for a full description. Pay particular attention to gluten, a protein found in most grains, because it can be very irritating to the intestinal lining. Individuals extremely sensitive to gluten will develop a condition known as Celiac sprue or gluten enteropathy. Those already suffering from poor regulatory systems (many FMS and CFS patients) might benefit from avoiding gluten altogether.

- **Supplement with good intestinal bacteria:** acidophilus, bifidobacteria, and lactobacilli.

- **Supplement with 2,000 mg. of L-glutamine** daily (remember to take amino acids on an empty stomach). I use a product especially developed for intestinal permeability known as GastroThera. Continue on L-glutamine or GastroThera for one–two months.

PARASITES

Parasites are organisms that live off of a parent host. Parasitic infections are the primary cause of many chronic illnesses, including autoimmune diseases, allergies, and Candidiasis.

Though parasitic infections are usually associated with third-world countries, world travel and increased immigration have contributed to their rise in the United States. One report submitted by a gastroenterology clinic showed that 74% of patient samples had parasites. At one time, Milwaukee's water supply was found to be contaminated with cryptosporidium, a parasite that caused 100 deaths and infected over 400,000 people. Every year, 1 million Americans become ill due to contaminated drinking water, and 10,000 of them die. The primary mode of transmitting parasites is by fecal to oral contamination (like when someone doesn't wash her hands after using the restroom or changing a diaper). However, water contamination is often the culprit, and most municipal water supplies carry some parasite.

In the United States, the most common parasites are *Giardia lamblia, Blastocystis hominis,* and *Dientamoeba fragilis. Giardia* is highly contagious and is carried by most animals, including dogs and cats. It has infested most of the ground water in North America. Children in day care are especially vulnerable to *Giardia* and *Dientamoeba.* It is estimated that 21–44% of children in day care are infected with one or both of these parasites. These parasites can then be spread to the rest of the family.

Other parasites include nematodes (intestinal worms). Nematodes include *Enterobius vermicularis, Ascaris lumbricoides, Trichuris trichiura, Nector americanus,* and *Strongyloides stercoralis. Trichinia spiralis* are worms that may contaminate uncooked pork. Pinworms are the most common intestinal worm. Tape worms, round worms, and hook worms are common in third-world countries. Roundworms are prevalent in the Appalachian Mountains.

The good news is that humans and parasites are able to co-exist as long as the intestinal tract lining is intact. A permeable intestinal lining allows parasites to penetrate into the body.

Symptoms and conditions associated with parasitic infection include:

- abdominal pain

- anorexia

- autoimmune disease

- chronic fatigue

- constipation

- fever
- bloating, gas, and indigestion
- headache
- nausea and vomiting
- diarrhea
- colitis
- irritable bowel syndrome
- Crohn's disease
- arthritis
- weight loss
- bloody stools
- rash
- skin and rectal itching
- low back pain
- food allergies
- malabsorption syndrome
- intestinal permeability

Notice how many of these symptoms are found in individuals with FMS and CFS. Anyone with a chronic illness, especially those with a weakened immune system (including FMS and CFS patients) should be tested for intestinal parasites.

Testing for Parasites and Dysbiosis

Most local laboratories don't specialize in stool testing and may miss parasitic infections. I recommend using a lab like Great Smokies Diagnostic that does specialize in stool testing. Great Smokies provides our patients with a take-home stool-test kit. Patients send their samples directly to Great Smokies where it is tested for parasites and bacterial and yeast overgrowth. For more information, see page 275.

Treating Parasites with Prescription Medications

Metronidazole (Flagyl) is usually used for amoeba, *Blastocystis,* and *Giardia* infections. Side effects may include nausea, headache, dry mouth, metallic taste, occasional vomiting, vertigo, diarrhea, parathesia, and rash. Rare side effects include seizures, encephalopathy, pseudo-membranous colitis, peripheral neuropathy, and pancreatitis.

Iodoquinol (Yodoxin) is also used for amoeba and *Dientamoeba* parasites. Side effects may include rash, acne, nausea, diarrhea, and cramps. Rare side effects include optic atrophy, loss of vision, and peripheral neuropathy after prolonged use (months).

Paramomycin (Humantin) is used to treat amoeba infections. Side effects may include GI disturbances and occasional auditory nerve damage or renal damage.

Quinacrine HCL (Atabrine) is mainly used for treating *Giardia*. Side effects may include dizziness, headache, vomiting, diarrhea, occasional toxic psychosis, psoriasis-like rash, and insomnia. Rare side effects include acute liver disease, convulsions, and severe exfoliative dermatitis.

Treating Parasites with Natural Remedies

Citrus seed extract is used throughout the world to treat a variety of viral, bacterial, fungal, and parasitic infections. It is not absorbed by the body but works within the intestinal tract. It is quite safe and relatively nontoxic, even when used for months at a time.

Artemisia annua (wormwood) is a Chinese herb that I find extremely effective in treating most parasitic infections. Artemisia can be toxic if used in large doses or for long periods of time. It works best when combined with other natural parasite supplements.

Allium sativum (garlic) is a perennial plant used as food seasoning throughout the world. It is also used in treating such health conditions as cardiovascular disease, immune deficiencies, and viral, bacterial, fungal, and parasitic infections. Garlic is a potent remedy for most intestinal parasites, especially round and hook worms.

Berberine is the active ingredient in goldenseal, Oregon grape root, and barberry. It is effective against a variety of parasites.

In one study cited in *The Textbook of Natural Medicine,* 40 children, ages 1–10, who were infected with *Giardia* received either metronidazole, berberine, or a placebo. After six days, those on berberine had reduced their symptoms by 48%, and 68% were clear from *Giardia* (according to stool samples). All those taking metronidazole were free of infection. However, they had enjoyed a modest 33% reduction in their symptoms. This study demonstrates that berberine is more effective in eliminating the symptoms of *Giardia*. Perhaps a larger dose administered over a longer period of time would have yielded results identical to the metronidazole.

AVOIDING PARASITES

- Always wash your hands after using the bathroom, handling animals, or working in the yard.
- Use bottled, filtered, or distilled water.
- Always wear shoes outside.
- Don't allow pets to lick your face.
- Deworm your pet as recommended by your veterinarian.
- Wash fruits and vegetables before eating them.
- Don't eat raw fish or meat. Thoroughly cook all meats.
- Don't drink from lakes, streams, or rivers without treating the water.
- Take digestive enzymes with each meal.

THE LARGE INTESTINE

The colon, or large intestine, receives the unusable chyme from the small intestine and begins to solidify it for evacuation. This semisolid material, known as feces, is propelled by muscular contractions and should produce a bowel movement within 36 hours. Healthy individuals should be having two or more bowel movements a day. Anything less increases the risk of fecal toxins being reabsorbed and leaking back into the bloodstream.

A poorly functioning colon can cause autoimmune disorders, arthritis, skin disorders including eczema and psoriasis, muscles aches, bad breath, offensive body odor, headaches, nausea, and even mood disorders.

Keeping Your Colon Healthy

Acidophilus, though found in milk and yogurt, is actually a bacterium. Along with over 400 other species of bacteria and yeast, they inhabit the intestinal tract. These good bacteria help keep potentially harmful bacteria and yeast in check. Acidophilus has proven to be effective in treating irritable bowel syndrome, *H. pylori,* diarrhea, and colitis. It's especially helpful in treating yeast overgrowth. It's also known as *Lactobacillus acidophilus* or *L. acidophilus.*

Dietary fiber helps to keep your digestive system clean. It regulates bowel movements, lowers cholesterol, detoxifies the body, reduces varicose veins, rids the body of excess water, regulates glucose-insulin levels, prevents gallstones and certain cancers, and assists with weight loss. Without it, constipation can result, increasing the risk of hemorrhoids and an unhealthy colon environment. There are many sources of natural fiber, including the following:

- **Cellulose** is a nondigestible carbohydrate that makes up the outer layer of fruits and vegetables. It is found in apples, carrots, pears, broccoli, green beans, grains, and Brazil nuts.

- **Hemicellulose,** a nondigestible complex carbohydrate, helps with weight by absorbing excess water. It is found in apples, beets, corn, bananas, and pears.

- **Lignin** is found in Brazil nuts, carrots, green beans, peas, tomatoes, peaches, strawberries, and potatoes. This form of fiber binds with bile acids and so aids in lowering cholesterol and prevents gallstone formation.

- **Glucomannan** is found in the tuber amorphophallis plant. It removes excess fat from the colon walls and may help with weight loss. It is a bulk-forming laxative that helps curb the appetite.

- **Psyllium** is a good intestinal cleanser and stool softener. It is a bulk-forming laxative and can help with colitis and other intestinal conditions.

Some herbs have a laxative effect as well. I recommend you not use Casa Cara or Senna for extended periods, since both of these herbs can cause dependency.

A PLAN FOR HEALING

If you suspect you have malabsorption syndrome, intestinal permeability, yeast overgrowth, or a parasite infection (most people with FMS/CFS have at least one of these), follow these steps:

- Obtain a Great Smokies test kit. See page 275.
- Eat plenty of fiber-rich foods and adequate protein.
- Begin using Intestamine, six capsules twice daily, for one–three months.
- Take probiotics daily for one–three months.
- Take a natural antiparasitic medication, or consult your doctor for a prescription.
- Treat any constipation with magnesium. Magnesium relaxes muscles, including the muscles of the colon, and FMS and CFS patients are usually deficient in magnesium. Most patients taking my Essential Therapeutics CFS/Fibromyalgia formula start to experience normal bowel movements within two–three weeks. Individuals extremely deficient in magnesium may need additional amounts. Start with the CFS/Fibromyalgia formula, and if your bowel movements don't normalize, add an additional 140 mg. of magnesium citrate a day until you start to have loose bowel movements. Then simply reduce the magnesium until you are having a normal bowel movement once again.

Notes
[1]Joseph Pizzorno, ND and Michael Murray, ND. *Encyclopedia of Natural Medicine.*

Resources
- GastroThera and digestive enzymes are available online at www.drrodger.com or by calling (205) 879-2383.
- Digestive enzymes are also available at many health food stores.

For Further Reading
- *Functional Assessment Resource Manual,* Great Smokies Diagnostic Laboratory; 1999
- *Total Wellness: Improve Your Health by Understanding the Body's Healing Systems* by Joseph E. Pizzorno, ND; 1996
- *The Human Body* by Isaac Asimov; 1992
- *Healer Within* by Steven Locke, MD; 1986
- *The Parasite Menace* by Skye Weintraub; 1998
- *Tired or Toxic* by Sherry A. Rogers; 1990
- *Missing Diagnosis* by Dr. C. Orian Truss; 1985
- *Dr. Jensen's Guide to Better Bowel Care* by Bernard Jensen; 1998
- *Enzymes the Fountain of Life* by M. Miehlke; 1994

18

Toxic Waste Sites

We've peeled away several layers of the onion, and we're getting to the core. Here's where some people have to peel a little deeper than others, investigating the health of their detox system.

THE LIVER

The liver is the largest organ in the body. Located on the right side of the abdomen, it is the first to process the nutrients delivered by the bloodstream. It filters two quarts of blood every minute, removing about 99% of all unwanted toxins and bacteria. The liver also secretes a quart of bile each day. Bile is necessary for absorbing fat-soluble substances, including certain vitamins. It helps eliminate toxic chemicals and is mixed with dietary fiber and voided through daily bowel movements.

We are constantly exposed to potentially dangerous toxins through the food we eat, the air we breathe, and the water we drink. An optimally functioning detoxification system is necessary for providing good health and preventing disease. Many diseases, including cancer, rheumatoid arthritis, lupus, Alzheimer's, Parkinson's, and other chronic age-related conditions are linked to a weakened detoxification system. It can also contribute to allergic disorders, asthma, hives, psoriasis, and eczema and is associated with CFS, FMS, depression, and systemic Candidiasis.

TWO-PHASE DETOXIFICATION

Unwanted chemicals, including prescription and non-prescription drugs, alcohol, pesticides, herbicides, and metabolic waste products are neutralized by the liver's enzymes. There are two enzymatic pathways, phase I and phase II.

Phase I Detox

Phase I detoxification enzymes are collectively known as cytochrome P450. The cytochrome P450 system is made up of 50–100 enzymes that attempt to neutralize toxic chemicals by transforming them into a less toxic form. Each enzyme is specially suited to certain types of toxins. Chemicals that can't be neutralized are changed into an intermediate form. As the phase I enzymes neutralize toxins, they spin off free radicals. If there aren't enough antioxidants to counter these free radicals, the liver may be compromised.

Phase I detoxification is inhibited by antihistamines, NSAIDs, azole drugs (antifungals), tranquilizers such as Valium and Klonopin, and antidepressants such as Prozac and Celexa. (Is it any wonder that FMS and CFS patients are told that their condition is "all in their head" when drugs may make them sicker?)

Phase I is responsible for neutralizing most over-the-counter and prescription drugs, caffeine, hormones, yellow dyes, insecticides, alcohol, and histamine.

Phase II Detox

Phase II detoxification enzymes go to work on the toxins that the phase I enzymes turned into intermediate form. They do this by attaching minute chemicals to the structures. This process is called conjugation, and it neutralizes the toxins, making them more likely to be excreted through urination or defecation. Unfortunately, many of these intermediate forms are more toxic and potentially more damaging than in their original state. So an inadequate phase II detoxification system can cause all sorts of chronic illnesses.

A person suffering from poorly functioning phase II and overactive phase I detoxification is known as a pathological detoxifier. These individuals fill up doctors' offices on a regular basis, because they suffer from a variety of ailments that seem to never go away. One illness is replaced by another as the patient tries one prescription after another. Neither the doctor nor the patient realizes that a compromised detoxification system is being further aggravated by toxic prescription medications.

Phase II is responsible for neutralizing acetaminophen, nicotine, and insecticides. It is comprised of the following conjugation processes:

- **Glutathione conjugation** requires vitamin B_6 and the tripeptide (made from three amino acids) glutathione.

- **Amino-acid conjugation** requires the amino acid glycine. Low-protein diets and deficient digestive enzymes inhibit this process. Individuals with hypothyroidism, arthritis, hepatitis, and chemical sensitivities may suffer from poor amino-acid conjugation.

- **Methylation** requires S-adenosyl-methionine (SAM). SAM is synthesized from the amino acid methionine and dependent on folic acid, choline, and vitamin B_{12}. Methylation detoxifies estrogen, testosterone, thyroid hormones, acetaminophen, and coumarin.

- **Sulfation** requires the amino acids cysteine and methionine and the mineral molybdenum. Sulfation is involved in processing steroids, thyroid hormones, food additives, certain drugs, and neurotransmitters. Individuals who can't take certain antidepressants or have reactions to certain sulfur-containing foods may benefit from taking extra molybdenum, taurine, cysteine, and methionine. (All these are included in our CFS/Fibromyalgia formula.)

- **Acetylation** requires acetyl-CoA and is inhibited by a deficiency in vitamin C, B_2, or B_5. This pathway is responsible for eliminating sulfa drugs, so individuals with sulfa allergies may benefit from extra vitamin C, B_2, or B_5.

- **Glucuronidation** requires glucoronic acid and detoxifies acetaminophen, morphine, benzoates, aspirin, and vanilla. Aspirin inhibits this process. Signs of deficiency include yellowish pigment in the eyes or skin not caused by hepatitis.

- **Sulfoxidation** requires molybdenum and detoxifies sulfites and garlic. You may be deficient in this enzyme if you have allergic reactions to sulfite foods or garlic, asthmatic reactions after eating, or a strong urine odor after eating asparagus. Individuals with a sluggish sulfoxidation pathway may benefit from taking additional molybdenum.

Fish oils, SAM, broccoli, Brussels sprouts, and cabbage all stimulate phase I and phase II reactions. Choline, betaine, methionine, vitamin B6, folic acid, and vitamin B12 (altogether known as lipotrophic factors) stimulate bile production and its flow to and from the liver. Lipotrophic factors also increase SAM and glutathione, which in turn spare the liver free-radical damage.

FREE RADICALS

Free radicals are unstable atoms or molecules with an unpaired electron in the outer ring. They fill the void by taking an electron from another molecule, which then becomes unstable, needing another electron of its own. This sets up a destructive cycle that can cause damage to our bodies inside and out.

Internal metabolic activities, including immune and detoxification processes, generate free-radical molecules, but sometimes they come from our environment. External sources include radiation, alcohol, tobacco, smog, medications, and pesticides. Free radicals have been implicated in such conditions as rheumatoid arthritis, Alzheimer's, Parkinson's, cancer, and heart disease.

Believe it or not, oxygen is responsible for the creation of most toxic free radicals. Just like it causes rust on a car, excessive oxygen can cause premature aging and dysfunction in the body. That's why antioxidants, including vitamins A, E, and C, and beta carotene, are so important. Along with the amino acids cysteine, methionine, glycine, and glutathione (tripeptide), they help deter the effects of free-radical damage.

Have you ever cut open an apple and then left it out awhile? If so, you've witnessed free-radical damage. The once white inner meat of the apple turns brown when exposed to the oxygen in the air. Sprinkling lemon juice on the apple will turn the brown back to its normal color. This is an example of an antioxidant at work.

TOXIC WATER

A study released in 1988 by Ralph Nader's Center for Study of Responsive Law in Washington, DC, shows that much of the nation's drinking water is unsafe: Tests conducted in 38 states found over 2,000 toxic chemicals in the drinking water. About 10% of these chemicals are associated with causing cancer, cell growths, neurological damage, and birth defects. Thousands of chemicals found in our water supplies have never even been tested for safety.

A joint study by the EPA and the National Academy of Sciences has attributed 200–1,000 US deaths each year to the inhalation of chloroform from water while bathing.

"No longer can anyone assume the 500 chemicals in the average US municipal water supply are without side effects on the body....We now know, for example, that when the brain is unable to detoxify some of these chemicals, it actually manufactures chloral hydrate in the brain...[producing] the symptoms of brain fog." —Sherry Rogers, MD[1]

So what's in the water Americans are drinking? Here is a partial list of the unwelcome additions that have been found in drinking water.

• **arsenic:** a known carcinogen and poison

• **asbestos:** a known carcinogen

• **cadmium:** causes arteriosclerosis, kidney damage, and cancer

• **lead:** causes learning disabilities in children

• **mercury:** causes nervous system and kidney damage

• **nitrites:** possible carcinogen that interferes with body's oxygen metabolism

• **viruses and bacteria**

• **toxic chemicals**

- **1,1,1-trichloroethane:** causes liver damage and depression

- **1,1-dichlorethylene:** causes depressed central nervous system and cancer

- **benzene:** causes chromosomal damage in humans, anemia, blood disorders, and leukemia

- **chloroform**: causes cancer

- **dioxin:** extremely toxic carcinogen

- **ethylene dibromide:** causes male sterility and cancer

- **polychlorinated biphyls [PCB]:** causes liver damage, skin disorders, and GI problems; highly suspected of causing cancer

Do I really need to continue? I think you get the message. Our drinking water is not safe! A hot shower or bath can increase your exposure to toxic chemicals by 400 percent. One thousand deaths occur every year from chloral hydrate poisoning while taking a shower.

What You Can Do

- **Have your water tested.** Several companies will run a laboratory test to see if your water is safe. Look in your local phone book under "water quality" or "laboratories, testing" or write to Water Test Corporation at 33 S. Commercial Street, Manchester, NH 03108.

- **Invest in a reverse osmosis system.** This is the most effective way to remove unwanted chemicals. It does have its drawbacks though; prices start at $350 dollars and can go above $1,000 dollars. Activated carbon filter systems, either above or below the sink, remove impurities. Block and granular filter systems are superior to powdered filters.

- **Buy bottled water, preferably in glass bottles.** Plastic bottles can emit harmful chemicals. The best water is distilled spring water. Buying bottled water can get expensive, and you should always question the bottling source.

TOXIC "FOODS"

We are a social experiment in the making. Never in the history of mankind have we been exposed to so many man-made chemicals. We have traded good, wholesome foods for grocery store convenience. I don't deny the convenience of walking into a store and purchasing next week's dinner, but to be oblivious to the damaging chemical preservatives in our foods is myopic. Try setting a fruit or vegetable on your back porch, and notice it will be consumed in a matter of days, if not hours. Do the same with a lump of margarine, and it's still there a week later—no sane animal would touch it!

Tons of toxic industrial wastes, including heavy metals, are being mixed with liquid agricultural fertilizers and dispersed across America's farmlands.

Artificial dyes and preservatives are used in most of our processed foods. They are even found in both prescription and nonprescription drugs. Asthmatics are often allergic to sulfites, for instance, but some asthma inhalant medications actually have sulfites in them as a preservative! Examples of dangerous additives are benzoates, yellow dye [tartrazine], nitrites, sorbic acid, and sulfites. Allergic symptoms associated with them include hives, angioedema, asthma, sinusitis, headache, anxiety, depression, and chronic fatigue. The most notorious culprits are aspartame, monosodium glutamate, hydroxytoluene, and butylated hydroxyanisole.

Aspartame can be found in most diet sodas and in other artificially sweetened food products. Commonly known as NutraSweet or Equal, it is broken down by the body into methanol and formaldehyde. Toxic levels of methanol are linked to systemic lupus and now Alzheimer's disease. Methanol toxicity also causes depression, brain fog, mood changes, insomnia, seizures, and similar symptoms associated with multiple sclerosis. As for formaldehyde, it is grouped into the same class of drugs as cyanide and arsenic.

When the temperature of aspartame exceeds 86 degrees F, the wood alcohol in the product is turned into formaldehyde and then into formic acid. Formic acid is the poison contained in the sting of a fire ant.

The amino acid aspartic acid makes up 40% of aspartame. Aspartic acid is an excitatory amino acid and often contributes in children to attention deficit disorder. I always encourage my

ADD patients to get off and stay off diet colas. There are over 92 documented symptoms from the use of aspartame.

Monosodium glutamate is often added to soups, stews, and Chinese food.

Benzoates, toluenes, and butylated hydroxyanisole can be found in pickles, jams, jellies, and some sodas and cakes.

Sulfites are added to salad bars, beer, frozen french fries, dried fruit, shampoos, conditioners, and some cosmetics.

Nitrites are used to preserve luncheon meats, hot dogs, and other ready-to-eat meats.

WHAT YOU CAN DO

- **Avoid foods containing artificial dyes and preservatives.** If the ingredients list is hard to pronounce, it's probably even harder on your body. Organic meats are becoming more available at grocery stores around the country. See page 277 for information on resources.

- **Consume whole, live foods.** Fruits, vegetables, and whole, unprocessed grains (unless you are gluten sensitive) are the healthiest foods to eat. These foods are loaded with antioxidant, cancer-fighting, and immune-boosting phytonutrients. They are easy on the digestive system and allow the body to generate more energy to fight diseases and build immunity.

TOXIC PRODUCTS: HEAVY METALS

Toxic chemicals don't have to enter through the mouth. Many of the products we use on a daily basis in the form of shampoos, conditioners, lotion soaps, deodorants, and cosmetics are contaminated with toxic chemicals, especially heavy metals. Many of these metals have been implicated in causing or contributing to such conditions as Alzheimer's, ADD, depression, headache, hypertension, kidney failure, hearing loss, FMS, CFS, and tingling in the extremities.

Aluminum toxicity has been linked to Alzheimer's disease and mental dementia. Aluminum is found in some antacids, baking flours, baking soda, processed cheeses, toothpastes, shampoos and conditioners, deodorants, prescription and non-prescription drugs, and aluminum cans, pots, and pans.

Arsenic can cause central depression, headache, high fevers, decreased red blood cells, fatigue, diarrhea, and even death. Municipal or well water may get contaminated with arsenic.

I once treated a woman who had been diagnosed with multiple scherosis, only to find through hair analysis and other testing that she had actually been poisoned with arsenic.

Cadmium levels, when elevated, are associated with hypertension, kidney failure, loss of coordination, numbness or tingling in the hands or feet, and loss of hearing. Common environmental sources include tobacco smoke and oil-based paints. A zinc deficiency exacerbates the effects of cadmium toxicity. If you are a smoker, please, please quit this destructive habit immediately. Many of my patients have had success with subliminal tapes and/or hypnosis. See page 275 for resources.

Lead toxicity effects are numerous and include neurological disorders in children, chronic anemia, learning disturbances, and fatigue. Common sources of lead in the environment are lead-based paints, drinking water, industrial contaminants, airborne emissions, and occupations involving metal work and printing. It is also found in some personal care products. Lead absorption is higher when calcium intake is deficient.

Mercury toxicity can cause a wide variety of health problems: CFS, FMS, stunted growth, confusion and dementia, numbness in the extremities, depression, muscle and joint pain, allergies, chronic infections, and possibly brain damage. Mercury can suppress selenium absorption. Selenium blocks mercury absorption by binding with competing sulfur enzyme centers. Mercury can turn normal bacteria pathogenic (disease causing) and block the function of the nerve cells in the brain and peripheral nervous system. Mercury can also trigger autoimmune responses. Detoxifying from mercury requires oral herbs, mineral supplements, and prescription oral or intravenous medications.

One source of chronic, low-level mercury exposure is the eating of predatory fish. Mercury enters the water as a natural process of off-gassing from the earth's crust and as a result of industrial pollution. It is then routinely found in large predatory fish, such as swordfish, shark, salmon, and tuna.

Most of the mercury in our patients comes from the fillings in their teeth. Dental amalgams (silver fillings) contain a highly absorbable form of mercury that vaporizes at room temperature. And while mercury is poorly absorbed if taken orally, its vapors are readily absorbed through the lungs and quickly pass the blood-brain barrier. Once inside a cell, mercury is usually there to stay, so it accumulates in the kidneys, neurological tissue (including the brain), and the liver. Evidence of high mercury exposure have also been found in the heart, thyroid, and pituitary tissues of dentists. Animal research has shown that within 24 hours of having a silver filling placed, an animal has detectable levels of mercury in the spinal fluid, and in the brain within 48 hours. Patients with symptoms of mercury toxicity should have all dental amalgams removed by a dentist with knowledge of mercury poisoning. Some patients have had a worsening of their symptoms when their fillings were removed without the proper measures to prevent increased mercury exposure.

Other sources of mercury include the use of fossil fuels, fungicides, and some paints, and the production of chlorine, paper, and pulp.

Nickel is not as toxic as many of the other metals. It's associated with headache, diarrhea, blue gums and lips, lethargy, insomnia, rapid heart rate, and shortness of breath. It is found in some personal care products.

Copper toxicity has been implicated in learning and mental disorders and may contribute to increased systolic blood pressure. It is found in some personal care products.

WHAT YOU CAN DO

- **Use stainless steel pots and pans.** Also avoid aluminum- and lead-lined cans.

- **Switch to natural toothpaste, hair products, and deodorants.** Visit your local health-food store or browse online; you should find a wide selection of natural body products. Read the labels.

- **Never take antacids that contain aluminum.** Not only do they contain toxic aluminum, they block hydrochloric acid, preventing the body from synthesizing essential nutrients like vitamin B12. A deficiency of vitamin B12 can cause dementia, Alzheimer's, depression, and fatigue. Antacids also don't allow you to absorb calcium. So if you are taking Tums as a source of calcium, you have been duped by their marketing team.

- Conduct a hair analysis. These inexpensive tests can be done at home and are an accurate first step in uncovering heavy metal overload. See Appendix C for resources.

TOXIC BODIES

The body does its best to dispose of toxins by neutralizing them or voiding them in the urine or feces. The lungs help through respiration, and the skin through sweat. But whether they come from heavy metal poisoning, pesticides, artificial food additives, or metabolic activities, these chemical toxins are neutralized at a price: the creation of more free radicals.

WHAT YOU CAN DO

- **Explore alternatives to long-term prescription drugs** like nonsteroidal anti-inflammatories. Work with your doctor.

- **Severely reduce or eliminate alcohol, nicotine, allergic foods, and preservative rich foods.**

- **Supplement with antioxidants** to combat free radicals. Antioxidants to include are vitamins A, E, and C, the mineral selenium, and pycnogenol.

- **Enjoy foods from the Brassica family:** broccoli, cabbage and Brussels sprouts. They contain phytochemicals that stimulate phase I and phase II detoxification pathways.

- **Supplement with a formula containing an amino acid blend.** (Our Essential Therapeutics CFS/Fibromyalgia formula is a good choice for this.) Glutathione is the most abundant and important liver-protecting antioxidant. Although it is readily absorbed from fruits, vegetables, and meats, depletion may occur during high or sustained exposure to toxins. Glutathione supplements are not readily absorbable, so supplement with its building blocks instead: cysteine, methionine, and glycine.

- **Supplement with silybum marianum (milk thistle).** The silymarin complex, particularly the silibinin component of milk thistle, protects the liver from free-radical damage. It prevents certain toxins from entering liver cells and stimulates regeneration of damaged liver cells.

Medical use of milk thistle can be traced back more than 2000 years. Over 30 years ago, intensive research on the liver-protecting properties of milk thistle began in Germany. Extensive research also may have led to the approval of a standardized milk thistle extract in Germany for the treatment of alcohol-induced liver disease and other diseases of the liver.

Milk thistle extract protects liver cells, both directly and indirectly. It is able to regenerate liver cells that have been injured, prevent fibrosis or fatty liver, bind to the outside of cells and block entrance of certain toxins, and even neutralize toxins that have already penetrated the liver. Milk thistle treatment can be effective even several hours after initial poisoning occurs, such as in the case of poisoning by death cap mushrooms. And there are no side effects.

Silymarin may also prevent the damage caused by certain drugs such as acetaminophen, antidepressants, and antipsychotic, cholesterol lowering, and anticonvulsive drugs. One study showed that increasing the antioxidants in patients receiving psychotrophic drugs reduced the production of potentially damaging free radicals in the liver.

Silymarin has been shown in animal studies to raise the glutathione levels in liver cells by as much as 50%. It also increases the activity of another antioxidant known as supraoxide dismutase (SOD).

Milk thistle may someday be the main treatment for hepatitis, a chronic viral infection of the liver that can lead to liver damage and, in some cases, liver failure. During a six-month treatment period in patients with chronic alcohol hepatitis, liver function test results normalized and liver enzymes improved over controls using placebo.

The normal dose is 420 mg. in three divided doses (80% silymarin content) daily.

- **Test your liver.** I recommend phase I and phase II detoxification testing to my patients who can't seem to get well (talk to your doctor; see page 275.) Individuals plagued with unrelenting poor health are usually saturated with poisonous chemicals.

- **Supplement with alpha lipoic acid.** This powerful antioxidant compound helps recycle glutathione. It is both fat and water soluble, so it works in both mediums. Manufactured by the body in small amounts, it needs to be also obtained through the diet. It can help prevent and repair damage to liver cells and is being studied for its regenerative properties in neurological diseases including Alzheimer's, multiple sclerosis, Lou Gehrig's disease, and Parkinson's disease. To increase liver detoxification and boost cellular energy, take between 200–400 mg. of ALA daily. I recommend Essential Therapeutics Liver Detox Formula, which contains both ALA and milk thistle. To order, see page 274.

- **Supplement with coenzyme Q10.** CoQ10 is also known as ubiquinone, because of its nature to exist in all living matter. It is most abundant in the organs requiring the most energy: the heart and liver. It is a vital catalyst for energy; without it, the process of cellular energy ceases (which spells d-e-a-t-h). CoQ10, along with ALA, gives the spark to the power plants of the cells, the mitochondria.

CoQ10 plays a direct or indirect role in most systems of the body. Experiments have shown that supplementing the diet with CoQ10 can extend the lifespan of mice by 50%. It acts as a powerful antioxidant, helps stimulate white blood cells, protects heart muscle from disease, reduces blood pressure, boosts the metabolism, helps prevent periodontal disease, and protects the liver. Studies have shown that CoQ10 can raise the brain energy level by over 29%. This is good news for those with fibro fog, and the reason why we included CoQ10 in our CFS/Fibromyalgia formula.

Notes
[1]*Tired or Toxic,* 1990

Resources
• Milk thistle and alpha lipoic acid are contained in Dr. Murphree's Essential Liver formula, available online at www.drrodger.com or by calling (205) 879-2383.

For Further Reading
• *Functional Assessment Resource Manual,* Great Smokies Diagnostic Laboratory; 1999
• *Total Wellness: Improve Your Health by Understanding the Body's Healing Systems* by Joseph E. Pizzorno, ND; 1996
• *Tired or Toxic* by Sherry A. Rogers; 1990
• *The E.I. Syndrome: An Rx for Environmental Illness* by Sherry A. Rogers; 1988
• *The Ultimate Nutrient: Glutamine* by Judy Shabert and Nancy Ehrlich; 1994
• *Textbook of Natural Medicine* by Joseph E. Pizzorno, ND, (ed.) and Michael T. Murray (ed.); 1999

19

The Role of Hypothyroid in Chronic Illness

Most of my FMS/CFS patients are suffering from low thyroid function, and traditional blood tests have failed them. Low (hypo) thyroid could be causing many of your symptoms, too.

Many of the symptoms associated with low thyroid are identical to those of FMS and CFS: fatigue, headache, dry skin, swelling, weight gain, cold hands and feet, poor memory, hair loss, hoarseness, nervousness, depression, joint and muscle pain, and burning or tingling sensations in the hands or feet.

A study of thyroid function showed that 63% of FMS patients studied suffered from some degree of hypothyroidism, a percentage much higher than of the general population. Some researchers claim that thyroid hormone deficiency might be a key factor in FMS, as patients have responded well to thyroid hormone treatment (as part of a comprehensive regimen). They state that nearly all FMS and CFS sufferers "dramatically improve or completely recover from the symptoms with this regimen. As long as the patient does not take excessive amounts of thyroid hormone there are no adverse side effects."[1]

It's been estimated that 1% of the population is suffering from hypothyroidism, but this number is widely disputed.

Many scientists, researchers, and physicians believe the number to be as high as 40%.

A SHORT COURSE ON THYROID HORMONES

The hypothalamus stimulates the pituitary gland (both are contained in the brain) to produce thyroid-stimulating hormone (TSH). TSH then stimulates the thyroid to produce and release thyroxine (T4). T4 is then converted into triiodthyronine (T3), which is vital for life and four times more active than T4. This conversion of T4 to T3 takes place in the cells. (T4 can also be converted into reverse T3, which is physiologically inactive.)

WHAT CAN GO WRONG?

The enzyme 5-deiodinase converts T4 into T3 and reverse T3. This enzyme can be inhibited by prolonged stress, acute and chronic illness, steroids (stress hormones or cortisol), and poor nutrition.

The body works best at the optimal temperature of 98.6 degrees. Higher temperatures (fevers) speed up the metabolism and allow the body to fight off infection. A temperature of 90 degrees or below qualifies as hypothermia, a medical emergency. But it doesn't have to go that low to affect health, because most of the biochemical reactions that occur in the body are driven by enzymes, and these enzymes are influenced by metabolic temperature.

EUTHYROID SYNDROME

Euthyroid is a medical term for patients who have normal thyroid blood tests but have all the symptoms associated with hypothyroidism: fatigue, low metabolism, headache, etc. Euthyroid patients often have a problem with T4 converting into active T3, even though blood tests show normal levels. Individuals might take synthetic thyroid hormones (like Synthroid, which contains T4 only), but since the T4 is not converting efficiently, they continue the symptoms of low thyroid.

A majority of FMS and CFS patients complain of low thyroid symptoms. They relate that they, and sometimes their doctors, suspected a thyroid problem only to have their blood work return normal. Most physicians, in this case, won't recommend thyroid replacement therapy. Many don't know about (or they choose to ignore) well documented studies that show that low body temperature is indicative of euthyroid hypothyroidism.

BODY TEMPERATURE, METABOLISM, AND THYROID HORMONES

Blood tests for thyroid function measure the amount of TSH, T4, and T3 in the bloodstream. But thyroid hormones don't operate within the bloodstream; the action takes place in the cells themselves. What good is a blood test that only shows what is racing around the bloodstream one second out of a day? It's inadequate for measuring true thyroid hormone levels.

Self-test for Low Thyroid

Dr. Broda Barnes was the first to show that a low basal body temperature was associated with low thyroid. His first study was published in 1942 and appeared in *The Journal of the American Medical Association.* This study tracked 1,000 college students and showed that monitoring body temperature for thyroid function was a valid if not superior approach to other thyroid tests.[2]

The test for low thyroid function, according to Dr. Barnes's protocol, starts first thing in the morning. While still in bed, shake down and place the thermometer (preferably mercury; digital thermometers are not as accurate) under your arm and leave it there for 10 minutes. Record your temperature in a daily log. Women who are still having menstrual cycles should take their temperature after the second and third days of their period. Menopausal women can take their temperature on any day. A reading below the normal 98.2 strongly suggests hypothyroid. A reading above 98.2 may indicate hyperthyroidism (overactive thyroid).

Treatment for Hypothyroid According to the Barnes Method

Dr. Barnes recommends patients take a desiccated glandular (derived from pigs) prescription medication known as Armour Thyroid, which was used before synthetic medications such as Synthroid were introduced. Armour Thyroid and other prescription thyroid glandulars (including Westhroid), contain both T4 and T3.

Synthroid and other synthetic thyroid medications contain T4 only. Since some individuals have a difficult time converting inactive T4 to active T3, these medications may not work at the cellular level. Individuals may take T4 medications for years and never notice much improvement.

WILSON'S SYNDROME

Wilson's Syndrome was first described by E. Denis Wilson, MD. He was refining some of the pioneering clinical research first performed by Dr. Barnes. Dr. Wilson showed that symptoms of low thyroid function could be present with normal thyroid blood tests. The group of symptoms that he studied he called Wilson's syndrome.[3]

These symptoms can include severe fatigue, headache and migraine, PMS, easy weight gain, fluid retention, irritability, anxiety, panic attacks, depression, decreased memory and concentration, hair loss, decreased sex drive, unhealthy nails, constipation, irritable bowel syndrome, dry skin, dry hair, cold and/or heat intolerance, low self-esteem, irregular periods, chronic or repeated infections, and many other complaints.

A lot of symptoms for such a little hormone problem, huh? Perhaps the greatest obstacle Dr. Wilson has had to overcome in his attempts to be recognized by mainstream medicine is the vast symptoms associated with Wilson's Syndrome. Yet all these symptoms can be seen in hypothyroid patients.

Causes

The symptoms tend to come on or become worse after a major stressful event. Childbirth, divorce, death of a loved one, job or family stress, chronic illness, surgery, trauma, excessive dieting, and other stressful events can all lead to hypothyroidism.

Under significant physical, mental, or emotional stress the body slows down the metabolism by decreasing the amount of raw material (T4) that is converted to the active thyroid hormone (T3). This is done to conserve energy. However, when the stress is over, the metabolism is supposed to speed up and return to normal. This process can become derailed by a buildup of reverse T3 (rT3) hormone. Reverse T3 can build to such high levels that it begins to start using up the enzyme that converts T4 to T3. The body may try to correct this by releasing more TSH and T4 only to have the levels of rT3 go even higher. A vicious cycle is created where T4 is never converted into active T3.

Certain nationalities are more likely to develop Wilson's syndrome: those whose ancestors survived famine, such as Irish, American Indian, Scotch, Welsh, Russian. Interestingly, those patients who are part Irish and part American Indian are the most prone of all. Women are also more likely than men to develop Wilson's syndrome.

Testing

Like with Dr. Barnes's protocol, patients suspected of Wilson's syndrome monitor their body temperature. Those with Wilson's syndrome have temperatures that run below 98 degrees, with 97.8 being typical. The temperature is taken three-four times daily over a five-seven day period. Patients are instructed to shake down and place a thermometer (preferably mercury) under their tongue for 10 minutes. An average day's temperature plotted over five-seven days will reveal if Wilson's syndrome is present.

Treatment

The way the cycle of Wilson's syndrome is stopped and the problem corrected is by reducing the rT3 levels so that T4 can convert to active T3.

A specially compounded form of timed-released T3 is used in gradual increments. Body temperature is monitored, and when it returns to normal, the patients gradually wean themselves off the medicine.

A big advantage of this over other hormone replacement therapies is that Wilson's syndrome patients are usually able to correct their low thyroid problem and eventually discontinue the medicine.

Wilson's protocol can be hard for patients to follow, but it often yields results when Armour and Westhroid therapies fail. We've used both protocols and gotten dramatic results for many of our patients.

Some of our patients have been on synthetic thyroid medications for years with very little or no improvement. So I'm often amazed at the turnaround they experience when taking thyroid medication. Many of them enjoy a newfound energy and metabolism, and it's common for them to lose weight that couldn't be lost, sleep better, rid themselves of chronic infections, and think clearly for the first time in years.

GLANDULAR THYROID SUPPLEMENTS

Thyroid glandulars can also be used to correct low thyroid function. Thyroid bovine glandulars have been used since the beginning of thyroid treatment. Dr. Barnes used Armour Thyroid, available by prescription. However, over-the-counter thyroid glandulars are also available. I like American Biologics brand.

Since these raw thyroid tissue concentrates contain T4 and T3, they can be used as a first line of treatment for low to moderate euthyroid dysfunction.

Notes

[1]*Life Extension Foundation's Disease Prevention and Treatment Protocols, 3rd edition*

[2]*Hypothyroidism: The Unsuspected Illness* by Broda Barnes, MD, and Lawrence Galton; 1976

[3]*Wilson's Thyroid Syndrome* by Denis Wilson, MD, 1991

Resources

• Glandular thyroid supplements are available online at www.drrodger.com or by calling (205) 879-2383.

For Further Reading

• www.wilsonssyndrome.com
• www.brodabarnes.org
• *Hypothyroidism: The Unsuspected Illness* by Broda Barnes, MD, and Lawrence Galton; 1976
• *Wilson's Thyroid Syndrome* by Denis Wilson, MD; 1991
• *Fibromyalgia Syndrome: A Practitioner's Guide to Treatment* by Leon Chaitow; 1999
• *Alternative Medicine: The Definitive Guide* by Burton Goldberg et al; 2002
• *Doctor's Guide to Natural Medicine* by Paul Barney, MD; 1998

20

Yeast Overgrowth Syndrome

Studies have shown that up to 90% of FMS/CFS patients have a yeast overgrowth. Could yeast be contributing to your symptoms? Probably. Take our yeast symptoms profile, page 253.

An overgrowth of the usually benign *Candida albicans* in the gastrointestinal tract is now recognized as a complex medical syndrome called chronic Candidiasis, or yeast overgrowth syndrome. Although it has been clinically defined for some time, it was not until recently that the public and many physicians realized the magnitude of the problem. As many as one-third of the Western world's population may be affected by Candidiasis. And unfortunately, there is no shortcut to getting yeast under control.

WHAT IS CANDIDIASIS?

Candida albicans is a yeast that can be found living in the intestinal tracts of most individuals. Yeasts cohabitate there in a symbiotic relationship with over 400 healthy bacteria. These bacteria help with digestion and absorption of certain nutrients, and they keep the yeasts in check. When these good bacteria die or are suppressed, the yeasts are allowed to grow to unhealthy levels, causing Candidiasis.

SIGNS AND SYMPTOMS

Candidiasis commonly infects the ears, nose, and the urinary and intestinal tracts. Typical symptoms are constipation, diarrhea, irritable bowel, abdominal pain, bloating, gas, indigestion, rash, bladder spasms and infection, and ear and sinus infections.

Yeast overgrowth is similar to allergies in that there are a plethora of symptoms. This can lead to skepticism in many doctors; the symptoms are tough to define. It's not uncommon for yeast overgrowth to cause or contribute to such complex conditions as depression, asthma, fatigue, mental confusion, weakened immunity, allergies, chemical sensitivities, hyperactivity, chronic ear and sinus infections, and adrenal fatigue.

Like most opportunistic infections, *Candida* and other yeasts may increase during times of stress. This overgrowth leaks toxins into the bloodstream or other tissues, allowing antigens (foreign invaders) to set up residence in various bodily tissues. Antigens then trigger complex allergic reactions. (This might explain why most individuals with chronic yeast overgrowth develop food, inhalant, and environmental allergies). Allergic reactions can manifest in a variety of symptoms: fatigue, brain fog, depression, joint and muscle pain, digestive disorders, headache, rash, and breathing problems. Inflammation of the nose, throat, ears, bladder, and intestinal tract, can lead to infections of the sinus, respiratory, ear, bladder and intestinal membranes. In an attempt to arrest these infections, your physician might prescribe a broad spectrum antibiotic. Such antibiotics promote yeast overgrowth and often times, additional symptoms.

CAUSES

The most common cause of Candidiasis is medication overuse, especially of antibiotics but also of birth-control pills and corticosteroids. These can suppress the immune system and the good intestinal bacteria. When used appropriately, antibiotics and corticosteroids save lives, but if you are taking these medications, check with your doctor about possible alternatives.

A minor increase in intestinal yeast is usually not a problem, leading possibly to infection of the mouth (thrush) or vaginal lining (vaginitis or "yeast infection"). The body's immune defenses are usually strong enough to keep the yeast from taking over the intestinal tract.

However, if yeast overgrowth is left unchallenged, more sinister symptoms appear. Yeasts can change into an invasive mycellial fungus with rhizoids (tentacle-like projections) that penetrate the lining of the intestinal tract. These projections can cause intestinal permeability and leak toxins across the cellular membranes. Penetration by these rhizoids and the resulting intestinal permeability cause a disruption in the absorption of nutrients and finally nutritional deficiencies. Deficient nutrients lead to reduced immunity and further weakening of the body's defense systems. This can lead to fatigue, allergies, decreased immunity, chemical sensitivities, depression, poor memory, and digestive complaints.

Your resistance to yeast overgrowth may be compromised by allergic reactions, more antibiotics, stress, fatigue, and poor nutrition. This sets the stage for environmental sensitivities. As the liver and adrenal glands become chronically overwhelmed, tolerance to the fumes of certain environmental chemicals is reduced: gasoline, diesel, other petrochemicals, formaldehyde, perfumes, cleaning fluids, insecticides, tobacco, pesticides, household cleaners, etc.

TREATMENT

The relationship of *Candida albicans* to many common health disorders was first described by a Birmingham, Alabama, physician, C. Orian Truss, MD. Dr. Truss is the author of *The Missing Diagnosis,*[1] which reveals how a yeast-free, low-sugar diet, along with antifungal medications, helped many of his chronically ill patients get well. His book is definitely recommended reading.

Proper treatment of yeast overgrowth requires a comprehensive multidimensional approach. Used alone, prescription drugs or natural antiyeast supplements rarely produce significant long-term results.

Step 1: Eliminate yeast-nourishing foods. A number of dietary factors appear to promote the overgrowth of *Candida.*

Try eliminating all the foods below for three months.

- **Sugar** is the chief nutrient for *Candida albicans,* so restricted sugar intake is absolutely necessity to effectively treat chronic Candidiasis. Avoid refined sugar, honey, maple syrup, fruit juice, milk, white potatoes, corn, processed or bleached (white) flour, bakery goods, muffins, cereals, and anything containing sugar. Ice cream, cake, cookies, and other sweets should be avoided for at least three months.

- **Fruits** should also be avoided, along with fruit juice (except the fruit juice taken with 5HTP if that has been prescribed for you). After the initial two weeks, try introducing apples and pears to see if you have any reactions. (Reactions might include fatigue, depression, aches and pain, rectal itching, itching of the ears or nose, and digestive disturbances.) If not, then try berries: strawberries, blueberries, blackberries, and raspberries. Avoid all other fruits.

- **Alcoholic beverages** should be avoided, as should malted-milk or other malted products.

- **Mold- and yeast-containing foods** are best avoided for two–three months. These include peanuts, dried fruits (including prunes, raisins, and dates), vinegar, pickled vegetables, sauerkraut, relishes, green olives, vinegar-containing salad dressings, catsup, mayonnaise and, pickles.

- **Dairy products** don't end up causing a problem for most people, with the exception of milk. But avoid all dairy for two weeks just to make sure.

- **Most vitamin and mineral supplements** purchased at a drug store are contaminated with yeast. Look for yeast-free products, though even some of these vitamins contain yeast because the B vitamins were derived from yeast-fermenting processes. All of the protects I recommend, including the Essential Therapeutics CFS/Fibromyalgia formula, 5HTP, Liver Formula, etc. are yeast free.

Step 2: Improve digestion. Gastric hydrochloric acid and pancreatic enzymes help keep *Candida* from overgrowing in the small intestine.

- **Supplement with pancreatic enzymes** (such as Ultra-Zyme). Take one or two with each meal.

- **Supplement with betaine hydrochloric acid** with each meal. Yeast can't live in an acidic environment.

Step 3: Replace good bacteria, such as *Lactobacillus acidophilus, L. bulgaricus, L. catnaforme, L. fermentum,* and *Bifidobacterium bifidum.* These normally inhabit vaginal and gastrointestinal tracts; help digest, absorb, and produce certain nutrients; and keep potentially harmful bacteria and yeast in check. Use probiotics to replace these bacteria when taking antibiotics, but not at exactly the same time of day.

L. acidophilus has proven to be effective in treating irritable bowel syndrome, *H. pylori,* diarrhea, and colitis. And it's especially helpful in treating yeast overgrowth.

Yogurt contains certain strains of good bacteria, but it isn't standardized for a particular amount. Also, most yogurts are made from *L. bulgaricus* or *Streptococcus thermophilus.* Both are friendly bacteria, but neither will help colonize the colon. So it's best to use live organisms that are shipped on ice and then kept refrigerated until purchase. Live *L. acidophilus* and *B. bifidum* powders or capsules are preferred.

- **Supplement with probiotics** for three months: 5–10 billion organisms daily. Or take up to 20 billion if taking antibiotics. Some extremely resistant yeast infections may need continuous probiotic replacement therapy.

Step 4: Consider prescription medications as indicated by a stool test (talk to your doctor about this test; see page 275). Typical choices are Nizoral, Nystatin, and Diflucan. Nystatin is the safest of the three, because it doesn't penetrate the intestinal lining. It should be used when there is a choice, but yeast overgrowth that's escaped the intestinal lining will need to be treated otherwise.

Most prescription antifungals, including Nizoral and Diflucan, have potentially serious side effects and should be used with caution. Those with yeast overgrowth must weigh the benefits and risks, but treating a raging infection with anything other than prescription medication might be futile.

- **Take medication as your doctor prescribes,** usually for three–six weeks. (Nystatin may be used longer.) Always take milk thistle and alpha lipoic acid when taking antifungal medication.

Step 5: Supplement with natural remedies as indicated by the stool analysis or recommended by your physician. Use natural remedies either by themselves or in combination with prescription medications. Most of our patients start with prescription medications for about three weeks and then switch to herbal antifungal supplements for one–two months. However, I've had lots of success just using herbals and diet to treat yeast overgrowth.

Patients not taking a prescription medication
should use a natural remedy listed below or one of
our combination formulas for at least three months.
Difficult cases of yeast overgrowth will require
longer treatment of six months or more.

For information on ordering natural remedies, see page 274.

- **Caprylic acid** is a naturally occurring fatty acid and a potent antifungal medicine. It should be taken as an enteric-coated timed-release capsule. Dosage is 500–1,000 mg. three times daily with food.

- **Berberine or Barberry** *(Berberis vulgaris)* has a wide range of antimicrobial properties. It is a proven herbal medicine used successfully to treat fungal, bacterial, and parasitic infections. Dosage of standardized extract (4:1) is 250–500 mg. three times daily with food.

- **Garlic** has been used for medicinal purposes for centuries. It is an effective treatment for the overgrowth of *Candida albicans* and other yeasts. It has shown to be more potent than Nystatin for *Candida albicans*. Dosage of standardized garlic (1.3% alliin) is 600–900 mg. two–three times daily with food.

- **Goldenseal** *(Hydrastis Canadensis)* is another berberine-containing plant. Dosage of standardized extract (4:1) is 250–500 mg. three times daily on an empty stomach.

- **Citrus seed extract** is a broad spectrum antimicrobial used to successfully treat yeast and bacterial parasites. Dosage is 100–200 mg. twice daily after meals.

- **Tanalbit** is used to treat intestinal parasites and yeast overgrowth. It should be taken in capsule form. Dosage is one capsule three times daily with food.

- **Fructo-oligosaccharide (FOS)** is a short-chain poly-saccharide used in Japan for dozens of years. It isn't digested by humans but does stimulate the growth of good bacteria within the intestinal tract. It also helps with liver detoxification, lowers cholesterol, and eliminates various toxins. Dosage for powder is 2,000–3,000 mg. daily.

Step 6: Supplement with Essential Therapeutics Liver Detox Formula when taking antifungals, especially prescription medications. At the minimum, take milk thistle, two capsules a day.

IF YOU GET WORSE AT FIRST

Sometimes, when a lot of *Candida* organisms are killed off during initial treatment, a sudden release of toxic substances results in an immune response and intensified symptoms, called the herxheimer reaction. The body becomes extremely acidic. Some doctors call this a die-off reaction; others call it a healing crisis. It normally lasts no longer than a week and is frequently confused as an allergic or adverse reaction to the antifungal treatment. Symptoms can be minimized by taking Alka-Seltzer Gold, or 2 tablespoons baking soda in 8oz. of water, as a buffering agent two to three times daily as needed.

If the reaction is severe, you might need to reduce your antifungal medications—or take them every other day—for several days. I usually recommend that patients half the dosage for a week and then return to the original dose. Patients should then continue their antifungal medications for a minimum of three months. If treatment is discontinued too early, symptoms will gradually return.

Once fungus overgrowth has subsided and the yeast have returned to a normal level (at least three–four months), medications and supplements can be gradually decreased over six–eight weeks, and the patient can gradually add previously forbidden foods to her diet. Be vigilant in monitoring your sugar and simple carbohydrate intake.

THE LINK TO INTESTINAL PERMEABILITY

Yeast overgrowth can cause intestinal permeability and contribute to food sensitivities or allergies. These should be addressed once treatment for yeast overgrowth has been successfully completed. Intestamine (L-glutamine), a special formula to repair intestinal permeability, should be started along with the elimination diet (see page 98) and adhered to for three–four weeks.

Notes
[1]2nd edition published 1986

Resources
• Supplements discussed in this chapter are available at many health food stores.

For Further Reading
• *Fibromyalgia Syndrome: A Practitioner's Guide to Treatment* by Leon Chaitow; 1999
• *Doctor's Guide to Natural Medicine* by Paul Barney, MD; 1998
• *The Yeast Connection and the Woman* by William G. Crook, MD, et al; 2003
• *Missing Diagnosis* by Dr. C. Orian Truss; 1985

21

Arthritis: Same Pain, Different Causes

Though it might feel like one, FMS isn't a joint or connective tissue disease. It's not arthritis, but it often accompanies it. For that reason, arthritis is an important layer for us to peel away.

Over 50 million Americans suffer from arthritis. It is associated with pain, stiffness, inflammation, and decreased range of motion. There are over 100 different forms of arthritis, but osteoarthritis is the most common.

OSTEOARTHRITIS

Sometimes wear and tear of the boney cartilage of the body causes bone spurs or calcium deposits to form on the ligaments surrounding the joint. This leads to inflammation, pain, and decreased joint motion. This is osteoarthritis.

What Causes It?

Osteoarthritis is usually caused by trauma or joint injury. Many of my patients can trace the onset of their arthritis to a car accident, but some don't remember anything that could be causing their neck or low back pain.

Some individuals develop osteoarthritis from repetitive motions, poor posture, or from simply carrying more weight than their joints can handle. Losing weight can often provide dramatic relief to those with weight-bearing osteoarthritis of the knees and hips. That's because these joints bear loads 2.5–10 times a person's weight. For a 200-pound individual, this can translate to one ton of pressure.

Heredity also plays a role in osteoarthritis.

Symptoms

Osteoarthritis is characterized by early morning stiffness or pain that eases up as the day goes on, only to return again in the evening. This form of arthritis generally affects the joints of the knees, hands, feet, and spine. It develops gradually over several years and usually doesn't cause joint redness, warmth, or swelling like rheumatoid arthritis.

NUTRITIONAL SUPPLEMENTS
FOR TREATING OSTEOARTHRITIS

- **Glucosamine sulfate** is an excellent approach to eliminating the destruction of osteoarthritis. A growing body of research supports the use of this natural supplement. Studies done in Milan, Italy, showed that glucosamine reduced arthritis symptoms by one half in 73% of the group, and 20% enjoyed total symptom relief. A Portugal study involving 1,208 patients and 252 physicians showed glucosamine to be quite effective in eliminating pain and stiffness caused by the disease. A study of patients with osteoarthritis of the knee, performed at the National Orthopedic Hospital in Manila, Philippines, showed that patients who were administered glucosamine had an 80% reduction in pain.

  Other studies have demonstrated that glucosamine is more effective than ibuprofen (Motrin, Advil, or Nuprin) in relieving the symptoms of osteoarthritis. Glucosamine is not only superior to nonsteroidal anti-inflammatory drugs such as ibuprofen, it is also free of the side effects of most arthritic medications. More importantly, glucosamine and chondroiten sulfate actually slow or arrest the destruction of cartilage.

Glucosamine, which is made up of glucose and the amino acid glutamine, actually helps repair damaged articular joint tissue. It does this by stimulating collagen cells within the articular cartilage to produce more proteoglycans. Proteoglycans are responsible for forming a protective netting within the articular cartilage, which helps prevent its destruction.

Glucosamine can be found at your local health-food store. Dosage is 500 mg. three times daily. You should see improvement in three–four weeks. Treatment should continue for a minimum of three months and, since there are little or no side effects, long-term therapy might be advisable.

Susan, a patient of mine, is a very active 50-year-old nurse who spends hours on her feet attending to patients. She first visited my office with the complaint that her lower back and knee pain had recently become worse and—out of desperation—she came to see me as a last resort before agreeing to surgery. I began treating her with weekly chiropractic adjustments, and I prescribed glucosamine sulfate, along with some other nutritional supplements. In three weeks, she reported that she was now completely free of the pain in her back, which had plagued her for years. The arthritis pain in her knee, which she has also endured for years, is nearly gone as well.

- **Chondroiten sulfate** is composed of a large number of sugar molecules. It attracts fluid into the proteoglygan molecules, and this fluid acts as a shock absorber. Chondroiten inhibits certain enzymes that can damage cartilage, while stimulating the production of proteoglycans and other molecules needed for healthy new cartilage growth.

Studies performed at the University of Genoa, Italy, show chondroiten sulfate to be an effective therapy in

eliminating the pain and stiffness associated with
osteoarthritis. Another study, this time in France,
showed patients who received three months of chondroiten therapy had actually repaired a significant
portion of their degenerated joint tissues.[1]

Chondroiten can be found at your local health-food
store. Dosage is 800–1,200 mg. daily. You should see
improvement in three to four weeks. Treatment should
continue for a minimum of three months and, since
there are little or no side effects, long-term therapy
might be advisable.

- **Niacin** (vitamin B3) may decrease the pain associated
  with osteoarthritis, especially in the knee. Dr. Abram
  Hoffer, author of *Orthomolecular Medicine For
  Physicians,*[2] writes: "I suspect vitamin B3 is necessary
  for everyone for tissue repair, and that one of the earli-
  est symptoms of deficiency is a decrease in the rate of
  repair." Begin with 100 mg. daily, and slowly increase
  until one gram three times daily can be tolerated.
  Caution: high doses of niacin can cause nausea and elevated liver enzymes, though elevated enzymes caused
  by high niacin are not a concern, according to Dr.
  Hoffer.

- **S-adenosyl-l-methionine** (SAM) acts as a natural
  anti-inflammatory with none of the side effects associated with NSAIDs. This supplement can be found at your
  local health-food store, or see page 274 for ordering
  information. Dosage is up to 1,200 mg. daily.

- **Shark cartilage extracts** may also be beneficial for
  arthritic sufferers. Several double-blind studies show
  that individuals on cartilage-extract therapy see a significant improvement in pain and stiffness. Animal
  cartilage contains a protein that inhibits tumor growth.

RHEUMATOID ARTHRITIS

Rheumatoid arthritis is an autoimmune disease in which the
body actually attacks itself. Antibodies develop in joint tissues
and cause pain. Women are three times more likely to develop
this arthritis than men. 1–3% of the population are afflicted.

What Causes It?

The definitive cause of rheumatoid arthritis is not known. It appears to result from a variety of triggers:

- **Malnutrition** plays a role. Nearly three-fourths of Alabama rheumatoid patients were shown to be suffering from malnutrition. Compared to other individuals with musculoskeletal disorders, those with rheumatoid arthritis were significantly malnourished. This suggests that individuals with rheumatoid arthritis are not properly digesting their foods.

- **Hydrochlorhydria** is associated with rheumatoid arthritis patients. Hydrochloric acid is needed for proper digestion, so individuals with known allergies, including arthritis, asthma, eczema, and psoriasis, should supplement their diets with 400–800 mg. of hydrochloric acid before each meal, but not if you suffer from peptic or gastric ulcers. (To order, see page 274.)

- **Zinc deficiency** is common in rheumatoid arthritis patients. And the worse the inflammation, the less zinc seems to be in the blood. Supplementing with zinc may help relieve the pain, swelling, and stiffness.

- **Essential fatty acid deficiency** is also a culprint. A double-blind study conducted on 49 patients—all taking NSAIDs—showed a 100% reduction in symptoms while taking a mixture of 90% evening primrose oil and 20% fish oils. And 94% of these patients were able to completely eliminate or cut in half their NSAID dosage.

Symptoms

Rheumatoid arthritis usually affects the knuckles, wrists, elbows, and shoulders with painful, warm, red swelling. Unlike osteoarthritis, which tends to be unilateral (one sided), rheumatoid attacks joints bilaterally (both sides).

TRADITIONAL ARTHRITIS TREATMENTS

Nonsteroidal anti-inflammatories (NSAIDs) such as aspirin, Tylenol, indocin, sulindac, tolectin, ibuprofen, Daypro, naprosyn, Celebrex, and Vioxx can cause intestinal permeability. They cover up the symptoms but do not address the cause, and they can actually cause further joint destruction.

Studies in Norway show that patients taking indocin, a powerful NSAID, suffered more hip degeneration (as seen on X-ray), than did those not on drug therapy.

Corticosteroids are strong hormonal drugs that can have serious side effects: peptic ulcer, osteoporosis, diabetes, glaucoma, depression, acne, water retention and weight gain, insomnia, facial hair growth, hypertension, and depressed immunity.

Methotrexate is an immune-suppressing drug used to treat psoriasis, psoriatic arthritis, adult and juvenile rheumatoid arthritis, and Reilers disease. It is a toxic therapy that can cause kidney failure and severe liver damage.

Gold injections can cause serious side effects: damage to the liver and kidneys, stomach disorders, anemia, headache, neuritis, and ulcerations of the mouth and gums.

A PLAN FOR HEALING RHEUMATOID ARTHRITIS

- **Consider an intestinal permeability test.** It's inexpensive and gives you a starting place for wellness. Many of our patients have enjoyed a reduction or elimination of arthritic symptoms after repairing their leaky gut.

- **Strongly consider food allergy testing.** Rheumatoid arthritis was absent in prehistory, when cereals and dairy products were not part of a daily diet. Some researchers believe that our bodies have simply not yet adapted to our modern eating habits.

- **Avoid nightshade foods.** These include tobacco, eggplant, bell peppers, tomatoes, and white potatoes. Nightshade foods have been linked to an increase in arthritis symptoms.

- **Treat any yeast or bacterial overgrowth** of the intestinal tract. Food elimination diets and/or food allergy testing (ELISA or FICA) are recommended for individuals with rheumatoid arthritis.

- **Supplement with glucosamine sulfate and chondroiten sulfate.** They have been proven quite effective in reducing osteoarthritis symptoms and rebuilding degenerated joint cartilage. Try 500 mg. of glucosamine and 400 mg. of chondroiten, three times daily. Continue for three months. By then, depending on the severity of your arthritis, the supplements should be reduced or discontinued (work with your health care professional).

- **Supplement with essential fatty acids.** Everyone should (see chapter 14) but especially arthritis sufferers. EFA therapy is probably ineffective in patients taking large doses of steroids or NSAIDs, though they may be able to reduce their dosages by using EFA therapy.

  A combination of omega-3 fish oil (eicosapentaenic acid) and omega-6 evening primrose oil (gamma-linolenic acid) is superior to one or the other by itself. Research suggests that the therapy must be continued for a minimum of 4–12 weeks before results are seen, and large doses of these oils are needed for the desired result: 3,000–6,000 mg. of evening primrose oil (GLA) and 3,000–5,000 mg. of fish oil (EPA).

- **Correct intestinal permeability if present.** This is necessary in order to reduce inflammatory reactions.

- **Supplement with digestive enzymes, hydrochloric acid, and pancreatic enzymes** (pepsin, amylase, lipase, etc.) on a periodic basis. Because the body produces less digestive enzymes as we grow older, take them regularly if you are 50 or older. Read more about hydrochloric acid on page 166 and pancreatic enzymes on page 164.

- **Receive regular chiropractic adjustments.** These help millions of Americans with osteoarthritis every year. **Deep tissue massage** can also help relieve aching, locked, or immobile joints. When combined together, these two disciplines are extremely successful in reducing and arresting the ravages of osteoarthritis.

- **Exercise to keep the joints moving.** Walking on a daily basis helps keep you limber and fit. Many of the back pain patients that I see are shocked to discover that they can severely reduce or eliminate the back problems they've had for years by simply walking 30–60 minutes a day.

Essential Therapeutics Arthritis Formula

I've developed an arthritis formula that has helped hundreds of patients over the years. The Essential Therapeutics Arthritis Formula contains:

- **glucosamine sulfate:** 1,500 mg.

- **chondroiten sulfate:** 1,200 mg.

- **boswelia:** one of the oldest herbs in Indian ayurvedic medicine. Studies show it to be a potent pain-relieving anti-inflammatory. Boswellia helps shrink inflamed tissue, build cartilage, increase blood supply, and repair damaged blood vessels.

- **bromelain:** a protein-digesting enzyme derived from pineapple. There is considerable research (over 200 medical journal articles) on its effectiveness in treating such conditions as inflammation, pancreatic insufficiency, and respiratory diseases. It blocks inflammatory chemicals called kinins. It also digests excess fibren, a chemical implicated in osteoarthritis, sciatica, ankylosing spondylitis, and scleroderma. As an anti-inflammatory, bromelain needs to be taken on an empty stomach. If taken with food, it acts as a digestive enzyme.

- **tumeric (curcumin):** a perennial plant found in eastern Asia and parts of India. It is a popular arthritis remedy in India and a powerful pain-relieving anti-inflammatory. It is as strong as hydrocortisone without the side effects.

- **devil's claw:** a perennial vine native to South Africa. It is a potent anti-inflammatory and pain reliever. Studies in Germany have shown this herbal medication to be very effective in relieving lower back pain and associated sciatica.

Notes
[1]Source: *The Arthritis Cure* by Jason Theodosakis et al, 1997
[2]1997

Resources
- Dr. Murphree's Essential Therapeutics Arthritis formula is available online at www.drrodger.com or by calling (205) 879-2383.

For Further Reading

- *Arthritis* by Anthony Di Fabio, MA and Gus J. Prosch, Jr., MD; 1997
- *Functional Assessment Resource Manual,* Great Smokies Diagnostic Laboratory; 1999
- *Textbook of Natural Medicine* by Joseph E. Pizzorno, ND, (ed.) and Michael T. Murray (ed.); 1999
- *Prescription for Herbal Healing* by Phyllis A. Balch; 2002
- *Essential Fatty Acids in Health and Disease* by Edward N. Siguel; 1995
- *Eating Well For Optimum Health* by Andrew Weil; 2001
- *Orthomolecular Medicine for Physicians* by Abram Hoffer; 1997
- *Dr. Braly's Food Allergy and Nutrition Revolution* by James Braly, MD; 1992

22

Mental Fatigue, Fibro Fog, and Depression

FMS/CFS doesn't just affect the body; it sabotages normal brain function. This "layer of the onion," though, usually responds quickly to consistent deep sleep and nutritional supplementation.

Anyone with fibromyalgia knows that it isn't just a disease of the body, but of the mind. But contrary to some opinion, depression does *not* cause FMS or CFS! Depression can lead to similar feelings and psychosomatic symptoms. But victims of these debilitating syndromes need so much more than to "cheer up." Of course, depression is a possible consequence of having a misunderstood chronic illness, not to mention constant pain and fatigue.

SHORTCOMINGS OF ANTIDEPRESSANTS

Antidepressants are sometimes helpful for my patients, because they correct low serotonin levels, but they usually don't correct the cause of the deficiency. And while prescription drugs have helped millions of people overcome mental illnesses, their side effects can be life threatening. Prozac alone has been associated with over 1,734 suicide deaths and over 28,000 adverse reactions. Prescription antidepressants can cause depression, addiction, suicidal tendencies, tardive dyskinesia (involuntary muscle spasms), and tardive dementia (senility). These side effects are due to drug-induced nutritional deficiencies and poor liver function—most of my patients have these anyway.

Prescription antidepressants attempt to improve the brain's use of specific neurotransmitters. Prozac, for instance, is classified as a serotonin reuptake inhibitor (SSRI). It inhibits the destruction of serotonin, allowing more time for it to circulate in the brain. But no one ever got fibromyalgia from a Prozac deficiency—it's serotonin they need! As I said on page 65, using SSRIs is like adding a gasoline additive to an empty tank. Most of my patients have been running on fumes (low serotonin) for years. A gasoline additive isn't going to help. There is a better way: correct the nutritional deficiencies. Pour in the gasoline. Fill up the tank.

NUTRITIONAL DEFICIENCIES

Metabolizing antidepressants uses up essential vitamins, minerals, and amino acids and can create nutritional deficiencies. These deficiencies then lead to further symptoms, including depression. Some individuals do notice an improvement for a period of time but then their nutritional deficiencies begin to rob them of what little serotonin they have left. Once their serotonin is used up, they are left to try yet another antidepressant.

Medical science has now determined that how we feel is largely controlled by the foods we eat and how well these building blocks are converted into neurotransmitters. (Remember that neurotransmitters are brain chemicals that control our moods.) The brain needs adequate amino acids for the production of neurotransmitters.

OUR HAPPY HORMONES

Serotonin, created from the amino acid tryptophan, elevates mood, reduces food cravings, increases pain threshold, promotes deep sleep, relieves tension, and calms the body.

Dopamine and norepinephrine are synthesized from the amino acid phenylalanine. They increase mental and physical alertness, reduce fatigue, and elevate mood.

Gamma-aminobutyric acid (GABA) is a tripeptide made from three amino acids. It has a calming affect on the brain. You may have heard of prescription antidepressants called MAOIs, such as Nardil and Marplan. These work by increasing the effectiveness of GABA. (This is another example of a gasoline additive. Why not just use GABA?)

A New Kind of Medicine

A group of progressive-minded physicians have helped pioneer a new way of treating mental disorders.

In 1968, Nobel Prize winner Linus Pauling, PhD, originated the term "orthomolecular" to describe an approach to medicine that uses naturally occurring substances normally present in the body. "Ortho" means correct or normal, and orthomolecular physicians recognize that, in many cases of physiological and psychological disorders, health can be reestablished by properly correcting—normalizing—the balance of vitamins, minerals, amino acids, and similar substances within the body. Like their more conventional colleagues, orthomolecular physicians acknowledge that mental disorders originate from faulty brain chemistry. However, they rely less on prescription medications and more on treating nutritional deficiencies, restoring nutrients to optimal levels to correct neurotransmitter dysfunctions.

The premise of orthomolecular medicine extends back to the 1920s, when vitamins and minerals were first used to treat illnesses unrelated to nutrient deficiency. During that time, it was discovered that vitamin A could prevent childhood deaths from infectious illness, and that heart arrhythmia (irregular heartbeat) could be healed by dosages of magnesium.

Today, orthomolecular medicine is making some of its greatest contributions to a controversial area of medicine, psychiatric disorders. Psychiatrist and a founding father of orthomolecular medicine, Abram Hoffer, MD, along with Humphrey Osmond, MD, began using large doses of niacin to supplement traditional medical therapy when treating schizophrenics. Their treatment doubled the number of recoveries in a one-year period.

Still, many physicians neglect the role proper nutrition plays in relation to our health. The prevalent notion is that a balanced diet supplies all the nutrients needed for the body to work properly. This draconian idea flagrantly ignores the research showing up in our very own medical journals. The majority of American diets are deficient in many of the vital nutrients needed for good health. Complicating the matter is our reliance on the recommended daily allowance (RDA) for proper vitamin and mineral doses. The RDA originated in the 1940s and has had only minor increases since its beginning. Yet individuals in the 2000s are bombarded with over 500 toxic chemicals on a daily basis. And much of our food supply is processed and grown in nutritionally depleted soil. We need more nutrients to keep ourselves healthy!

And each of us is a special creation; we have different nutritional needs. Although the RDA for nutrients may prevent severe deficiency disease, orthomolecular physicians say that these levels do not provide for optimal health, and people may need many more times these levels. For example, studies of guinea pigs show a twenty-fold variation in their vitamin C requirements. Similar studies have been done in humans: children have been shown to have varying needs for vitamin B6.

Orthomolecular medicine, used alone or with prescription medications, can provide quick and lasting relief from dozens of stubborn health problems. Orthomolecular medicine relies on nutrition first; drug treatment is reserved for conditions unresponsive to nutrient therapy alone.

Orthomolecular physicians realize biochemical individuality and place no value in across-the-board RDA guidelines. Instead, megadoses of nutrients may be required to overcome dietary deficiencies.

ARE MEGADOSES SAFE?

Some argue against megavitamin treatment ("megadoses"), noting that high doses of certain vitamins can cause adverse reactions. A major study, however, that compared overdose fatalities and adverse reactions showed that too much prescription medication is cause for over 106,000 deaths a year. In comparison, the total number of deaths from vitamin/mineral therapy between 1983 and 1990 was zero.

Problems can occur with megavitamin or herbal therapy, but if symptoms arise, reducing or stopping the therapy will almost always terminate any side effects. It's important to work with a physician who specializes in vitamin/mineral or herbal therapies. In the three years we've been using ortho-molecular doses of vitamins, minerals, and amino acids—both intravenously and orally—we have not seen a single major side effect.

WHAT CAUSES MENTAL DISTRESS?

Depression, mental fatigue, and mental confusion share several underlying causes.

- **Poor sleep** depletes mood-controlling neurotransmitters, including serotonin. Decreased serotonin leads to depression, mental fatigue, lowered pain threshold, and sugar cravings.

- **Low protein diets, poor digestion, and malabsorption syndromes** contribute to amino acid deficiencies. Remember, amino acids—along with certain vitamin and mineral cofactors—create the neurotransmitters.

- **Nutritional deficiencies** are quite common in America. In one study, up to 50% of patients admitted for hospital care had nutritional deficiencies.[1]

- **Magnesium deficiency** affects 50% of the population.[2] Magnesium and vitamin B6 are cofactors in the production of dopamine, GABA, and serotonin.

- **A chromium deficiency,** which is especially common among those taking cholesterol-lowering drugs, can cause hypoglycemia and mood disorders.

- **A deficiency in any of the B vitamins** can lead to depression, brain fog, and mental fatigue.

- **Birth control pills and Premarin** can deplete vitamin B6.

- **Vitamin C deficiency** hurts the production of dopamine, norepinephrine, and serotonin. Vitamin C plays a major role in the production of the adrenal "fight-or-flight" hormone, adrenaline. A deficiency in adrenal function can contribute to fatigue, depression, and confusion.

- **A deficiency of any of the essential nutrients** can create a chain reaction leading to all sorts of mood disorders, anxiety, depression, and panic disorders.

ALLERGIC DISORDERS

Food and chemical sensitivities can cause all sorts of symptoms. Allergic inflammation of the intestinal tract causes irritable bowel. Allergic inflammation of the nasal membranes creates sinusitis. Allergic reactions in the respiratory tissue creates bronchial spasms (asthma). Allergic reactions can also occur within the brain, creating mental confusion, depression, anxiety, and other mood disorders.

AMINO ACIDS AND ORTHOMOLECULAR MEDICINE

The amino acids tryptophan, phenylalanine, and glutamine can all be used to successfully treat depression, anxiety, and mental fatigue.

If you suffer from any of these, the following Amino Acid Brain Chemistry Profile is a great tool in evaluating which orthomolecular treatment(s) would work best for you. Into which group(s) do *you* best fit? Each group description suggests an amino acid supplement to treat your particular deficiency.

The "O" Group

If three or more of these descriptions apply to your present feelings, you are probably part of the "O" group:
   • Your life seems incomplete.

   • You feel shy with all but your closest friends.

   • You have feelings of insecurity.

   • You often feel unequal to others.

   • When things go right, you sometimes feel undeserving.

   • You feel something is missing in your life.

   • You occasionally feel a low self-worth or -esteem.

   • You feel inadequate as a person.

   • You frequently feel fearful when there is nothing to fear.

The "O" Group is named for the **opioid neurotransmitters** contained in the hypothalamus gland. These neurotransmitters have two primary functions:

First, opioids are released in small bursts when we feel a sense of urgency (stress). Some individual seem to feed off of this adrenaline rush. A sense of urgency can also help us get out of bed in the morning or get the kids off to school. However, if you can never turn this sense of urgency off, you'll eventually deplete the opioids, along with other vital hormones including cortisol and DHEA.

As a way to turn off the constant mind chatter, those in the "O group" use stimulants and mind numbing chemicals (alcohol, marijuana, food, etc.) to escape the constant pressure they place on themselves to be more, do more, have more. These chemicals can temporarily relieve the anxious feelings associated with opioid overload by providing artificial opioids. Unfortunately, these artificial opioids also cause the opioid manufacturing cells in your brain to reduce their output. These cells then lose their ability to produce the needed opioid neurotransmitters. You then crave the artificial opioids, and an addiction has been born.

Second, when you exercise, your body releases extra opioids. This takes away the pain of sore muscles and may provide a feeling of euphoria. The opioids play an important role in pain modulation, so a deficiency of opioids can lower our pain threshold and make us more sensitive to painful stimuli.

DL-phenylalanine (a special form of the amino acid phenylalanine) can be extremely helpful in restoring proper opioid levels.

Start with 1,000mg of DL-phenylalanine one–two times daily on an empty stomach. If you don't seem to notice any benefits, keep increasing the dose, up to 4,000mg twice a day. If you experience a rapid heart beat, agitation, or hyperactivity, reduce or stop taking DL-phenylalanine. L-glutamine increases the effectiveness of DL-phenylalanine, so take 500mg of L-glutamine one–two times daily on an empty stomach.

Phenylalanine can increase blood pressure. If you already have high blood pressure, consult your doctor before taking any form of it. Phenylalanine can be stimulating and shouldn't be taken past 3:00 in the afternoon.

The "G" Group

If three or more of these descriptions apply to your present feelings, you are probably part of the "G" group:

- You often feel anxious for no reason.
- You sometimes feel "free-floating" anxiety.
- You frequently feel "edgy," and it's difficult to relax.
- You often feel a "knot" in your stomach.
- Falling asleep is sometimes difficult.
- It's hard to turn your mind off when you want to relax.
- You occasionally experience feelings of panic for no reason.
- You often use alcohol or other sedatives to calm down.

The "G" group symptoms are from the absence of the neurotransmitter **gamma-aminobutyric acid (GABA)**. GABA is an important neurotransmitter involved in regulating moods and mental clarity. Tranquilizers used to treat anxiety and panic disorders work by increasing GABA.

GABA is made from the amino acid glutamine. Glutamine passes across the blood-brain barrier and helps provide the fuel needed for proper brain function.

A shortage of L-glutamine can reduce IQ levels. L-glutamine supplementation has been shown to increase IQ levels in some mentally deficient children. That's because L-glutamine is brain fuel! It feeds the brain cells, allowing them to fire on all cylinders. A deficiency in L-glutamine can result in foggy thinking and fatigue. Individuals with fibro fog may benefit tremendously from supplementing this essential amino acid.

Even a small shortage of L-glutamine will produce unwarranted feelings of insecurity and anxiousness. Other symptoms include continual fatigue, depression, and occasionally, impotence.

Usually only a small dose of GABA is needed, 500–1,000mg twice daily. Some individuals may need to take it three–four times a day. Like most amino acids, GABA needs to be taken on an empty stomach.

The "D" Group

If three or more of these descriptions apply to your present feelings, you are probably part of the "D" group:

- You lack pleasure in life.

- You feel there are no real rewards in life.

- You have unexplained lack of concern for others, even loved ones.

- You experience decreased parental feelings.

- Life seems less "colorful" or "flavorful."

- Things that used to be fun aren't any longer enjoyable.

- You have become a less spiritual or socially concerned person.

Dopamine is a neurotransmitter associated with the enjoyment of life: food, arts, nature, your family, friends, hobbies, and other pleasures. Cocaine's (and chocolate's) popularity stems from the fact that it causes very high levels of dopamine to be released in a sudden rush.

A dopamine deficiency can lead to a condition known as anhedonia. Anhedonia is the lack of ability to feel any pleasure or remorse in life. It also reduces the person's attention span. The attention span of a person who has taken cocaine for some time is often reduced to two–three minutes, instead of the usual 50–60 minutes. Learning, for such a person, is nearly impossible.

Brain fatigue, confusion, and lethargy are all by-products of low dopamine.

The brain cells that manufacture dopamine use the amino acid **L-phenylalanine** as raw material. Like most cells in the hypothalamus, they have the ability to produce four–five times their usual output if larger quantities of the raw materials are made available through nutritional supplementation.

Start with 1,000mg of L-phenylalanine one–two times daily on an empty stomach. If you don't seem to notice any benefits, keep increasing the dose, up to 4,000mg twice a day. If you experience a rapid heart beat, agitation, or hyperactivity, reduce or stop taking L-phenylalanine. L-glutamine increases the effectiveness of L-phenylalanine, so take 500 mg. of L-glutamine one–two times daily on an empty stomach.

Phenylalanine can increase blood pressure. If you already have high blood pressure, consult your doctor before taking any form of it. Phenylalanine can be stimulating and shouldn't be taken past 3:00 in the afternoon.

The "N" Group

If three or more of these descriptions apply to your present feelings, you are probably part of the "N" group:

- You suffer from a lack of energy.
- You often find it difficult to "get going."
- You suffer from decreased drive.
- You often start projects and then don't finish them.
- You frequently feel a need to sleep or "hibernate."
- You feel depressed a good deal of the time.
- You occasionally feel paranoid.
- Your survival seems threatened.
- You are bored a great deal of the time.

The neurotransmitter **norepinephrine,** when released in the brain, causes feelings of arousal, energy, and drive. On the other hand, a short supply of it will cause feelings of a lack of ambition, drive, and/or energy. Deficiency can even cause depression, paranoia, and feelings of apathy.

Norepinephrine is also used to initiate the flow of adrenaline when you are under psychological stress.

The production of norepinephrine in the hypothalamus is a 2-step process. The amino acid L-phenylalanine is first converted into tyrosine. Tyrosine is then converted into norepinephrine. Tyrosine, then, can be supplemented to increase norepinephrine (and dopamine). But too much tyrosine can cause headaches, so I usually recommend **L-phenylalanine** replacement first.

Start with 1,000mg of L-phenylalanine one–two times daily on an empty stomach. If you don't seem to notice any benefits, keep increasing the dose, up to 4,000mg twice a day. If you experience a rapid heart beat, agitation, or hyperactivity, reduce or stop taking L-phenylalanine. L-glutamine increases the effectiveness of L-phenylalanine, so take 500 mg. of L-glutamine one–two times daily on an empty stomach.

Phenylalanine can increase blood pressure. If you already have high blood pressure, consult your doctor before taking any form of it. Phenylalanine can be stimulating and shouldn't be taken past 3:00 in the afternoon.

The "S" Group

If three or more of these descriptions apply to your present feelings, you are probably part of the "S" group:

- It's hard for you to go to sleep.
- You can't stay asleep.
- You often find yourself irritable.
- Your emotions often lack rationality.
- You occasionally experience unexplained tears.
- Noise bothers you more than it used to; it seems louder than normal.
- You flare up at others more easily than you used to; you experience unprovoked anger.
- You feel depressed much of the time.
- You find you are more susceptible to pain.
- You prefer to be left alone.

Serotonin is a hypothalamus neurotransmitter necessary for sleep. A lack of serotonin causes difficulty in getting to sleep as well as staying asleep. It is often this lack of sleep that causes the symptoms mentioned above.

Serotonin levels can easily be raised by supplementing with the essential amino acid L-tryptophan, but dietary supplements of L-tryptophan are banned in the United States. (For more on this, see page 69.) However, **5-hydroxytryptophan (5HTP),** a form of tryptophan, is available over-the-counter and works extremely well for most patients.[3]

Start with 100mg of 5HTP, 30 minutes before bed. Take on an empty stomach along with 4oz. of juice (apple or grape). You may need to increase this dose, up to 200mg per night. If you feel hungover the next day, decrease your dose. Individuals who don't have trouble sleeping at night but do have other symptoms of the "S" group might want to take 50 mg. of 5HTP two–four times daily. More than 50 mg. at a time may cause sleepiness. Always take 5HTP on an empty stomach along with 4oz. of juice. To order 5HTP, see page 274.

OTHER HELPFUL SUPPLEMENTS

The following supplements aren't amino acids, but they are definitely worth a try, no matter what group(s) you fit into.

- **St. John's wort** is a perennial plant native to Great Britain and northern Europe. It has antibacterial, antidepressant, antiviral, and anti-inflammatory abilities but has received the most attention for its use in treating depression. (It's been described as "natural Prozac.") Hypercin, along with other chemicals contained in St. John's wort, acts as both a weak MAOI and an SSRI.

  A review of 23 studies shows St. John's wort to be as or more effective as several prescription drugs (Elavil, Zoloft, and Tofranil) in treating depression. Each year, over 60 million prescriptions for St. John's wort are written in Germany alone. Dosage is standardized (.3% hypericin) 300 mg. 3 times daily.

  St. John's wort should not be taken along with prescription antidepressant medications, unless you are working with a knowledgeable physician. It may also increase the potential for sunburn, especially if taken with Propulsid, Previcid, Feldane, or sulfa drugs. You may wish to consult your physician about taking St. John's wort along with Ultram. St. John's wort may decrease the effectiveness of certain medications, including digoxin, Coumadin, theophylline, birth control pills, and cyclosporine.

- **S-adenosyl-methionine (SAM)** is involved in regulating the brain's neurotransmitters. Normally the brain manufactures all the SAM it needs from the amino acid methionine. However, low-protein diets, malabsorption, and deficiencies can create a need for SAM replacement. SAM has been shown through several well designed studies to be one of the best natural antidepressants available. Only its relatively high cost keeps it from replacing other natural remedies.

  Start with 200 mg. twice daily, and gradually build up to a maximum of 400 mg. four times daily. Not everyone will need to take the maximum dose. To reduce the amount of SAM needed, combine it with amino acids or St. John's wort.

PRESCRIPTION MEDICATIONS

- **Effexor** raises norepinephrine and serotonin levels.
- **Wellbutrin** increases norepinephrine and dopamine levels.
- **Prozac, Zoloft, Celexa, Luvox, and Paxil** increase serotonin levels.
- **Selegiline** is a MAOI that stimulates dopamine production.

REDUCING FIBRO FOG

- **L-acetylcarnitine (LAC)** reduces brain fog. It is a more active form of the amino acid carnitine. Studies have shown it to be valuable in helping decrease depression and increase mental acuity, especially memory enhancement.

  LAC tends to be expensive, and you might want to try a formula that contains several brain-boosting nutrients. ProThera makes a product called NeuroThera, which I recommend. NeuroThera contains phosphatidylserine, phosphatidylcholine, LAC, ginkgo biloba, and other brain-boosting nutrients.

- **Phosphatidylserine** reduces brain fog and is the major phospholipid in the brain. It regulates the fluidity of the brain cells, allowing nutrients in and toxins out. It plays a key role in allowing brain cells (neurotransmitters) to communicate with one another. A deficiency of SAM will create a deficiency of phosphatidylserine.

  Like LAC, phosphatidylserine can be expensive, so I recommend NeuroThera (described above) instead.

- **Malic acid** is found in a variety of foods and is a vital nutrient needed for the production of cellular energy. Malic acid is one of the essential nutrients in the Krebs cycle (a highly sophisticated process of supplying cellular energy), and its supplementation boosts the efficiency of mitochondria. Malic acid also helps reduce achy muscles by supplying a needed energy boost to remove unwanted toxic waste productions occurring in the muscles of individuals with FMS/CFS.

SEASONAL AFFECTIVE DISORDER (SAD)

Seasonal affective disorder (SAD) is linked to the short days of winter. For more information, see page 69.

FINAL THOUGHTS

Brain fog, mental fatigue, and depression can be caused by poor diet, deficient nutrients, food allergies, Candida yeast overgrowth, intestinal permeability, and chemical sensitivities. It is important to address the whole body and correct any and all of these potential causes. To do so...

- Take a good digestive enzyme.

- Eat plenty of protein.

- Take a good multivitamin and mineral formula with plenty of B6, B1, B3, vitamin C, magnesium, CoQ10, and essential fatty acids.[4]

- Take a free-form amino acid formula.

- Make sure you get a good night's sleep each night. If needed, take 5HTP or a prescription medication.

- Supplement with amino acids (as indicated by the Brain Chemistry Profile), SAM, or St. John's wort as recommended. I prefer to use the amino acids first. However, if you are on prescription medication, you might want to try SAM first. Don't combine prescription and natural antidepressants or stop taking any of your prescription medications without first consulting your medical doctor.

- Working with your medical physician, wean off your prescription medications and try the amino acids or St. John's wort.

- Keep your DHEA levels in the "high-normal" range.

- Consider thyroid glandular or prescription medications if your temperature is low (see chapter 19).

- Uncover and avoid any food allergies.

> "After 26 years in medicine, if I had to choose the number one food that has caused the most depression, it would be sugar." —Sherry Rogers, MD

Notes

[1]Source: Roubenoff R et al. "Malnutrition among hospitalized patients: problems of physician awareness." *Arch Intern Med;* 1987

[2]Source: *Tired or Toxic?* by Sherry A. Rogers; 1990

[3]Natural sources of L-tryptophan include milk, cheese, meat, ham, peanuts, and cottage cheese. All of these are very high in calories and cholesterol. So, if you want to use food sources, supplement *small* amounts, along with the serotonin-production catalysts: calcium, magnesium, and trace chromium.

[4]If you aren't dreaming at night, you're probably deficient in B6. If you're taking up to 250 mg. of B6 in the form of pyridoxine and still not having dreams (whether you remember them is not important), switch to taking 50–150 mg. of pyridoxal-5-phosphate (an easier-to-absorb form of B6).

Resources

• The supplements discussed in this chapter are available online at www.drrodger.com or by calling (205) 879-2383.

• To obtain prescription medications discussed in this chapter, see your doctor.

For Further Reading

• *Nutrition and Mental Illness: An Orthomolecular Approach to Balancing Body Chemistry* by Carl Curt Pfeiffer; 1988

• *The Ultimate Nutrient: Glutamine* by Judy Shabert and Nancy Ehrlich; 1994

• *Healing the Mind the Natural Way* by Pat Lazarus; 1995

• *Anxiety Epidemic* by Billie J. Sahley; 1994

• *Essential Guide to Psychiatric Drugs* by Jack M.Gorman, MD; 1998

• *Botanical Influences on Illness* by Melvyn R. Werbach, MD, and Michael T. Murray, ND; 2000

• *Orthomolecular Medicine for Physicians* by Abram Hoffer; 1997

23

The Incredible Benefits of Exercise

Daily exercise helps boost the immune system, counter stress, raise serotonin and dopamine levels, and improve self-esteem. Most FMS/CFS patients benefit from daily exercise.

ONE STEP AT A TIME

If you don't have any energy to start an exercise program then the first place to start is simply walking around the block. Start with five minutes a day. Then after a few weeks, begin increasing the time you walk each day. While step aerobics, StairMasters and cross-country ski machines may be more glamorous, walking is the easiest form of exercise to maintain on a consistent basis. Long after the stationary bike, the treadmill, and the Soloflex have been abandoned, walking will still be in vogue, and it takes only commitment and a good pair of shoes to get started. Plus, it can be done anywhere, any time, alone or with a group.

A moderate pace burns 300 calories per hour. Walking six days a week will burn over two pounds of fat a month. That's 26 pounds a year! A faster pace burns even more calories, and running burns 600 calories per hour. (Step aerobics and other high-intensity workouts can burn even more calories per hour, but I don't recommend step aerobics for most individuals recovering from FMS/CFS.)

THE CASE FOR GETTING MOVING

Here's more good news: your metabolism will continue to burn calories even after you're through exercising. Your basal metabolism determines the speed and efficiency at which calories are burned for fuel, and it remains elevated for several hours after a workout.

Exercise decreases triglycerides (fats) and LDL (bad) cholesterol while increasing the HDL (good) cholesterol. Systolic and diastolic blood pressure numbers are decreased. The heart becomes stronger and increases its efficiency at pumping more blood per beat. Exercise increases the diameter of coronary arteries which greatly reduces the risk of having a heart attack (and helps you to bypass a bypass)! Research shows that exercise can reduce the risk of having a second heart attack. Those who chose not to exercise were over twenty times more likely to have another heart attack compared to those who did exercise.

Exercise is a wonderful stress reducer and mood elevator. It helps relieve mild depression by generating endorphins. Endorphins are the body's natural pain killers and are associate with the "runners high." Some researchers say that exercise can raise norepinephrine levels by 200 percent. Epinephrine and norepinephrine are neurotransmitters associated with drive, ambition, energy, and happiness.

Exercise also stimulates important neurotransmitters that help us combat insomnia, depression, irritability, fatigue, and food, alcohol, and tobacco cravings. Blood glucose and insulin levels are decreased with exercise. This is extremely beneficial for carbohydrate-intolerant individuals and type-2 diabetics.

Exercise stimulates brown fat to burn more calories. (Brown fat is found at the posterior base of the neck and shoulders. It's what allows bears to hibernate in the winter, and humans also have varying amounts of brown fat, which burns calories to provide needed body heat.

Exercise increases human growth hormone, which helps burn fat, builds muscle, and stimulates the thymus gland, the master gland of the immune system.

Allergy sufferers benefit from regular exercise as well. It raises norepinephrine and cortisol levels, and these natural hormones reduce inflammation and allergic reactions. Many of my asthmatic patients notice a drastic reduction in the frequency and severity of their attacks after being on a consistent exercise program that's medically right for them.

Exercise helps detoxify the body by ridding it of waste products, including carbon monoxide. It enhances the delivery of oxygen and nutrients to the cells. The benefits of exercise are numerous. Just take it slow, and don't overdo it.

And please, don't attempt and exercise program without repairing your adrenal glands, first. See chapter 7.

24

Chiropractic and Other Physical Medicine

chapter cowritten with Margaret Arthur, MD

Nearly half of FMS patients who have tried chiropractic care rate it as moderately to extremely helpful in treating their symptoms.

CHIROPRACTIC CARE

Chiropractic health care is a 100-year-old profession, licensed and practiced in all 50 states as well as most countries around the world. Chiropractic health care originated in America in 1895. It is the third largest (and the fastest growing) health profession in the country, serving over 25 million Americans each year.

Daniel David Palmer, a successful, self-taught healer in Davenport, Iowa, founded Chiropractic as a health profession distinct and separate from conventional medicine. This was a pretty dark time for health care and medicine in particular. Medicine hadn't yet discovered antibiotics, and blood letting and folk medicine ruled the day. Palmer founded chiropractic to emphasize a more natural approach. Early chiropractic was based on a one cause, one cure philosophy. Palmer taught that nerve interference or "nerve tone" was the cause of disease. Finding misalignments (subluxations) in the spinal column and then correctly realigning (adjusting) them helped restore proper nerve flow.

Chiropractic later doggedly overcame an aggressive campaign by the American Medical Association to contain and eliminate chiropractic care. Through sheer determination, a sometimes militant belief that chiropractic should stay separate from medicine, and the popularity chiropractic enjoyed among its ever-growing crowd of supporters, it prevailed.

In the 1980s, the US Supreme Court upheld a previous verdict stating that the AMA had, for political and economic reasons, illegally and maliciously sought to destroy the chiropractic profession. Later, the AMA rescinded its ban on referring to chiropractors. Today, chiropractic and the medical profession work together at many of the medical facilities around the country. Dozens of hospitals have chiropractors on staff, and most insurance companies, including Medicare, cover chiropractic services.

TODAY

A minority of chiropractors still believe in a one cause, one cure philosophy. However, most of today's chiropractors focus on musculoskeletal conditions, primarily low back pain, sciatica, neck pain, and headaches.

95% of today's chiropractic treatments are for musculoskeletal problems. There are more randomized clinical trials of spinal manipulations (chiropractic adjustments) for spine-related disorders than any other single approach. Affirmative backing by such highly respected organizations as the US Agency for Health Care Policy and Research (AHCPR), the RAND corporation, the Canadian Government, and others have allowed chiropractic to continue to grow and be accepted around the world.

Along with chiropractic adjustments, chiropractors may incorporate diet, exercise, nutritional supplements, and physical therapies to treat most musculoskeletal conditions. Still a firm believer that the power that made the body heals the body, today's chiropractor is often a leading thinker in 21st century medicine. This medicine integrates conventional with alternative therapies that have been clinically proven effective.

For low back pain and leg pain, both acute and chronic, scientific studies recommend chiropractic as the first line of management.

"THE SKY IS FALLING"

Some critics would have the public believe that chiropractors are witch doctors. But chiropractic has proven itself through numerous studies and inquiries to be the safest health profession when compared to dentistry and traditional medicine. The studies strongly show the safety of chiropractic care. There are 0.000001 incidences of severe complications from spinal manipulation. 94% of these complications occurred from osteopaths, medical doctors, and physical therapists attempting spinal manipulation procedures. Compare this to the staggering amount of patients who die each year from medical complications. Deaths from medical treatments is now the fourth leading cause of death in the US.

Used properly, manipulation can help a range of health problems including low back pain, sciatica, neck pain, headaches, carpal tunnel syndrome, and symptoms of FMS/CFS.

EDUCATION OF CHIROPRACTORS

Doctors of chiropractic are not only trained in problems of the spine but are formerly educated in clinical examination and diagnosis of the entire human body. Chiropractic students receive about the same amount of total educational hours as medical students. There are 18 chiropractic colleges located in the US. Over 70% of those entering chiropractic college already have one or more college degrees. The chiropractic degree bestows the tittle of doctor of chiropractic (DC). It usually takes four–five years and 4,805 clinic and classroom hours to complete chiropractic college. See below a comparison of chiropractic educational hours with those of a typical medical school student in nine important subject areas.

Subject	Chiropractic hrs.	Medical hrs.
Anatomy/Embryology	456	215
Physiology	243	174
Pathology	296	507
Chemistry	161	100
Microbiology	145	145
Diagnosis	408	113
Neurology	149	171
Radiology	271	13
Orthopedics	168	2

Choosing the Chiropractor for You

This isn't always easy. Sometimes the doctor or the therapy just doesn't connect with the patient. When this happens, just find someone else that you feel comfortable with. You didn't agree with every medical doctor you've seen, but that didn't stop you from utilizing the benefits of medicine. You simply found a doctor you liked.

Some chiropractors specialize in family medicine, some in nutritional, and some in sports chiropractic. Although I've not found many chiropractors who specialize in FMS/CFS, I do see that this is beginning to change. This shouldn't stop you from seeing a chiropractor who isn't a specialist in FMS/CFS.

Chiropractic treatments should never *hurt*. Occasionally, your chiropractic physician might need to use certain techniques that can leave you sore for a few days. However, this shouldn't be a common occurrence.

I like what applied kinesiology (AK) has to offer for FMS/CFS patients. This technique, when carried out in conjunction with other gentle adjusting techniques, has benefitted the majority of my patients.

I've found that my FMS/CFS patients can't handle a lot of force or pressure applied to their spine. Unless they have an acute joint misalignment, gentle techniques result in the best responses. (I can only speak from my experience and this is somewhat clouded by the fact that the majority of my patients come to me as a last resort. By this time they've have had FMS/CFS for many years.)

Just remember that you are the consumer, and the doctor provides the service. If something is not going right, tell your doctor. An open dialogue is extremely helpful and appreciated. See Appendix C for resources.

Massage Therapy

Massage therapy is one of the oldest health care therapies in existence. Chinese medical texts show massage techniques have been used for over 4,000 years. Modern massage therapy was introduced in America in the mid-1800s. Massage therapy uses soft tissue body manipulations to help restore proper musculoskeletal function. It is made up of hundreds of different techniques. Massage therapy continue to grow and now plays an important role in today's health care.

There are many different types of massage therapy, but some are better known than others in the US:

- **Swedish massage** is based on the therapist using long gliding strokes along stressed muscles. This form of massage is rarely uncomfortable and is probably for everyone, including those with FMS/CFS.

- **Deep tissue massage** is used to release chronic patterns of muscular tension. It uses slow and sometimes very firm pressure to restore normal muscle function. It is usually not comfortable for individuals with FMS/CFS, though there are always exceptions.

- **Neuromuscular massage** is deep massage applied to an individual muscle. It may be too uncomfortable for individuals with FMS/CFS.

- **Acupressure** is based on Chinese meridians and is administered by applying finger- or thumb-pressure to specific locations around the body.

- **Shiatsu** is a form of acupressure.

- **CranioSacral therapy** is a method for finding and correcting disturbances in the flow of spinal fluid. This form of therapy is extremely gentle, and in the hands of an experienced therapist, patients are known to experience tremendous relief.

- **Myofascial release technique** seems to offer a good deal of relief for our FMS/CFS patients. An excellent addition to the treatment protocol is to find a therapist trained in myofascial release as taught by John Barnes, PT. He has trained many thousands of therapists around the world about a system of our body ignored in medical training: the fascial system. Dysfunction of this system can cause great pain

Myofascial Release (MFR) Technique

MFR might be for you if you suffer from any of these:

headaches	myofascial pain syndromes
TMJ syndrome	chronic fatigue syndrome
fibromyalgia	neck pain
chronic pelvic pain	low back pain

Myofascial release is a gentle hands-on therapy used to remove unwanted fascial restrictions. Fascia is a densely woven connective tissue. It's actually an interconnected tissue that exists from head to toe without interruption, similar to nylon tights, or a spider's web. The fascia system covers every cell as well as all the nerves, arteries, veins, brain, spinal cord, muscles, organs, and bones.

Fascia also plays an important role in supporting the muscles and bones that contribute to our posture. The bones would not be able to remain upright without this structure that is able to tighten to a tensile strength of 2000 pounds per square inch and also relax and reshape itself.

In a normal healthy state, the fascia is relaxed and has the ability to stretch and move without restriction. Physical trauma, scars, poor posture, spinal misalignments, stress, and inflammation cause the fascia to tighten. It then becomes restricted and creates unwanted tension on the rest of the body. Repetitive traumas and stress have a cumulative effect. They can cause the fascia system to exert excessive pressure that creates inflammation and pain.

Fascial restrictions can cause sudden or chronic pain syndromes including headaches, carpal tunnel syndrome, frozen shoulder, sciatica, tennis elbow, and neck, back, knee, foot, and hip pain.[1]

Myofascial release, as taught by Barnes, is designed to find and release any fascial restrictions that may be contributing to the patient's pain. Many patients describe this therapy as a gentle but effective massage. The therapist analyzes the patients posture, palpates and locates fascial restrictions, then through gentle techniques, releases restrictions.

When the fascia is touched through the skin, this sets up a piezoelectric effect where mechanical touch affects the physical tissue and the cellular energy. A therapist, utilizing the gentle, sustained pressure of myofascial release through compression, stretching, or twisting of the myofascial system, generates a flow of bioenergy (information) throughout the mind/body complex. This flow starts at the cellular level and is transferred to large areas of tissue through a tubular system, recently discovered to also carry neurotransmitters. The result is that sometimes places where we have been injured carry memories of that event, and they are released with the treatment.

Often patients ask, "How often will I need treatment?" Every individual is different, depending on the length of time the problem has been present and the patient's desire to do home treatment. In general, pain and fascial restrictions that are new or less than several months old may resolve in one to several treatments. Conditions that have developed over a number of years benefit from two–three MFR treatments per week. When you are limited to one treatment per week and your fascial restrictions are extensive, you may tighten again. Home stretching with self-treatment MFR techniques shown to you by your therapist will minimize this phenomenon.

If you hurt during a treatment, let the therapist know. It is important for the therapist to ease the pressure, because pain will result in the fascia tightening even more to protect the body. Soft, gentle pressure allows the fascia to return to a normal state. Sometimes you may feel pain for one–two days after treatment. As the fascia is opened, the metabolic waste that was trapped can be released, so drink lots of water to flush the system.

Many massage therapists are given some training in myofascial release, but the technique described above is a system developed over a number of years that requires gentle sustained holds of at least two–three minutes.

If you have any of these conditions, MFR is not recommend as a therapy for you:

malignancy	acute rheumatoid arthritis
cellulitis	sutures
febrile state	hematoma
localized infection	healing fracture
osteoporosis	acute circulatory condition
osteomyelitis	anticoagulant therapy
aneurysm	advanced diabetes
obstructive edema	hypersensitivity of skin
open wounds	

Craniosacral therapy is included in Barnes's MFR training. John Upledger, DO, has also trained thousands of therapists in craniosacral therapy. The craniosacral system is a physiologic system that includes: (1) the tissue surrounding the brain and spinal cord; (2) the fluid that surrounds the spinal cord and brain (cerebrospinal fluid) and (3) the structures related to production of this fluid. Many systems of the body influence and are influenced by the craniosacral system including the brain, spinal cord, and all other nerves, the muscles, blood vessels, and endocrine and respiratory systems. Just as our heart beats 68–72 beats per minute (on average), our fluid throughout this system flows at a 6–12 cycle per minute rate. TMJ syndrome (with its constant clinching) can especially alter this system as can fibromyalgia in general. This therapy requires gentle techniques with hands resting on various parts of the head and sacrum.

If you have any of these conditions, craniosacral therapy is not recommend as a therapy for you:

acute intracranial hemorrhage
brain aneurysm
herniation of the base of the brain (medulla oblongata)
recent skull fracture
acute systemic infectious conditions

Many people describe their experience of craniosacral therapy as very relaxing or "floating." For online information, visit www.myofascialrelease.com

Notes
[1]Currently there are not diagnostic tests that demonstrate this phenomenon. However, MRI may someday be able to demonstrate the restrictions that cause you so much pain.

For Further Reading
- *Healing Ancient Wounds: The Renegade's Wisdom* by John Barnes, PT; 2000
- *Waking the Tiger* by Peter A. Levine; 1997

25

Feeding the Spirit

We can't separate the mind from our health any
more than we can separate our eyes from
seeing. The connection between the mind and
health is profound and undeniable.

Psychoneuroimmunology is the study of the interrelationships between the mind, brain, and immune system. Four decades of ongoing research is just now making its way into the medical and public arena. This research shows how the brain uses the nervous system to communicate with every system in the body, including the immune system. But more importantly, this research leads to an understanding of how thoughts, emotions, and the experiences they create, influence our overall health.

Just how does the mind control our health? Well, let's look at how the body, brain, and mind interact. Think of the brain as a musical instrument and the mind as the musician. The instrument is played by the musician. Nothing happens until he picks up the instrument and begins to play. In the same way, the brain is an instrument (in this case, an "organ") under the influence of the mind.

A person's inner spirit is the conductor of the symphony. This inner spirit influences what the mind says to the body.

Like the conductor, your spirit has the ability to control every note played by the body. Some people may call this inner spirit our innate intelligence, some the Holy Spirit or Holy Ghost.

Although every one of us has an inner spirit, most don't fully tap into its incredible positive energy. When you do tap into this energy through prayer, meditation, or times of pure mental clarity, you know that, without a doubt, you've experienced bliss.

Since our minds undoubtedly influence our bodily functions, it is only logical to ask, "How can we control our minds?" The self-help movement has already educated us on positive thinking, affirmations, resolutions, goal setting, and mission statements. These are all valid tools to help you write your life script. Your life script is a combination of genes, environment, thoughts, beliefs, and experiences. These make up your reality, your own little world. For instance, if you lived alone with a group of pygmies, you'd feel like a giant. You might think you're more attractive, stronger, or more powerful than everyone else. Or just the opposite, you might feel inferior, because you look so different. It is all about our beliefs, which turn into our reality.

For as a man thinketh in his heart, so is he.
—Bible Proverb 23:7

WRITE A NEW LIFE SCRIPT

Rewriting your script from one of poor health, despair, and helplessness is crucial in overcoming your illness! Your illness is an opportunity to evaluate what was (and probably still is) not working in your life. We rarely question what is truly important in our lives. *Why are we here? For what purpose?* Normally, we live each day as the day before, sometimes "sleepwaking" through entire portions of our lives. Major life challenges are often the catalyst for re-evaluating life. We may seek solace by tapping into our inner spirit. We may turn to God and ask for his guidance. (If we fail to recognize this opportunity, God will usually give us additional chances!)

Your script might have read like this: "hard working, perfectionist, responsible for everybody around her. Long work hours, poor diet, too much real or imagined responsibility, negative thoughts, unmanaged stress."

A twenty-year study by George Engel, professor of medicine at University of Rochester, showed that 70–80% of all chronically ill patients had experienced extended periods of feeling helpless before the onset of their disease.[1]

True Health is a Triangle

True health is made up of three pillars: physical, chemical, and spiritual. Picture a triangle in which each of these pillars interacts and supports one another. Our inner spirit makes up the bottom pillar (or line of the triangle). The other two pillars, physical and chemical health, join together at the pinnacle.

Physical health involves the mechanical aptitude of various moveable body parts, how well the muscles and joints move. How strong are the various bones that support our posture? Our dexterity, flexibility, and stamina are all associated with physical health.

Chemical health involves the nutrients, enzymes, hormones, white blood cells, neurotransmitters, and other biochemicals that perform the countless functions needed to run the body.

Our inner self (conscious and unconscious mind) and our higher self (spirit, soul, God within us, Universal intelligence, The Holy Ghost, etc.) act as the rudder that steers every facet of our lives, including the state of our health. This is the spiritual pillar.

If any one side of the triangle is removed or ignored and weakens, the structure collapses into itself.

The Healer Within

Our subconscious mind (autonomic nervous system) controls how fast our heart beats, the rate of our breathing, how we walk, how we stand, and how fast blood pumps through our veins. We are born with an innate ability to heal ourselves. If this were not true, we would quickly succumb to the millions of deadly microbes (viruses and bacteria) that inhabit our lungs and digestive tracts. These bugs are monitored and kept in check by the inner healer, which coordinates all functions of the body, including the immune system. Do you have to think about breathing or healing a broken bone? No. Your inner self maintains a constant vigil, overseeing every bodily process. We are truly amazing healing organisms.

You have a new stomach lining every three days. The actual cells that contact food are renewed every five minutes. You have a new liver every six weeks, and 98% of the atoms in our bodies are renewed every year. The power that made the body is ultimately the power that heals the body.

Understanding this concept can be intimidating. Medicine has been blinded by science and has largely neglected the profound influence of our higher self. Health professions are known as the 'healing arts," yet the art of medicine has been too often replaced with brain scans and drug therapies. But true health is more than the absence of disease. True health is optimal physical, chemical, and spiritual well being.

I suggest a new paradigm, one that considers the role of our inner self in determining our state of health.

Mind Chatter and Responsive Thoughts

Our minds never stop chattering. We take in and consciously or subconsciously sort, analyze, and respond to billions of thoughts each day. This constant chatter, if not checked, begins to take its toll on our mental and physical well-being. Negative thoughts create a blueprint for the subconscious mind to rely on. A few negative thoughts a day aren't so bad. Thirty years of incessant worry and negative thoughts, however, shapes who we become as people, our personality. The script is being written and rewritten every day by every thought you have.

We are what we think. All that we are arises
with our thoughts; with our thoughts we make
our world. —Gantama Buddha

I could write a lengthy chapter about all the mind-body studies and how they relate to emotional, mental, spiritual, physical, and chemical health, but I think it's really this simple. Do you feel better or worse when you are laughing and smiling than when you are frowning and scowling? It doesn't take a scientific study filled with brain scans and heart monitors to know. Without a shadow of a doubt, we feel better and are healthier when positive emotions or actions (some would say reactions) are the dominating force in our lives.

Have you ever tried to stay sad or angry when smiling at yourself in the mirror? You can't do it. This is because the muscles in the face, when contracted into a smile, trigger the brain to release happy hormones. I've found I feel and look my best when I'm physically and mentally rested. When I make the time to tone down the mind chatter and begin to listen to my inner voice, health, vitality, and joy are the rewards.

> *The greatest discovery of my generation is that human beings can alter their lives by altering their attitudes of mind.* —William James

I'm not implying that you can think, meditate, or even pray yourself to be free of all ailments. I know first-hand how debilitating FMS and CFS can be. These are not illnesses to be taken lightly! However, finding and tapping into your inner self only increases the chances of getting and being well in its truest sense.

Sometimes we have to dig deep to find the courage to overcome life's tragedies. Consider Christopher Reeve. He has never given up on using his paralyzed legs. He continues to inspire millions of people around the world. What about Stephen Hawking, the famous physicist who has no use of his arms or legs? Some would give up and be content to slowly die.

> *Everything can be taken from a man but one thing:*
> *The last of the human freedoms—to choose one's*
> *attitude in any given set of circumstances, to choose*
> *one's own way.* —Victor E. Frankl

We can't always control life's obstacles, only how we respond to them. Neglecting your inner self, your life essence while attempting to overcome something as potentially life squelching as FMS/CFS is like trying to use a magnifying glass to watch a big screen movie. Remove the magnifying glass, and take in the big picture. Focusing on covering up symptoms with chemicals or physical therapies ignores the third pillar, the very foundation of optimal health. Can you have optimal health without personally experiencing love and inner peace on a daily basis?

In order to heal yourself, you must begin to realize that true health comes from within. Your state of health is largely determined by how well you recognize this concept and your willingness to listen and trust your inner self.

> *Those who are at peace with themselves and their immediate surroundings have far fewer serious illnesses than those who are not. The simple truth is happy people don't get sick.* —Bernie Siegel, MD, author of *Love, Medicine and Miracles*

THE HEALING POWER OF PRAYER

Although 95% of Americans believe in God, most doctors are uncomfortable discussing spiritual matters. This is in light of the fact that 60% of the population would like to discuss spiritual issues with their doctors and 40% would like for their doctors to pray with them.

The effects of prayer are numerous: less anxiety, stress, and anger; lowered resting pulse rate and blood pressure; increased production of happy hormones; and increased pain threshold. In addition, prayer provides an important link to our spirituality. Dr. Larry Dossey, in his book, *The Power of Prayer,* reveals just how impactful prayer can be. Dr. Dossey discusses research that validates the power of prayer in eliminating human illness. Several double-blind studies are cited that show the impact prayer has on individuals with illnesses. The power of prayer was effective whether the patient knew he was being prayed for or not.

Prayer and other spiritual practices tap into the mind-body connection. These practices have a calming effect that involves every system in the body, including the nervous system, immune system, endocrine (hormonal) system, digestive system, and cardiovascular system. One study involving individuals with HIV showed that participation in religious or spiritual activities substantially increased immune function.

One of the most talked about studies evaluating the positive benefits of prayer was published in *The Southern*

Medical Journal in 1988. This study involved 393 hospitalized patients who were equally divided into two groups. One group served as the control and was treated with traditional medical care alone. The second group received prayer along with traditional medical care. Neither group, nor their doctors, knew who was receiving prayer from a third party. The group receiving prayer had these remarkable results: had fewer congestive heart failures (8 versus 20), needed less diuretics (5 versus 15), experienced fewer cardiac arrests (3 versus 14), had fewer episodes of pneumonia (3 versus 13), were prescribed fewer antibiotics (3 versus 17), and required less medication than the control group who received no prayer.

TAPPING INTO YOUR INNER SELF

One of the healthiest things we can do in this lifetime is to learn to rise above the constant mind chatter by quieting the mind and allowing our inner self to flourish. As you begin to tap into your inner self, you'll start to realize how negative and self-destructive thoughts sabotage your innate desire to be healthy. Life's true game may be more about learning to let go of unwanted negative thoughts—much like shedding layers of clothes when entering a warm room. The ability to control our minds by understanding, acknowledging, and choosing which thoughts, emotions, and feelings serve us best is perhaps the key that unlocks optimal health. Below are just a few ways to quite the mind and tap into your inner self.

CONSCIOUS BREATHING

Conscious breathing is a way to integrate mind and body. Focusing on breathing, using mantras (repetitive sounds), and/or visualizing a word or soothing scene are central to most meditative practices. In basic breathing exercises, all you need is a quite place and a willingness to quiet the mind. Conscious breathing reduces stress and allows you to filter out the constant mind chatter. Quieting the mind offers the opportunity to get in touch with your inner self.

An Exercise in Conscious Breathing

This exercise can be done any time of day and as often as you wish. It can be a powerful stress-busting tool. Use it when you are feeling overwhelmed.

Bring your attention to your breathing. Notice the flow of breath in and out of your lungs. Take a deep breathe in through your nose. Allow the breath to fill your lungs. Slowly exhale through your mouth. Observe the rhythm that naturally occurs. Acknowledge any distracting thoughts, and simply let them go when they appear. Return your attention to the rhythm of your breathing. Continue to take deep breathes in and out. When it feels natural, try allowing more time between each breath. Pause when appropriate, and feel the inner peace. Enjoy the freedom from mind chatter.

Refocusing Technique

This is a technique designed to allow you to get in control of your mind. Too often we find ourselves at the mercy of our emotions and have knee-jerk reactions that don't serve our higher self. When facing a stressful situation that threatens to overwhelm your best intentions, stop and take time to consider the wisdom of your inner self. This allows you to avoid being at the mercy of old negative habits and to write a new positive script that serves you better.

1. **Stop.** Call time out. Give yourself time to take several deep breaths. Remind yourself that you can tap into your inner self. With the help of your inner self, you can take control of any situation.

2. **Look.** Rise above the situation and just be an observer. Notice how you feel, your thoughts, your surroundings, any other people involved. Be objective. Take it all in.

3. **Listen.** Take a few minutes to focus on your breathing. Listen to what your inner self is saying. Pay attention to your chest area. Notice how you feel. Is this how you want to feel? Listen deeply. What is inner self, your inner voice, telling you about this situation?

4. **Choose.** Make an affirmative statement about what you wish to choose in light of this situation "I choose to feel calm, balanced, and open to positive experiences".

5. **Let it go**. Choose happiness, peace, and serenity over having to be right. Choose acceptance of not knowing over having to understand. Choose love over hate. Choose thoughts of improving health over nagging reminders of disease.

MEDITATION

Meditation can generally be divided in two categories: concentration methods, which emphasize focusing on your breathing or a specific object, and mindfulness meditation, which usually uses chants, focused breathing, or repetitive thoughts. The goal in either case is to allow thoughts, feelings, and emotions to appear moment by moment without placing any attention on them. Simply let the thoughts enter. Acknowledge them and let them go, allowing yourself to tap into your inner self.

Meditation may be especially helpful for chronic pain. Others studies have shown the effectiveness of meditation for anxiety, substance abuse, skin ailments, and depression.

YOGA

Yoga is thought to have first reached America in the 1890s, but it has been practiced in India for over 6000 years. Hatha yoga is the best-known form in America. It's based on a system of physical postures. Yoga means "yoke," or union of the personal self with the Divine source. Others describe yoga as a way to join mind, body, and spirit to enrich one's life. Yoga has made its way into several large hospitals around the country and continues to gain in popularity. Used on a regular basis, yoga offers a unique way to exercise and tone the physical body while at the same time quieting the mind.

THE HOUR OF POWER

Taking time on a daily basis to quite the mind is a crucial component of living the lives we want to live. I try to find an hour of power every day. My hour of power involves prayer, meditation, and exercise. I also use some of this time to listen to positive subliminal tapes on such topics as abundant energy, laughter and happiness, and stress management.

One of my favorite artists, Brian Andreas, has captured this witticism on one of his pieces, *Before Dawn:*

> *I've always liked the time before dawn, because*
> *there's no one around to remind me who I'm*
> *supposed to be, so it's easier to remember who I am.*

You can review Brian's imaginative and insightful works at www.storypeople.com.

Notes

[1]Source: G. Engel. "A Life Setting Conductive to Illness: The Giving Up-Given Up Complex." *Bulletin of Menninger Clinic*, 1968

For Further Reading

- *Feelings Buried Alive Never Die* by Karol K. Truman; 1991
- *There's a Spiritual Solution to Every Problem* by Wayne W. Dyer; 2001
- *Power vs. Force: The Hidden Determinants of Human Behavior* by David R. Hawkins, MD, PhD; 2002
- *Yoga and You* by Esther Myers; 1997
- *The Bigness of the Fellow Within* by B. J. Palmer; 1949
- *Creating Health: How to Wake Up the Body's Intelligence* by Deepak Chopra, MD; 1995
- *Anatomy of the Spirit: The Seven Stages of Power and Healing* by Caroline Myss; 1997
- *Why People Don't Heal and How They Can* by Caroline Myss, PhD; 1998
- subconscious life-enhancing tapes (to order, see page 275)

26

Putting it All Together

"Progress, however, of the best kind, is comparatively slow. Great results cannot be achieved at once; and we must be satisfied to advance in life as we walk, step by step." —Samuel Smiles

Discovering and correcting the causes of fibromyalgia and chronic fatigue syndrome take time and commitment. Remember, you are peeling away dysfunction and its symptoms—one layer at a time. There will usually be several peaks and valleys along the way, and it's easy to get discouraged.

As you probably realize, I pay a lot of attention to proper diet and nutrition, and rightly so. Without the essential chemicals, the human organism will always be in a state of declining health. Vitamins, minerals, amino acids, and essential fatty acids provide the building blocks you need to get well and stay well. Remember, FMS and CFS are biochemical problems that manifest themselves as physical ailments.

I'm convinced you *cannot* get well without replacing vital nutrients through supplements. What's more, you should stay on these supplements, especially a comprehensive multivitamin and mineral formula, for months, maybe years, to restore nutrients to proper levels. So don't stop taking supplements when you start to feel better!

I understand how anxious you are to feel good again. I also know you've been to several doctors, most who couldn't help you. It's easy to lose faith.

> *Victory becomes, to some degree, a state of mind.*
> *Knowing ourselves superior to the anxieties,*
> *troubles, and worries which obsess us, we are*
> *superior to them.* —Basil King

You will feel better, but it will take time—months, maybe longer—before you correct your homeostatic mechanisms. Until you carry out these basic but essential 15 steps, there's little hope you'll get well. I know some of these steps are difficult. Avoiding certain foods, and giving up caffeine and sugar can be hard. But have faith in yourself, and go to work!

1. Get eight or more hours of deep restorative sleep each night. If you don't do anything else, start here! See chapter 6.

2. Restore optimal adrenal function. Use adrenal extracts and DHEA. See chapter 7.

3. Find, avoid, and slowly—with a rotation diet—reintroduce any allergic foods. The elimination diet is an important tool in restoring proper digestion and eliminating common and sometimes mysterious symptoms associated with FMS/CFS. See chapter 9.

4. Take a comprehensive multivitamin and mineral formula. See chapter 10.

5. Supplement with essential fatty acids. See chapter 14.

6. Supplement with an amino acid formula. See chapter 13.

7. Treat all opportunistic bugs, including viruses, parasites, bacterial, and yeast overgrowth. See chapters 9, 18, and 20.

8. Repair any abnormalities associated wit the digestive system including intestinal permeability and malabsorption syndrome. See chapter 17.

9. Supplement with digestive enzymes and probiotics!

10. Build up your immune system. See chapter 8.

11. Eat a healthy diet. A diet built around healthy principles goes a long way towards increasing your chances of being healthy. Avoid simple carbohydrates (see chapter 15). Increase your intake of good fats (see chapter 14). Eliminate alcohol, caffeine, nicotine, aspartame, and preservative-rich foods. A balanced diet devoid of blatant offenders lays the foundation for getting healthy and staying healthy. You can't get well until you change your dietary habits.

12. Test for and treat low thyroid with prescription or natural glandular extracts. See chapter 19.

13. Manage your daily stress! See chapters 3.

14. Find a chiropractor, physical therapist, and/or massage therapist who is knowledgeable about FMS/CFS. See chapter 24.

15. Find your inner self. What is this illness trying to show you? Is God giving you an opportunity to reevaluate your life? Read books on how to tap into your inner self. Become skilled in sifting through mind chatter, keeping the positive thoughts and responses and letting go of the negative disease-causing thoughts. See chapter 25.

Never, never, never give up! —Winston Churchill

I wish you joy, happiness, and optimal health.

www.drrodger.com
(205) 879-2383

Appendix A
Symptoms Profiles

Yeast Symptoms Profile

Check any of the symptoms below that you experience on a regular basis.

___ fatigue or lethargy

___ depression or manic depression

___ pain and/or swelling in joints

___ abdominal pain

___ constipation and/or diarrhea

___ bloating or excessive belching or intestinal gas

___ indigestion or heartburn

___ prostatitis

___ impotence

___ loss of sexual desire or feeling

___ endometriosis or infertility

___ cramps and/or menstrual irregularities

___ premenstrual tension (PMS)

___ attacks of anxiety (nerves) or crying

___ sore throat

___ recurrent infections or fluid in ears

___ cold hands or feet; low body temperature

___ hypothyroidism

___ chronic hives (urticaria)

___ cough or recurrent bronchitis

___ nasal congestion or postnasal drip

___ nasal itching

___ laryngitis (loss of voice)

___ eczema, itching eyes

___ sensitivity to milk, wheat, corn, or other foods

___ mucus in stools

___ psoriasis

___ shaking or irritability when hungry

___ cystitis or interstitial cystitis

___ incoordination

___ pressure above ears; feeling of head swelling

___ tendency to bruise easily

___ troublesome vaginal burning, itching, or discharge

___ rectal itching

___ dry mouth or throat

___ mouth rashes, including "white tongue"

___ bad breath

___ foot, hair, or body odor not relieved by washing

___ pain or tightness in chest

___ wheezing or shortness of breath

___ urinary frequency or urgency

___ burning upon urination

___ spots in vision or erratic vision

___ burning or tearing eyes

___ ear pain or deafness

If you checked more than five of the above symptoms, you might be suffering from a yeast overgrowth. See chapter 20.

Wilson's Syndrome Symptoms Profile

Check any of the symptoms below that you experience on a regular basis.

___ fatigue

___ abnormal throat sensations

___ headaches

___ sweating abnormalities

___ migraines

___ heat and/or cold intolerance

___ PMS

___ low self-esteem

___ irritability

___ irregular periods

___ fluid retention

___ severe menstrual cramps

___ anxiety

___ low blood pressure

___ panic attacks

___ frequent colds and sore throats

___ hair loss

___ frequent urinary infections

___ depression

___ lightheadedness

___ decreased memory

___ ringing in the ears

___ decreased concentration

___ slow wound healing

___ decreased sex drive

___ easy bruising

___ unhealthy nails

___ acid Indigestion

___ low motivation

___ flushing

___ constipation

___ frequent yeast infections

___ irritable bowel syndrome

___ cold hands or feet

___ inappropriate weight gain

___ poor coordination

___ dry skin

___ inhibited sexual development

___ dry hair

___ infertility

___ insomnia

___ hypoglycemia

___ falling asleep during the day

___ increased skin infections/Acne

___ arthritis and joint pain

___ abnormal swallowing sensations

___ allergies

___ changes in skin pigmentation

___ asthma

___ muscle aches

___ excessively tired after eating

___ itching

___ carpal tunnel syndrome

___ high cholesterol

___ dry eyes/blurred vision

___ ulcers

___ hives

___ increased nicotine, caffeine use

___ bad breath

If you checked more than five of the above symptoms, you might be suffering from Wilson's Syndrome. See chapter 19.

Brain Function Profile
(Also found on page 219)

The "O" Group

If three or more of these descriptions apply to your present feelings, you are probably part of the "O" group. Read about a deficiency of **opioid neurotransmitters** on page 219.

- Your life seems incomplete.
- You feel shy with all but your closest friends.
- You have feelings of insecurity.
- You often feel unequal to others.
- When things go right, you sometimes feel undeserving.
- You feel something is missing in your life.
- You occasionally feel a low self-worth or -esteem.
- You feel inadequate as a person.
- You frequently feel fearful when there is nothing to fear.

The "G" Group

If three or more of these descriptions apply to your present feelings, you are probably part of the "G" group. Read about a deficiency of **gamma-aminobutyric acid (GABA)** on page 221.

- You often feel anxious for no reason.
- You sometimes feel "free-floating" anxiety.
- You frequently feel "edgy," and it's difficult to relax.
- You often feel a "knot" in your stomach.
- Falling asleep is sometimes difficult.
- It's hard to turn your mind off when you want to relax.
- You occasionally experience feelings of panic for no reason.
- You often use alcohol or other sedatives to calm down.

The "D" Group

If three or more of these descriptions apply to your present feelings, you are probably part of the "D" group. Read about a deficiency of **dopamine** on page 222.

- You lack pleasure in life.
- You feel there are no real rewards in life.
- You have unexplained lack of concern for others, even loved ones.
- You experience decreased parental feelings.
- Life seems less "colorful" or "flavorful."
- Things that used to be "fun" aren't any longer enjoyable.
- You have become a less spiritual or socially concerned person.

The "N" Group

If three or more of these descriptions apply to your present feelings, you are probably part of the "N" group. Read about a deficiency of **norepinephrine** on page 223.

- You suffer from a lack of energy.
- You often find it difficult to "get going."
- You suffer from decreased drive.
- You often start projects and then don't finish them.
- You frequently feel a need to sleep or "hibernate."
- You feel depressed a good deal of the time.
- You occasionally feel paranoid.
- Your survival seems threatened.
- You are bored a great deal of the time.

The "S" Group

If three or more of these descriptions apply to your present feelings, you are probably part of the "S" group. Read about a deficiency of **serotonin** on page 224.

- It's hard for you to go to sleep.
- You can't stay asleep.
- You often find yourself irritable.
- Your emotions often lack rationality.
- You occasionally experience unexplained tears.
- Noise bothers you more than it used to; it seems louder than normal.
- You flare up at others more easily than you used to; you experience unprovoked anger.
- You feel depressed much of the time.
- You find you are more susceptible to pain.
- You prefer to be left alone.

Parasite Symptoms Profile

Check all that apply.

___ Have you ever traveled outside the United States?

___ Do you have foul-smelling stools?

___ Do you experience any stomach bloating, gas, or pain?

___ Do you experience any rectal itching?

___ Do you experience unexpected weight loss with increased appetite?

___ Do you experience food allergies that continue to get worse despite treatment.

___ Do you feel hungry all the time?

___ Have you been diagnosed with irritable bowel syndrome?

___ Have you been diagnosed with inflammatory bowel disease?

___ Are you plagued by an itchy nose, ears, or anus?

___ Do you have sore mouth and gums?

___ Do you experience chronic low back pain that's unresponsive to treatment?

___ Do you have digestive disturbances?

___ Do you grind your teeth at night?

___ Do you own a dog, cat, or other pet? Or are you frequently around animals?

If you checked three or more of the above symptoms, you might be suffering from a parasitic infection. See chapter 18.

Adrenal Fatigue Risk Profile

Social readjustment scale: Add up all points applying to the following events that have occurred in your life over the past 12 months.

Event	Points
1. Death of spouse	100
2. Divorce	73
3. Marital separation	65
4. Jail	63
5. Death of a close family member	63
6. Personal injury or illness	53
7. Marriage	50
8. Fired from work	47
9. Marital reconciliation	45
10. Retirement	45
11. Illness of family member	44
12. Pregnancy	40
13. Sexual difficulties	39
14. Addition of new family member	39
15. Business adjustment	39
16. Financial change	38
17. Death of a close friend	37
18. Change to a different line of work	36
19. Increased arguments with spouse	35
20. Large mortgage	31
21. Foreclosure of loan or mortgage	30
22. Change of work responsibilities	29
23. Your child leaving home	29
24. Trouble with inlaws	29

25. High personal achievement	28
26. Spouse begins or stops work	26
27. Beginning or end of school	26
28. Change in living conditions	25
29. Revision of personal habits	24
30. Trouble with boss	23
31. Change in work conditions	20
32. Change in residence	20
33. Change in schools	20
34. Change in recreation	19
35. Change in church activities	19
36. Change in social activities	18
37. Small mortgage	17
38. Change in sleeping habits	16
39. Change in number of family reunions	15
40. Change in eating habits	15
41. Vacation	13
42. Christmas	12
43. Minor violation of law	11

200 points or more in one year's time is indicative of a weakened immune system and increases the risk for serious illness. A score of 100 or above is enough to bring on adrenal fatigue, especially if any of the following apply:

___ I've been under stress for long periods of time.

___ I work or my spouse works over 50 hours a week.

___ I work full-time.

___ I have one or more children living at home.

___ I've been unhappy for more than two months.

___ I'm unhappy at work.

___ I'm overweight.

___ I have a chronic illness.

___ I have a nervous stomach.

___ I have been on a low-fat or low-calorie diet in the past year.

___ I don't exercise.

___ I exercise more than 14 hours per week.

___ I drink more than two cups of coffee per day.

___ I drink sodas on a daily basis.

___ I smoke.

___ I drink two or more alcoholic beverages per day.

___ I can't sleep at night.

___ I get fewer than seven hours of sleep each night.

___ I eat sugary foods on a regular basis.

___ I've had surgery in the past year.

___ I've had more than one surgery in the past two years.

___ I'm a professional or family caregiver.

___ My spouse doesn't understand my illness.

___ I take prescription or over-the-counter medicines to lift me up.

Read about adrenal dysfunction in chapter 7.

www.drrodger.com
(205) 879-2383

Appendix B
Tests, Results, and Normal Ranges

Listed below are many of the numerous medical tests used by Advanced Family Medicine for evaluating the health of fibromyalgia and chronic fatigue syndrome patients. This list is intended for general reference, and the descriptions are far from exhaustive. It should not be used to diagnose or treat any condition. An increased or decreased level in any area should not be assumed as an indication of illness. Your doctor will take many other factors into account before diagnosing you.

- **Complete Blood Count (CBC)**

    The CBC test usually includes a red blood cell (RBC) count, a white blood cell (WBC) count, hemoglobin, hematocrit, indices, platelets, and WBC differential.

- **WBC Count**

    The WBCs are the main defense against invading microorganisms. WBCs destroy most bacteria.

    Normal range: 5,000–10,000 cubic units. **Increased in** various infections, certain blood disorders, and emotional distress. **Decreased in** overwhelming infections.

- **WBC Differential**

    Neutrophils are active and increased in acute bacterial infections.

    Lymphocytes are particularly active in fighting off viruses. **Increased in** acute viral infections, lymphocytic leukemia, and multiple myaloma. **Decreased in** Hodgkin's disease.

    Eosinophils are increased in allergies and parasitic infections.

    Monocytes are active in chronic infections and Hodgkin's disease.

Basophils release heparin to prevent clotting in inflammation. **Increased in** polycythemia. **Decreased in** acute infections.

• RBC Count

The amount of RBCs per cubic millimeter is used to assess the degree or presence of anemia. **Increased in** polycythemia. **Decreased in** anemia.

• Hemoglobin

Hemoglobin is the oxygen-carrying portion of RBCs. **Normal range:** female: 12–15 mg.%; male: 13–16 mg.% **Increased in** polycythemia and dehydration. **Decreased in** all anemias and late pregnancy.

• Hematocrit

This is a measure of the volume of settled RBCs per 100 ml. of blood. **Normal range:** female: 40–48%; male: 42–50%. **Increased in** polycythemia. **Decreased in** anemia.

• Indices Mean Corpuscular volume (MCV)

MCV is calculated by dividing the hematocrit result by the RBC count. **Increased in** macrocytic anemia. **Decreased in** microcytic anemia.

• Platelet Count

Blood platelets strengthen the resistance of the vessel walls against trauma and are the initial factor in coagulation (clotting). **Increased in** trauma, blood loss, and polycythemia. **Decreased in** anemia, thrombocytopenia, and severe burns.

• Prothrombin Time

Prothrombin is produced in the liver and is converted

to thrombin in the clotting process. Therefore, clotting ability decreases with an increase in the Prothrombin time. **Increased in** Vitamin-K deficiency, liver and biliary disease.

• **Serum Glutamic Oxalacetic Tranaminase (SGOT)**

SGOT is an enzyme present in large amounts in muscle and liver tissue. It is also in heart muscle. It's primarily used as a marker for heart disease, but elevation may also be due to liver disease or muscular dystrophy.

• **Serum Glutamic Pyruvic Transaminase (SGPT)**

Primarily an indicator of liver disease (hepatitis) and myocardial infarction.

• **Triiodthyronine (T3)**

T3 is a thyroid hormone. **Increased in** hyperthyroidism. **Decreased in** hypothyroidism.

• **Thyroxine (T4)**

T4 is a thyroid hormone that is converted into T3. **Increased in** hyperthyroid. **Decreased in** hypothyroid.

• **Thyroid Stimulating Hormone (TSH)**

The pituitary gland is responsible for secreting TSH, which then prompts the thyroid gland to release thyroid hormones. **If T3 and T4 are low and TSH is elevated:** indicates hypothyroidism. **If T3 and T4 are low and TSH is also low:** indicates pituitary gland dysfunction (secondary hypothyroidism).

• **Uric Acid**

Increased in arthritic gout and kidney insufficiency. **Decreased in** acute hepatitis.

- **Erythrocyte Sedimentation Rate (ESR)**

  This test is used to detect inflammatory conditions. It is relatively nonspecific and is used as a screening tool. If levels are abnormal, further testing might be needed. **Increased:** heavy metal poisoning, all collagen diseases (autoimmune arthritis), some cancers, gout, infections, and other inflammatory diseases. **May be decreased in** sickle cell anemia and congestive heart failure.

- **Food and Inhalant Allergy Testing**

  Food and inhalant allergies have been implicated in a wide range of health problems. There are several ways to test for allergies, including blood tests, scratch tests, Electro acupuncture according to Voll (EAV), muscle testing or Applied Kinesiology (AK), provocation/neutralization, and elimination diets. I usually recommend blood tests that combine Radio Allergo Sorbent (RAST) testing with Enzyme-Linked Immunoabsorbant Assay (ELISA) testing. RAST testing is very useful in uncovering inhalant allergies like pollen, ragweed, and molds. ELISA testing is more accurate in measuring reactions to foods. See chapter 9.

- **Liver Detoxification Profile**

  This test evaluates the ability of the liver to properly detoxify foreign substances. Standard blood liver panels are used to uncover elevated liver enzymes and gross liver diseases. Functional medical tests like this one are designed to access the body's or organ's performance when challenged with a potentially harmful substance. The test uses saliva and urine samples to measure the liver's ability to detoxify potential harmful substances. Our liver's detoxification system can be measured by challenging it with caffeine, aspirin, and acetaminophen. See chapter 18.

• Adrenal Cortex Stress Profile

This test uses saliva samples taken throughout the day and night to measure levels of the adrenal hormones cortisol and dehydroepiandrosterone (DHEA). These adrenal hormones play a vital role in balancing a person's response to stress. They allow us to adapt to and manage stress appropriately.

Abnormal cortisol levels have been observed in patients suffering from CFS, FMS, depression, panic disorders, male impotence, infertility, PMS, menopause, and sleep disorders. **Low levels of DHEA** are associated with fatigue, insomnia, depression, decreased libido, and lowered immunity.

I like this test because it shows how these two hormones perform throughout the day—a single sample doesn't provide much information. Cortisol levels ebb and flow throughout the day in accordance with our circadian rhythms (sleep/wake cycle). I've found cortisol and DHEA to be extremely valuable in correcting many of the problems associated with CFS and FMS.

See chapter 7.

• Comprehensive Parasitology Profile

The Comprehensive Parasitology Profile checks for parasite as well as bacterial and yeast overgrowth. The test also uncovers harmful bacteria or yeast inhabiting the intestinal tract and measures the amount of good bacteria there. The test requires a stool sample.

Most people, including physicians, don't realize how common parasites infect Americans. We think of parasites as being a "third world" phenomenon, and that's true in a sense. Up to 99% of those living in undeveloped countries have one or more parasites. But world travelers have spread many of these parasites, and it is not uncommon for those in developed countries to be stricken with parasitic infections. In a study of outpatients at the Gastroenterology Clinic in Elmhurst, NY, a 74% incidence of parasites was found. Great Smokies Diagnostic Laboratory in Ashville, North Carolina, is arguably the stool-testing lab in the world. They report that 30% of all examined specimens are positive for parasites.

Parasites can cause a wide range of health problems, including irritable bowel, ulcers, gastritis, malabsorption, fatigue, autoimmune reactions, colitis, low back pain, irregular bowel movements, and abdominal cramps.

See chapter 18.

· Intestinal Permeability Profile

This is a functional medical test that measures the permeability of the cells that line the intestinal tract. These cells are known as mucosal cells. They act as a barrier to help prevent toxic substances from leaking into the rest of the body. **Increased permeability** of the intestinal tract is associated with a number of health problems, including food allergies, malabsorption, irritable bowel syndrome, and rheumatoid arthritis.

See chapter 17.

· Hair Elemental Analysis

This test should only be used to access the levels of heavy metals. It's not an accurate test for mineral levels and shouldn't be used to measure mineral stores. Still, an inexpensive screening test like a hair analysis is an ideal way to uncover any potential contributors to poor health.

Heavy metals include cadmium (in smokers), aluminum, lead, mercury, tin, silver, and arsenic. Heavy metal toxicity can present a host of unwanted symptoms, and we commonly find heavy metals in FMS and CFS patients.

See chapter 18.

- **Antinuclear Antibodies (ANA)**

  This is a blood test that measures autoimmune reactions. A positive finding may indicate rheumatoid arthritis, scleroderma, or lupus (if accompanied by glucoronic acid) in the liver. **Increased:** hepatitis (liver disease). **Decreased:** hemolytic (blood) disease.

- **Bilirubin**

  Bilirubin is the main bile pigment. Free bilirubin is released into the blood as a result of RBC breakdown and is the conjugated form.

- **Blood Urea Nitrogen**

  This blood test measures urea. Urea is the end product of protein metabolism and is formed in the liver. It is excreted by the kidneys. **Increased in** kidney damage or urinary tract obstruction. **Decreased in** liver failure or pregnancy.

- **C Reactive Protein**

  C reactive protein is a substance present in tissue destruction and inflammation.

  Positive may indicate rheumatic fever or myocardial infarction (heart disease). Also is a warning sign of increased risk for heart disease, cancer, and inflammation.

- **Creatinine**

  Creatinine is a waste product usually eliminated by the kidneys. **Increased in** possible kidney disease or urinary obstruction. **Decreased in** possible muscular dystrophy.

- **Fibrinogen**

  Fibrinogen is formed in the liver and, in the presence

of thrombin, is converted to fibrin as part of the clotting mechanism. **Increased in** kidney disease. **Decreased in** liver disease. Fibrinogen has been implicated as a possible contributing cause of FMS and CFS.

• Glucose

Glucose (blood sugar) can be measured by either a blood or urine test. **Normal test range:** 80–120 mg./dl. **Increased in** diabetes and Cushing's disease. **Decreased in** hypoglycemia and Addison's disease.

• Lipase

Lipase is a fat-digesting enzyme produced by the pancreas. **Increased in** inflammation of the pancreas (acute pancreatitis), obstructed pancreatic duct, and pancreatic cancer.

• Cholesterol

Cholesterol is transported through the blood while attached to lipoproteins. Lipoproteins (Lipo meaning fat) are broken down into very low density lipoproteins (VLDL), low density lipoproteins (LDL) and high density lipoproteins (HDL). VLDLs and LDLs are considered bad because they transport fats from the liver to the cells. HDLs are considered good because they carry fats from the cells to the liver. Cholesterol and its role in arteriosclerosis are being questioned. Many scientists and physicians (including yours truly) don't believe that cholesterol is the villain it's been made out to be. **Total cholesterol =** HDL + LDL+ VLDL. **VLDL =** triglycerides (fats) divided by 5.

Normal test ranges: total cholesterol below 220mg/dl; LDL below 130 mg./dl; HDL above 35mg/dl; triglycerides less than 150 mg /dl. The ratio of total cholesterol to HDL, and the ratio of LDL to HDL, are known as the cardiac risk factor ratios. The first should be no higher than 4. The second, no higher than 2.5.

• Epstein–Barr Virus AB and Cytomegalovirus Panel

This blood test measures the antibodies Immunoglobulin M (IgM) and Immunoglobulin G (IgG). IgM antibodies measure the acute (recent infection) phase of the virus. IgG antibodies measure the dormant (inactive) phase of the virus. The test also measures Epstein–Barr Nuclear Antigen (EBNA) antibodies.

We often see a reactivated virus in CFS patients. The person was exposed to the virus in the past and was able to get over the acute infection. But later in life, when the immune system was compromised, the virus became active again.

If IgM is normal (low) but the IgG is high and the EBNA is high: indicates that the virus is again active. (This criteria is also useful in testing for the cytomegalovirus.)

See chapter 5.

• Human Growth Hormone (HGH) and Insulin-like Growth-factor 1 (IGF1)

HGH helps increase muscle mass, decrease adipose (fat), repair damaged tissues (especially muscle), build stronger bones, increase energy, and improve sleep. Insulin-like growth factor-1 levels are an indication of how much HGH is circulating in the body.

I have found FMS and CFS patients improve much faster when HGH levels are over 200—over 250 is ideal. Restoring HGH to normal or above-normal levels can often provide dramatic relief for insomnia and the symptoms associated with it: fatigue, depression, and achy muscle pain.

· DHEA

Normal test range: 12–379 mcg./dl. This is a very broad range, and I like to see DHEA levels above 200. DHEA is a very important hormone, and most FMS and CFS patients are very low (less than 100 mcg./dl) and need replacement therapy. Treatment of females is usually 25 mg a day; of males, 50 mg a day. I prefer a special sublingual form of DHEA. I've tried several different types of DHEA, but sublingual (absorbed under the tongue) DHEA (and this brand in particular) seem to yield the quickest results.

· RA Latex Agglutination

Positive test: indicates rheumatoid arthritis

Appendix C
Supplements, Testing, and Other Resources

HOW TO ORDER SUPPLEMENTS, BOOKS, AND TAPES
- **Order online** at www.drrodger.com
- **Call** (205) 879-2383.

OUR MOST POPULAR FORMULAS
Nutritional Supplements
- Dr. Murphree's Essential Therapeutics CFS/Fibromyalgia Support Pack (one-month supply)
- Dr. Murphree's Essential Therapeutics Liver Formula (one–two months supply)
- Dr. Murphree's Essential Therapeutics Arthro Formula (one month supply)

Sleep Formula
- Dr. Murphree's 5HTP

Adrenal Boosters
- Adrenal Cortex
- DHEA sublingual

Digestion and Leaky Gut
- Dr. Murphree's Digestive Enzymes
- Dr. Murphree's GastroThera (leaky gut formula)

Amino Acids (for anxiety, depression, mental fatigue)
- GABA
- Dr. Murphree's NeuroThera

HEALTH NEWS YOU CAN USE NEWSLETTER
Write to Dr. Murphree at 3401 Independence Drive, Suite 121, Homewood, AL 35209, or visit www.drrodger.com for a free trial copy of *Health News You Can Use,* a monthly publication from Dr. Murphree containing the latest breakthrough therapies and ideas on fibromyalgia, CFS, and other health issues.

CONSULTATIONS AND SPEAKING ENGAGEMENTS

Dr. Murphree is available for conference and convention events and, as of printing, is still accepting new patients. To schedule a speaking engagement, telephone consultation, or visit to his Birmingham, Alabama, practice, call (205) 879-2383

DIAGNOSTIC TESTING

Great Smokies Diagnostic Laboratory

Your licensed healthcare provider may order liver detox, yeast stool, parasite stool, hair analysis, essential fatty acid profile, amino acid profile, adrenal cortex profile, and other tests.

- Write to   63 Zillicoa Street
                      Asheville, NC 28801
- Call 1-800-522-4762.
- Fax (828) 252-9303.
- Visit www.gsdl.com

ALLERGY TESTING

Immuno Laboratories

- Call 1-800-231-9197.

THYROID PROTOCOLS

Broda Barnes Research Foundation

- Call (203) 261-2101.
- Visit www.brodabarnes.org

WILSON'S SYNDROME

- Visit www.wilsonssyndrome.com

OTHER RESOURCES

The American Yoga Association

- Call (941) 927-4977.
- Visit www.americanyogaassociation.org

International Association of Yoga Therapists

- Visit www.iayt.org

American Chiropractic Association
- Call 1-800-986-4636.
- Visit www.acatoday.com

International Chiropractors Association
- Call 1-800-423-4690.
- Visit www.chiropractic.org

International Society for Orthomolecular Medicine
- Call (416) 733-2117.
- Visit www.orthomed.org

American Massage Therapy Association
- Call (847) 864-0123.
- Visit www.amtamassage.org

American Herbalist Guild
- Call (770) 751-6021.
- Visit www.americanherbalistsguild.com

Herb Research Foundation
- Call (303) 449-2265.
- Visit www.herbs.org

Insight Meditation Society
- Call (978) 355-4378.
- Visit www.dharma.org/ims

Center for Mind-Body Medicine
- Call (202) 966-7338.
- Visit www.cmbm.org

Organic Meats: Goose Pond Farms
- Call (256) 751-0987.

Index